GW00503714

FROM THREE WORLDS

By the same author:

Less Than Kin (1957)
What Is the Commonwealth? (1957)
Number 10 (novel 1966; play with Ronald Millar, 1967)
Special Relationship (novel, 1968)
Cataclysm: The North-South Conflict of 1987 (future
  history, 1984)

FROM THREE WORLDS

Memoirs

William Clark

SIDGWICK & JACKSON
LONDON

First published in Great Britain in 1986
by Sidgwick & Jackson Limited

Copyright © 1986 by Run of the Mill Productions

ISBN 0–283–99372–3

Phototypeset by Falcon Graphic Art Ltd
Wallington, Surrey
Printed in Great Britain by
Biddles Ltd, Guildford and King's Lynn

for Sidgwick and Jackson Limited
1 Tavistock Chambers, Bloomsbury Way
London WC1A 2SG

Contents

Illustrations

Unless otherwise stated, all the photographs come from the author's private collection.

Preface

On All Hallows Eve 1984 I left a meeting of the Parliamentary Group for World Government which I had been chairing in a stuffy office just off Westminster Hall, saying that I had to go to a medical appointment. The group continued the discussion on how to teach world affairs to 11-14-year-olds, while I walked up to the Middlesex Hospital, glancing at the newspaper billboards proclaiming that Mrs Gandhi had been shot, and all India was rioting. This was sufficiently dramatic to keep my mind off the nagging fear that my recent liver biopsy would reveal something nasty.

Dr Peter Ball, whom I had met only once two weeks before, inspired complete trust and I felt curiously grateful to him for telling me simply that I had an inoperable and so terminal cancer. Though I felt that I was falling down a lift shaft I asked how long the stay of execution would be. 'Six months to two years; it's rather bleak,' replied Dr Ball.

Of course being theatre time I could not get a taxi and had to walk back to my rooms at Albany, wanting all the time to shout at busy taxis, 'Hey, I am a dying man, drop everything and drive me home.' But I quickly realized that dying is not a very distinguished part of life.

At the top of three flights of stairs (eighteenth-century Albany does not run to lifts) I was out of breath. I found David Harvey – who had shared my Mill in the Chilterns for twenty-five years, and was now formally my literary partner in Run of the Mill Productions – awaiting expectantly my news. I gave it him as unvarnished as I had received it, and watched the colour drain out of his face. When I finished he responded immediately: 'That's the bad news, now the good news. Granada TV wants you to fly to Manchester to appear on a major programme tonight and over the weekend on India after Mrs Gandhi. The BBC Radio 4 wants you to record a piece for tonight's news. Third, this news gives you a perfect opportunity to concentrate on your memoirs and to tell the truth because you won't be here to be abused when the book appears. After you're dead you don't need to be respectful.'

I did the broadcast, taking a little private pride in my professional capacity to answer my old friend Richard Kershaw's questions calmly and without revealing my inner turmoils and terrors.

Once back in the quiet calm of Albany I quickly realized that I dared not yet face bed. I spent some hours thinking over the reasons for writing memoirs at all. I had long been planning them in my mind and had even resolved on a title, *Four Fathers*. This would tell of the dominating influences in my life: my natural father who was in his mid-sixties when I was born and my mother died. As the youngest of six children my relationship with him was distant and cool, but he created a pattern in my life which lasted: I looked to my father as the source of all personal promotion, and only by pleasing him could I hope to advance to a position where I might rival or even excel my elder brothers.

My father died late in 1937 a few months before I left for America with a Harkness Fellowship at the University of Chicago, so it was a strange new world that I sought for the familiar father substitutes. None was satisfactory, all were British.

The first was Bertrand Russell, who arrived at the University of Chicago as a visiting professor on the same day as I. During the following months from Munich to the outbreak of war we 'imported Englishmen' were thrown very closely together, and I remained a close friend of Bertie and his young third wife for many years. He taught me to question, in an adult way, most of what I had been taught to accept at home, school and university. But as a father figure he was lacking in authority; I did not feel that by following his exhortations I was necessarily going to be rewarded – if only because I could not help noticing that on some judgments of personality and policy Bertie could be both wrong and silly. But what he taught me, for which I am eternally grateful, was to think for myself and question the received wisdom of both the authorities and the anti-authorities.

Oddly, the next British visiting professor was R.H. Tawney and I quickly slipped into a father-son relationship with him. By then I was working in the British Information Services in Chicago though still living in the university area. When towards the end of the war I was transferred to the Embassy in Washington as Press Attaché, I lived for a time in their flat, since Harry Tawney had earlier become Labour Attaché, though listed at first in the Embassy as a typist. This was the beginning of a couple of years in Parnassus where I watched the creation of the post-war world and conversed with its British progenitors in that easy, slightly fake atmosphere of equality which characterizes a group of temporary exiles in a country that was definitely foreign – however friendly, supportive, and like-minded.

There were three men in particular in the Embassy at that time who turned my eye to the unlimited opportunities that lay before us as the war drew to a victorious close: Harry Tawney, Lord Halifax, and Maynard Keynes.

Harry Tawney saw the possibility of creating in Britain and Europe a dignified way of life without poverty, without degrading toil, but with full employment and adequate opportunities for education and leisure. This could only be achieved, he argued, by diminishing man's competitive, aggressive instincts and increasing his collaborative capacity. For this reason Tawney argued passionately in private for the abolition of the sovereign state at least in those areas – such as Europe – where the war had obligingly smashed it. 'I cannot believe that the peace treaties will restore all that prickly sovereignty which has caused Europe's downfall and left it a flattened corpse,' he once said to me and I have never forgotten that lost vision.

Edward Halifax. As a man who had been Viceroy of India, Foreign Secretary and was still a member of the War Cabinet while serving as Ambassador to the United States, he was a natural father figure for me and in the year that I knew him he became a good friend, and he too prepared my mind for post-war thinking. He was convinced that Britain's first post-war task was to bring America finally out of isolation to protect Europe from Russia on day one, and not in year three as in the two previous world wars. But he was deeply afraid that American isolationism would in fact turn into imperialism of the type that Harry Ince was proclaiming as the American Century. To avoid being overrun by this juggernaut Halifax spent much of his post-war years in Washington trying to smooth out the minor differences between Britain and America, negotiating not unsuccessfully but with many concessions from an extremely weak position. As Donald Meekam, then one of the rather critical First Secretaries put it: 'We must find good use for such an arch-appeaser.'

But Halifax used to talk to me privately about the press and radio and ask what I'd heard from the columnists and commentators, who he said were always so much more forthcoming and better informed than his informants – the Secretary of State and his minions. At the end of these debriefings we used to reverse roles and the Ambassador would tell me something about what he thought about the events of the time. His thoughts kept on coming back to India, not to his Viceregal days, but to much more recent events. He was certain that India must become politically independent and self-governing, and had worked very hard to this end with Stafford Cripps (and with President Roosevelt's covert support), but had been frustrated by the implacable opposition of Winston Churchill. As the war in Europe drew to a close he became more and more concerned about India, which he felt would be the crux of the final war settlement which would take place in Asia. Could Britain with its centuries of Asian experience show how there could be East-West co-operation between independent partners?

On India Halifax could become quite lyrical; he was convinced that it was a great nation, far more of a leader in Asia than Chiang Kai-shek's China which the Americans so greatly overvalued. From Edward Halifax I received this precious lifetime gift of a realization that the post-war world would not just be a consort of the Three Great Powers (USA, Great Britain and Russia) but would have to take full account of new and different nations – such as India. I must add that I learned at the San Francisco conference which founded the United Nations how determined the Churchill government was to prevent the UN having any say in the future of the British Empire. So I also learned that Halifax, whose wisdom about the great game of world politics had so impressed me, was not going to be a decisive influence in formulating British policy. As a father figure he lacked not authority but power.

The third of the trinity who shaped my approach to the world I was to live in was Maynard Keynes. He came to the Embassy during 1944 for what were known as Phase 1 negotiations which resulted in the establishment of the World Bank and International Monetary Fund, and then again in September 1945 for Phase 2 negotiations, which were to clear up the economic debris of the war, and resulted in the Anglo-America loan of 1946.

Preface

I did not work directly with him, but I met him often and because he had a don's delight in bright young minds, he encouraged me (unnecessarily) to talk or at least ask questions. From Keynes I received the strongest sense of the amazing opportunities that lay ahead of us in the post-war world. If only governments would see that by proper management of the economic levers of power they could not only avoid the slumps which had caused the war, but have a boom that would raise the standard of living of all Europe to the levels of America today. Yes, all Europe including Russia; they had shown that they could out-produce Hitler's war machine, and if that massive energy could be turned to peacetime uses Russia would soon be one of the great productive world powers.

India and the rest of the Empire? I asked once in Halifax's presence. Keynes's stern reply: that must wait until the reconstruction of Europe is much further advanced. All reconstruction costs money and only one country has money, America. But if they are as wise and generous in peace as they have proved in war, they can create a brave new world without beggars even in Calcutta.

This was a dizzying vision for a man in his twenties who found himself present at the creation of the era in which he was to live. Additionally I was given the task of creating public understanding in what appeared pre-eminently to be the capital city of the victors in the world war. The opportunities were unbounded, the determination to get things right this time seemed unshakable, the self-confidence of America under Roosevelt appeared invincible, and the bonds which linked American power and British experience were unbreakable.

It was under these happy auspices on a bright confident morning that I set out on my Odyssey.

1

Chicago
1939–44

It was in November 1944, in the Battle of the Bulge days, that I was taken into a room in the Willard Hotel, Washington, the headquarters of the British Economic Missions to the US, and shown a secret document on our national finances. It was labelled 'Very Secret' because, as I later learned, it was intended as a briefing for the Prime Minister and his entourage for a planned Churchill-Roosevelt meeting in advance of Yalta. It was a longish document which took me about half an hour to read and it can be summed up very succinctly as follows: the war had bankrupted Britain and while with lend-lease we could and should fight on, both on the Western Front and in the Far East, we must be aware that reconversion to peace and a restoration of our leading position as a world industrial and commercial power would need large sums of money injected over several years. This could only come from North America.

There was an accompanying note from a Treasury knight which said that there should be no publicity at all about this on the strict instructions of the Prime Minister who was determined that we should show no signs of thinking about the post-war world when we were pledged to fight to our last men with the United States, not only to imminent victory in Europe but even to the more distant prospect of a victory in Japan. But the Treasury needed to know what were the best ways of approach to the United States and what obstacles were apparent to those working in the field. Roger Stevens, who had shown me all this, had been our Consul in Denver and had known me when I was working in Chicago. We had become very good friends. I was very flattered that he should

1

ask my opinion as the expert on one of the most obvious and least understood obstacles, i.e. the Middle West, and the *Chicago Tribune* and its brand of isolationism.

On the sixteen-hour train journey back to Chicago (designed for long thoughts rather than sleep), I jotted down my impressions of the last five years and tried to make sense of the events which now presented us with the imminent possibility of victory in Europe and ruin in Britain.

It all began on my fourth day in Chicago when I had gone out to Libertyville in the suburbs with an introduction from an English friend to a young Chicago lawyer called Adlai Stevenson. By chance we listened together that night to the news from Munich. Adlai shook his head sadly at the end and said, 'I don't blame you for buying time on the never-never, but it will certainly cost you a lot in the end.'

I had gone out to the University of Chicago on a Harkness Fellowship, direct from Oxford, and had chosen Chicago because it seemed the least like Oxford or Cambridge of the universities on offer. It had, therefore, been something of a surprise to discover on campus not only a fairly exact model of King's College, Cambridge, but also of Magdalen Tower, Oxford, which was firmly attached to Christ Church Hall. One of the conditions of the fellowship was that the summer vacation should be spent driving around the United States, touching at least half of the individual states. It was this very wise condition that gave me an opportunity of seeing the whole United States in the last year of the Depression, and to form some judgments about its power and influence in the world. The abiding impression that I gained was of the vastness and impregnability of the continent. But 1929, the collapse of the boom and of the stock market, had desperately wounded the pride and the viability of the American people. In spite of all the latent power to survive I saw little that gave me the impression that America was going to involve itself in world affairs to any great extent. There was one exception to this, which was when I was sleeping out in the open on the hills above the Bay Bridge in San Francisco and saw the Pacific Fleet sailing at dawn out to battle stations from the safe haven of the San Francisco Bay. They were sailing, though I did not know it at the time, to their bases in Pearl Harbor, Hawaii, and Manila in the Philippines. Even that power was being exerted away from my centre of attention, which was Europe, towards the Far East and the Pacific Ocean.

2

Chicago 1939–44

The university where I had been spending the last few days was named Berkeley after the bishop who wrote a poem on 'the prospect of planting arts and learning in America'. It began:

> Westward the course of empire takes its way:
> The four first acts already past,
> A fifth shall close the drama with the day:
> Time's noblest offspring is the last.

Was this in fact true? Was California really the egg of a new world? I had already seen something of the spirit of California, and it had seemed somewhat exotic to me.

I had driven through the south-western deserts to Santa Barbara where I stayed for a few days with my old friends Bertrand and Patricia Russell. For my birthday party (28 July) we had gone down to stay with Aldous Huxley actually in Sunset Boulevard. They gave a magnificent party for me, at which I was able to satisfy myself that I had seen the best of Hollywood. But what particularly stuck in my mind was a post-dinner argument between Bertrand Russell, Aldous Huxley, Gerald Heard, and – of all people – Groucho and Harpo Marx. Groucho began a very lucid, indeed intellectual, attack on Neville Chamberlain for his policies of appeasement. He said that he was of course influenced by Hitler's persecution of the Jews, but he thought that Chamberlain had not only condemned a number of Jews to death by Munich, he had really delivered over the continent of Europe to Russia, and that form of Marxism was a heresy of the junior branch of his family. Bertie responded by saying that Hitler had to be stopped, but the difficulty was that modern war was an ineffective means of imposing law and order: 'We killed many millions of people in the period 1914–18, and I went to gaol because I thought that the whole idea was wrong. I was of course proved right because in spite of the millions we killed, we omitted to kill Mr Hitler.' He then went on to say that if America and Britain plus Western Europe were to exert all their pressure relentlessly on Hitler we might get him removed without a war and its incalculably horrific consequences. Groucho responded that it was certainly not beyond the powers of the Western Europeans to stop Hitler, especially in an alliance with Russia where the West Europeans could be the rider, not the horse, of that alliance.

Aldous Huxley, joined by Gerald Heard, then began to extol the

3

virtues of life on the rim of the civilized world (i.e. California) which had a good deal of space between it and the catastrophes that were about to fall on Europe. Aldous tended to believe that Europe was a lost cause, and even the eastern United States was likely to be severely damaged by the European conflicts. He went on to advocate a concentration on the spiritual, intellectual world, turning one's back on the barbaric behaviour of the European tribes. He told us something (which was the first I had ever heard of it) about the mind-stretching capacity of some drugs occurring in nature, like mescalin, and said he had hopes that a new, more peaceful civilization could be built on this western rim.

As the party broke up I asked the two Marx brothers – whom I had very much liked – whether we could talk further some time about the possibility of American influence being actively used to contain Hitler. Groucho said that that was not the American job in life, and that if the United States undertook to make it so, it would probably destroy the United States which was in a very fragile state owing to the Depression at that time. However, Harpo invited me to come and see him when I got to the East Coast in about a month's time when he would be spending part of the autumn in New Hampshire.

Driving up the West Coast into the magnificent scenery of the north-west around Spokane and through Montana and Wyoming I could not help wondering whether this was not God's own country from which a new Pacific civilization might not come. It certainly seemed to be almost totally cut off – both isolated and insulated – from the horrid affairs of Nuremberg rallies and digging trenches in Hyde Park.

Someone had given me a 'portable' radio for my birthday which I carried in the back of the car and I occasionally stopped to listen to the local radio stations. There was virtually no news about Europe on them. Then I turned up north into Canada at Winnipeg, and at once the atmosphere was completely different. The news was filled with the European crisis and Canadians talked about it as if they were part of the European scene. Almost immediately the news came through (23 August) of the Molotov-Ribbentrop pact, and the Canadian Broadcasting Corporation made it clear that war was likely to begin in a matter of days.

On 1 September I turned down across the US border into New Hampshire where I put myself up in a hotel in Berlin. There I heard the announcement of Hitler's invasion of Poland. I went

4

down the next day to Monty Woolley's house on Lake Bomoseen, where I found Harpo Marx and quite a large group of literary lions glad to be guests of the man who came to dinner. The conversation, to my surprise, was throughout tinged with relief that at last Hitler had put himself out of court; the Europeans were bound to turn on him and would put him out of business in very short order, as America had long recommended. There seemed to be no feeling that it might involve America.

I started early next day for the long drive up to Maine where I was to stay with my friend from the London School of Economics and, more recently, neighbour at the University of Chicago, David Rockefeller, in the family home on Mount Desert. There were quite a number of members of the family there, including David's parents and two of his brothers. It was a very different and much graver household at dinner that evening.

On Sunday morning, 3 September, we were roused early, and in dressing gowns sat round a radio set to hear Neville Chamberlain entering the Second World War. At the end of that, without saying a word more, we went upstairs, dressed, and came down to breakfast.

There was conversation about the meaning of these events right through the morning; conversation of a serious and responsible kind, particularly focusing on what was going to be the role of the United States. What struck me about the tenor of this conversation was that the family as a whole believed that the United States had considerable responsibilities to Britain and France to support them in their struggle with fascism. But they did not believe that major help of a military kind was likely to be necessary. They thought that there should be no war debts out of this war, and they believed that it would still be possible for the United States to supply a number of British needs without involving massive transactions across the exchanges. They were sure that now that Britain had decided to hit back at Hitler there would be a victory fairly soon, though there were doubts about the national unity of France and its capability of avoiding communist diversionary tactics to shake the national resolve. But for Britain they were unanimously confident in its capacity and will to defeat Hitler without any very great difficulty, though the possibility of devastating air raids remained in the forefront of their minds.

It was with this general air of confidence in Britain coming from some of the leaders of the East Coast establishment that I set off a few days later for New York City to register at the British Consulate-General. The offices were absolutely overwhelmed by those wishing to register their willingness to serve in almost any capacity – including quite a large number of non-British subjects who were given some literature but not asked to register. The courteous official who looked after me, noticing that I still had a slight limp from my football knee injuries, said very confidentially, 'Of course they won't be wanting the likes of you for some time, but put your name down here and perhaps by next summer we'll be able to find something for you to do.' Having found it rather difficult to make the decision to register and make myself available for repatriation I found this both slightly humiliating and faintly welcome. I asked if there was anything I could do in the city where I was working, which was Chicago, and was handed a card giving the name and address of the Chicago Consul-General.

Driving back to the Midwest I felt a certain real confidence that Britain had the full support of traditional East Coast America and that Britain was regarded by competent and serious observers as perfectly capable of dealing with the Hitler menace. This seemed from all the propaganda that came out of Britain at this time to be the view of the government itself. So in fact I did not worry about going round to the British Consul-General in Chicago for several weeks. However, the situation in the Midwest was quite different. The constant pressure on the US Administration from the *Chicago Tribune*, its radio stations, and many of the smaller newspapers that were on sale around the university began to make me wonder whether some response should not be made to set forth the British case and the British expectations.

When I called on Lewis Bernays, the Consul-General, I had already been warned by some English and American friends that he was rather a weak reed and something of a defeatist. That was not my conclusion from a warm and friendly talk that we had together in the Consul-General's office with its splendid view of the *Chicago Tribune* tower. I thought, in fact, that Lewis Bernays was a rather bumbling speaker who was, however, something of a realist. He told me that he did not think that Britain and France alone could overthrow the Axis powers of Hitler and Mussolini; he complained at the way David Low, the cartoonist, had made them figures of fun when they were in fact figures of powerful evil. He was particularly irritated by Charlie Chaplin's film *The Great Dictator*. 'All of this plays into the hands of the Colonel,' he said with a wave of his hand towards the *Tribune* tower. 'He is saying, a plague on all your houses, and don't let us get involved in the traditional quarrels of old-fashioned, monarchical Britain and Europe.'

Bernays went on to say that he thought America would eventually become a vital factor in the European struggle; the main obstacle to fulfilling its obligations and national needs towards Western Europe was the Midwest isolationism, which he found positively anti-British compared with the isolatedness of California and the states west of the Rockies. He said, further, that he was constantly putting this point of view to the Embassy and equally constantly hearing behind-his-back chatter about his being a defeatist, which was not true. 'I need to try and get this point of view across in the Embassy or we shall rue the day that we failed to recognize what obstacles lie in the way of a firm alliance. But in order to do so I need to have much more time and opportunity than any senior British official can have to discover just what opinion is in this area.'

I was flattered and delighted to be asked to do something of this sort, and from that date in early November 1939 till after the American entry into the war I made regular reports through the Consulate-General to the Embassy and, I was led to believe, ultimately to London. I was regarded formally by the University of Chicago, and so recorded in their university list, as 'On leave of absence for war service'. But as I still lived in the campus area I mixed with the faculty and students; I even did some desultory work on my PhD thesis on 'The Politics of the Anglican Church during the Restoration of Charles II', and in 1940–1 I was Lecturer in Humanities.

After the defeats of May and June 1940 (which were so represented, in all their bleakness, in the American press) we in the British and Commonwealth community recognized how important American support was to us, not necessarily by their declaring war – which seemed an impossible dream – but by America becoming the arsenal of democracy. The famous gift of destroyers by Roosevelt to Britain was hailed in the UK as a generous act which proved America's support for the embattled opponents of Hitler. But Congress had not gone to war and it exacted a price for the deal. The US was to take over a string of naval bases in the British Caribbean colonies to defend the United States. We believed that Roosevelt was wholly on our side, and that so was Wendell Willkie, the Republican candidate in the 1940 election; but, equally, we knew that Congress was on the whole opposed to America entering the war and so were a majority of the people to whom Roosevelt felt forced to make obeisance by reiterating his statement that he would send no American boy overseas to fight in European wars.

In this situation, clearly, the propaganda war, particularly in the Middle West, mattered tremendously. I felt that though I was playing a small part in this war, it was a highly significant part. Chicago was of great importance in the political life of America. The *Chicago Tribune*'s importance as the leader of isolationism was probably exaggerated but it was very significant. At the same time, the University of Chicago was a marvellous pressure point for finding out about and dealing with opinion in the multi-national communities which made up Chicago. Beneš and a good part of the Czech government overthrown by Hitler in March 1939 had found refuge at the university and my slight acquaintance with him gave me an *entrée* to the overrun European peoples so heavily represented in Chicago. In terms of population Chicago was the second largest Czech city in the world. It was also the second largest Polish city in the world, and amongst the largest of many other European nations. Through connections with the representatives of these communities in the university I was able to get lines into the peoples whose freedom we were claiming to fight for.

At the same time, I was presented with first-class connections with the more thoughtful members of the America First group which was publicizing the case against American involvement in the war. Both Robert Hutchins, the president of the university, and Bill Benton, the vice-president, were members of the America First grouping and both had been, and remained, good friends of mine. My best girlfriend (to whom I had given, in an odd American rite, my fraternity pin) had an uncle, Leon Stolz, who was the chief leader writer for the *Chicago Tribune*; he too, though with some difficulty on occasions, remained a real friend and a link with Colonel Robert R. McCormick himself. Through Benton, who had a home in Connecticut, I had met Charles Lindbergh who was considered the *éminence grise* of the America First movement, and his wife Anne Morrow Lindbergh (author of a rather Orwellian book called *The Wave of the Future* forecasting an authoritarian rightist future for most of the world). My best friends, liberals like Clifton Utley and Adlai Stevenson, thought such people demons, though they understood, without necessarily approving, my keeping up connections with them. I did not, in fact, find that the

America First group or even the McCormick isolationists were all that evil, but then they were not citizens of my country. The America First movement, for instance, was not generally pro-Nazi, there was no hint of treachery about those that I knew, though undoubtedly there were some people, mostly of German descent, who were genuine pro-Nazis and probably deserved the imprisonment that some were given after 1941. It seemed to me that the America First members were very chauvinist, but that was a common attribute in the United States. Their policy was primarily to keep the United States unspotted from the world – especially from a world driven mad by war (not unlike the CND movement in recent times).

My suggestions in my reports were that we should not worry too much about trying to catch these people out in false representations of fact but rather seize upon their false premises and expose them. Can it ever be safe for the United States to live with Nazism poisoning the rest of the world even if it seems inconceivable that it can defeat the United States militarily? I urged that we should try and nurture a sense of there being a Western community, with Britain in the front line of the fighting but giving some hope to the overrun people of Europe so heavily represented in Chicago. This became very much more difficult as an argument once Russia had entered the war on our side and had been welcomed by Mr Churchill.

I also had to report that one of the reasons for isolationist/anti-British feeling in the area was a strong anti-Empire feeling. This was kept going by the Irish but there were a number of other people, including Caribbeans and east Indians, who helped to fan the flames. Posters saying 'Mahatma Gandhi is India's George Washington' were plastered all over the British Consulate-General and on a number of buildings in the centre of Chicago. It was partly for this reason that I once or twice urged that we should have an office in the Chicago area of the British Press Service (the British Information Services, or BIS, as it became known).

The reports that I sent in seemed to please what I suppose I should have called my 'control' in the Embassy. I was paid nothing and I had asked for nothing, but I did get one or two trips to Washington to discuss issues that I had raised.

Eventually, at the beginning of the winter of 1941, the proposal to set up a British Press Office in the Consulate-General in Chicago was agreed in London and to my intense delight a brilliant and talkative journalist – Graham Hutton of the *Economist* – was put in charge of it. He had been told about my work and we became instant and lasting friends. He asked me if I would occasionally help with items that rather overloaded his tiny staff, and wondered if I would care to join his staff if he could get permission to make use of me.

It was in this rather betwixt and between situation that Graham asked me if I could look after an important journalist coming out from the *Daily Express* called Tom Driberg and see if I could introduce him around a bit while Graham himself was out of town. After artful intrigue through Leon Stolz I managed to get an invitation for lunch with Colonel McCormick not only for Tom Driberg but including myself for the coming Sunday, which was 7 December 1941. About a dozen of us sat down at 1.30 for lunch in what was a perfect parody of an Edwardian gentleman's family Sunday lunch in London at the beginning of the century. We had only just got through soup and were still being served with excellent beef when the butler (who was English) came up to Colonel McCormick with a small folded note on a silver salver. The Colonel, looking every inch a military man, read the slip, which was an Associated Press message, then rose to his feet and announced in his curiously booming but almost inaudible voice, 'The Japanese have bombed Pearl Harbor.' There was a pause, in which I was able surreptitiously to find out what Pearl Harbor was, then the Colonel said, 'I must leave my guests and write an editorial that will rally the nation against aggression.' He walked out of the room leaving a buzz of conversation which rapidly became a hubbub. He did indeed write an editorial rallying the nation to a united chauvinist front against the enemy in the Pacific, but in the first edition there was no reference to Europe, though after Hitler's bombastic denunciation this was inserted.

After lunch I walked the hundred yards to the British Consulate-General and took out a draft report on the situation in the Middle West that I had been preparing for Graham Hutton to pass on to the authorities. The main drift of this was that Roosevelt was losing in the Middle West in his battle for American intervention on the side of Britain against Hitler. All the evidence I could gather from the press and the broadcasts, all the opinion polls (which were less frequent and scientific then than now) seemed to indicate that the American people and the American Congress did not feel that it was in America's interests to get involved in the European war. The final proof of this seemed to be given by a vote in Congress the previous week, which had extended the military draft of young men for another six months by a margin of one vote, and that after most tremendous pressure by the Administration.

I added to this a last paragraph saying that the United States had now been pitchforked into the war against its will. The American people were certainly determined to win it and would succeed, but would their objectives be the same as Britain's or would they be primarily concerned with defeating the Japanese who had, after all, humiliated them by carrying the war into their naval harbours? Would their objectives include a root and branch victory over the Axis powers and the rebuilding of a new world order that found room for peaceful progress and some diminishment of sovereignty?

After Pearl Harbor our propaganda/public relations policy was not changed in any radical way, it was simply intensified. Since our loss of the battle for France in May-June 1940 Britain had had to prove that it could survive – which very many of its supporters in America did not believe was possible. After Pearl Harbor we had to prove that we too were fighting in the war, as well as the American forces. This was not much easier. There was a certain camaraderie between the two nations but the mainstream of news was very American and therefore concentrated on the Pacific war rather than on the unpopular sideshow in Europe. As one got away from the eastern seaboard this became more and more apparent, and therefore the Middle West became the real front line of the British effort to retain the respect and firm alliance of the United States.

I was sent for a few weeks to Washington and New York to learn how the machine worked, and to report to them what was needed on the front line. Soon I returned to Chicago with an official position as Graham Hutton's deputy and found myself put in charge of servicing a quite new team of consuls in posts which had never had a British consul before. In my area there was Minneapolis, Kansas City, Cincinnati, and new British Information Services officers in the old consulates of St Louis and Detroit. These consuls were the cream of the younger crop of the Foreign Office, all aged about forty and clearly marked out for a good career by their appointment to these front-line positions. I found that they added enormously to our knowledge of opinion in the US and were very helpful in the quite new art to them of press and radio relations. It must be said that some of the old breed of consul-generals chosen to fill the existing posts as they fell vacant were not so young or so adaptable. I remember one on the West Coast telling a group of his fellow officers that he really had no use for the Foreign Office now, they had let him down in his hour of need in May 1940 when he was in charge of an office in the Low Countries: 'As I realized the Germans were approaching closer and closer to our office I sent an urgent telegram to the Foreign Office demanding to know whether I should burn my ciphers and code books or simply sink them in the canals. I got no reply. After two days, when I could hear the German guns, I sent a most immediate telegram asking the same question, with a reference back to my earlier telegram. Still no reply . . . So, of course, when the Germans reached us, they got all the code books.'

Some of the older consuls deeply resented the sudden dominance of the United States in the world scene, but the Ambassador Lord Halifax – himself a member of the War Cabinet and former Foreign Secretary – made it perfectly clear to all his officials that this was the most important diplomatic front for Britain in the whole world. He set out to visit all the forty-eight states of the Union, and succeeded by the end of his term in fulfilling his pledge. This was in great contrast to the admirable Consul-General in New York City who used to boast that he had never left New York City nor in fact landed on the mainland of the United States. His office was on Manhattan Island, his town home was on Staten Island, and his summer home was on Long Island.

Very early on I became involved in the quite numerous visits that Lord Halifax paid to the Middle West. They were meticulously planned by his own rather personal staff, consisting of his cousin Angus McDonnell, a Falstaffian figure who could reduce any group of regional worthies to helpless laughter and won their hearts with ease. The second member was Archie Gordon from the Ministry of Labour where he had become a trusted protégé of Ernest Bevin. Archie took the low road of looking after the trade unions and the women's organizations on these travels. He once requested the BIS to produce a paper for publication on how much war work was being done by women in factories, agriculture, etc. It was an admirable pamphlet but someone entitled it 'British Women in Labour'. The cover was reprinted.

The Ambassador also requested information from the local consuls and, where there was one, the local BIS. I used to give him

12

long, detailed and slightly humorous biographies of the extraordinarily competitive and curious leaders in the press and radio field (they were not yet known as 'the media'). He often used to have questions to ask over the phone before he set off or when he arrived, and I felt that these were the best organized Progresses since he had left New Delhi. I must say that I learned a lot from this which was of considerable use to me in organizing those comprehensive black books for Bob McNamara when he was setting off as President of the World Bank on one of his many foreign trips.

I also used to try to prepare my friends amongst the press for how to get the best out of a meeting with the British Ambassador. The first question that I was always asked was, 'How do you address Lord Halifax? As My Lord or as Your Excellency or what?' My general rule was to say, 'Call him Ambassador or, if you like, Mr Ambassador. It saves you a great deal of effort in getting complicated titles right and to be Ambassador to the United States is such an honour that he certainly regards it as being on a par with being Viceroy of India.' Even this foolproof method did not quite succeed. At a dinner in the Indianapolis Club Lord Halifax was asked at the end of the meal by the vast black head waiter whether he would give him his signature on one of the menus which had been printed for the occasion. Lord Halifax did more than that; he wrote a warm message of thanks and signed it with a flourish, 'Halifax'. The head waiter looked at this for a long time and accusingly said to the Ambassador, 'Don't you have no first name?' After a moment or two's pause, Lord Halifax, who was not very keen about giving people the right to use his first name (for instance he suggested to his daughters-in-law that they should call him Lord Halifax), wrote 'Lord' before Halifax. This pleased the head waiter much more than a simple name like Edward and he left the table saying, 'Praise the Lawd!'

The Ambassador was not a very cosy man, but he was an earnest and well-informed man. As a result, his conversations with intelligent journalists and concerned politicians were usually a great success. At the same time, he brought more information about the state of mind of America into the Embassy than any other man there. I personally always tried to debrief him when he had been in our area and found his judgments extremely good, though at the time they seemed to be slightly pessimistic about America's long-term purposes.

By the summer of 1942 there started to be a flood of visitors from

Britain, which had been held in check in the past for fear they would be denounced as propagandists trying to entangle America in the war, but could now be represented as allies sharing experience. The first lot to come were the military who were intended to explain how much Britain had been doing in the past two and a half years. Unfortunately this tended to grate on American ears, suggesting that there had been a war going on before 7 December 1941, and that Britain had done comparatively well without any active participation by the United States. This was not intended by any of the visitors but it was an almost inevitable result of senior officers talking in relatively non-military areas of the country. I personally found them something of a trial because they all wanted to see Colonel McCormick of the *Chicago Tribune* just to explain to him, as they easily could in five minutes' talk, that he was wrong to have been an isolationist. We prevented most of these meetings. On discovering that Chicago had more than a dozen channels of radio and was within easy reach of 100 or more, they were all also determined to address the masses in the same informative way. This could usually be arranged at a time when little damage would be done and probably conveyed a fair amount of good information to people.

But there was one colonel from a Guards regiment who clearly proved to be one of the Midwest's main allergies. He talked by prearrangement to a group of journalists who considered themselves somewhat expert in the strategy of the Second World War (like Dr Strabismus of Utrecht Whom God Preserve, the greatest of Beachcomber's creations, they had a set of coloured pins and were making free use of large-scale maps of Burma and the Pacific and the beaches opposite Britain). The colonel offended them all by being very chauvinist and boastful about that small part of the United Kingdom from which he came. But that was not enough for him; he insisted that he should do a broadcast. I really tried to find a spot for him, but he had earned a reputation which meant real trouble. Eventually, when he was threatening to ring up Field Marshal Jumbo Wilson, I reached a point of desperation and got hold of Julian Bentley, the news editor on one of the most powerful and well listened to stations in Chicago, WLS, the Voice of the Prairie Farmer. Julian agreed to my plot and we took the colonel down to the station, showed him detailed maps of how many listeners at peak time WLS could reach in an area almost 150 miles around Chicago, and took him into a well-appointed studio with a well-informed engineer. We sat the colonel down in front of the microphone and let him go. He addressed the prairie farmers as such for about a quarter of an hour, giving a rather personalized account of how he had so far prevailed against the enemy throughout the war. At the end we gave him signals – two minutes, one minute, and then cut-off. He was duly released, full of high spirits. We even gave him one of those early wire recordings and explained to him how it could be played to his friends in England. What he never knew was that the broadcast did not go further than that bit of wire because the studio was not at that time plugged in to the broadcasting system.

But there were some superb visitors, and I shall never forget the first time (since Oxford) that I met Barbara Ward, by then a famous broadcaster and a writer on the *Economist*. She gave lectures around the Middle West which wowed her audience by their mixture of Roman Catholic morality, English pragmatism, and almost Shakespearean rhetoric. It was the beginning of a friendship for me that lasted till the end of her life. Our first meeting was not wholly happy. She had come into the Consulate-General, where the British Information Services offices were located, a few months after a new Consul-General with a passion for security had taken over. He had installed a most complicated system of steel doors and wires and buzzers, etc. which were designed to make us safe from military attack by the Wehrmacht as well as more likely threats. On the day that Barbara was sitting in my office a shot suddenly rang out. I went to the door and found a man writhing in agonies on the floor, holding his foot, and another man waving a revolver and talking to our lady receptionist, who remained completely calm. I managed to get the shooter to sit down and hand over his revolver to the receptionist.

It emerged that the reason two civilians were having a shoot-out in His Britannic Majesty's Consulate-General was that the man with the revolver, who was clearly a loony, believed that the name Churchill meant 'ill of the church', and he was determined to demonstrate to us that we must not allow ourselves to be involved in the ill of the church. While trying to demonstrate this to the receptionist he pulled the revolver out and threatened her. What no one had noticed was that there was someone standing in the corner, reading our files of the London *Times*. He attempted to intervene and was shot in the foot. What was worse, he was an employee of the *Chicago Tribune*, of British origin, who regularly came over to our office to read the English football results in our newspaper file. He had not identified himself as a *Tribune* employee.

Then the second disaster struck. The Consul-General, with admirable promptitude, had thrown the switch to prevent anyone entering or leaving our offices; but no one quite knew how this process was to be reversed. So we were all locked in the Consulate-General with a homicidal maniac – luckily disarmed – and a perfectly innocent *Chicago Tribune* employee who had been shot in the foot and urgently needed medical attention. After a few moments' consultation we decided there was only one thing to do, which was to get the Chicago police to break in. Even more humiliating, it turned out that they knew quite well how to open the doors, which consisted of nothing much more complicated than switching off the electricity which had locked them. The police luckily concentrated all their attention on the man who had done the shooting and took him off, while sending the victim off to hospital without ever getting him to reveal that he was an employee of Colonel McCormick visiting enemy territory.

The best visitors from Britain were either intellectuals like Barbara Ward or Ernest and Sheena Simon of Manchester University, or genuinely the common man, such as Mr Hodge the taxi driver, who had just written a book called *It's Draughty In Front* which had been a bestseller in Britain. He came to talk about everyday life in the Blitz to rapturous audiences in the Middle West. He did so well talking to a group in the *Chicago Tribune* (their building was only a stone's throw from our offices) that it was suggested that this remarkable and humorous English working-class man would be of interest to Colonel McCormick himself. The Colonel treated him with all the courtesy of a conquering general who was going to strike the shackles off the prisoners of the earlier regime. He told Mr Hodge how, when he was travelling around Britain as a very young man, he had found that people had treated him as an inferior just because he was an American. Hodge looked at him with wonderment in his eyes, laid his hand on the Colonel's knee and said, 'But Colonel, any real working man would recognize you for a toff.' According to one of the staff who was there, the Colonel was really rather flattered by this tribute and they went on talking for some minutes.

There were long periods when there were no visitors at all, but the war, with its news and its difficult situations between allies, continued all the time. It was then that the British Information

Services had to do its job with the working press and radio of the region, trying to reach a fair number of the people and explain why their sons were involved in a war in Europe which ought to have been won by the British, leaving the Americans free to fight their real enemy in the Pacific. We did this chiefly by a network of personal contacts and very heavy use of the telephone.

I started at this time to get a regular telex of the BBC's British press review of that morning's newspapers, which came in at about six in the morning and was copied to about 100 editors, commentators and radio stations. This was regular unofficial information for a quite broad sector of opinion, but I also tried to get around the region and talk to journalists and editors of relatively small-town papers, as well as the bigger ones where Graham Hutton made an *entrée* for me. Our object in talking to these opinion leaders in their community was to counter the inevitable chauvinist bias in the general news about operations by, it seemed, primarily American forces, which really was not true in 1942 and 1943 in Europe. The best way of achieving this was to talk around how we as old hands in the war, from an avowedly British position, saw the unfolding of the military effort. An editor like Bill Waymack of the very influential *Des Moines Register*, which really dominated the corn belt population, would be persuaded to write the occasional leading article or the occasional signed column making the point that America's allies were essential to her and took some of the burden off the shoulders of Iowa's gallant sons. We were much helped in doing this by a service from the Ministry of Information, carefully labelled 'For British officials only', and sent out by us with a letter explaining that use could be made of this but not attributed.

In particular we found it possible to help radio commentators who had virtually no news services outside the AP and UP wires, by giving them something that was exclusive in a personal sense and which could make them appear to have a deeper knowledge than the common listener. In Chicago we had the really brilliant Chairman of the Chicago Council of Foreign Relations, Clifton Utley, who became NBC's main commentator, with a fifteen-minute slot on the BBC Home Service once a month. He was a very old friend (who lived, as I did, in the university area) and gave the British point of view in addition to the American point of view, often being critical of both. A similar tower of strength in the newspaper trade was Carroll Binder, the foreign editor of the *Chicago Daily News*, who ran what was probably the best foreign news service in America at that time. We never could really complain that we did not get a fair deal from either of these important purveyors of news and opinion.

There were also some oddities amongst the radio commentators whom we cultivated. One was Captain Michael Fielding, late of the Indian Army, who could always be relied on to give explanations of the fighting on the China/Burma/India front, and a very favourable, even Kiplingesque, account of the Indian Army. Another was Gerhard Schacher, a fairly recent Jewish refugee from Danubian Eastern Europe, who had a faithful audience in the Chicago area, composed of the very large number of East Europeans who resided in the city. Schacher had from the very first day of Hitler's invasion of Russia predicted firmly and unwaveringly that Hitler would be defeated by the Russians, even when things were at their very darkest and Hitler at the gates of Moscow. For this he was not forgotten and we tried to keep him in mind of the contribution to Hitler's defeat that had been made also by the British effort. Though he often maddened me by his insistence that the only people who were really fighting Hitler were the Russians, I think that during the war he was a force for Allied unity which was very necessary in a cosmopolitan area like the Midwest.

Finally, after 1 December 1941, we had the constant anti-isolationist, anti-*Chicago Tribune* new newspaper founded by Marshall Field (himself the descendant of the founder of Chicago's most famous department store), which was named the *Chicago Sun* but was normally known amongst its friends and particularly journalistic supporters as McCormick's Grim Reaper. There I made very close friends with the editor, Ernest von Hartz (a third or fourth generation of pure German blood coming from New England), and was lucky enough to find that one of the main foreign affairs leader writers was Bob Lasch, a Rhodes Scholar from my own college Oriel. Again, the *Chicago Sun* kept the flag of Allied unity and Allied involvement in America's war flying high and visibly.

Yet as I watched public opinion in the Midwest from 1940–5 I could not really say that it had changed its basic suspicion, constantly fed by the *Tribune*, of Britain and particularly the British Empire. It was the act of cutting itself off from the British Empire which marked the foundation of the United States. It was – as a Congressman said in the middle of the war in a serious speech in the House – the foundation of one of two systems of running the world: the American system which was the system of freedom and individual opportunity in a classless society; and the British system of worldwide domination of subject peoples for the benefit of a relatively few British aristocrats who oppressed their own lower classes as well as the coloured masses of India and the colonies. This ancient grudge, which ran so deep not merely in populist thought in America but in a great deal of the more respectable right-wing thinking (for example it was an important part of John Foster Dulles's foreign policy make-up), we neglected at our peril and ultimate disaster. The *Chicago Tribune* and far more respectable middle-of-the-road Americans kept alive a chauvinist, almost xenophobic, anti-British Empire feeling. While there was virtually no criticism of the French, Belgian, Dutch or Portuguese empires, even the pro-British liberals and New Dealers led by Franklin Roosevelt participated in the resentment and malevolence towards the British Empire.

What was special, I think, about the Midwest's approach to these problems was rooted in the recollection that in 1776 the United States of America turned its back on Europe; a geographical move which left them facing the task of Opening the West, and when that was completed, opening the Pacific Ocean to America's expansion-ist drive. Therefore the result of being pitchforked into war was to make the old America Firsters the supporters of a Pacific Ocean anti-Japanese policy. America First in fact, without changing their name or their basic policies, took over America's war aims in the Pacific, using China as the Asian base, and the West Coast, Hawaii and the Philippines as their advance outposts. The objectives of this Pacific war were to put America's interests first and if that involved some strategic imperialism – the taking over of islands which had begun with Hawaii, the possession of permanent bases which had begun in the Caribbean with Cuba and was very considerably extended by the bases/destroyers deal of 1940 – this was forgiven as necessary for America's protection, the prime objective of the Pacific War Party which grew out of America First. As a result, by 1945 American war aims were being established below the presidential level by the old isolationists – an inapplicable term at this point – working through the armed services led by General MacArthur. It was supported by the mass of American business-men who were determined to prevent the return of the Depression by a global American export drive. It was these men whom Britain and other American allies faced in 1945–7 when the death of Roosevelt plunged the country into leadership by a weak, unpre-pared Administration, based on parochial Congressional rather than national interests.

---2---

D–Day to V–J Day
1944–5

The beginning of 1944 was dominated for us in the Information Services by an uncertain future event – D-Day, the invasion of Europe. It was ordained from on high that every effort must be made to ensure that the American public fully appreciated the large part that Britain would play in the invasion, and our firm determination to be alongside the American GIs when the invasion of Japan took place.

So as to make sure that I would be back on duty in time, I took my regular summer trip to Britain in the spring. The build-up for D-Day was at its peak. On board the 'fast opportunity' (as the two Queen liners, *Mary and Elizabeth,* were known to Security) were 24,000 troops and three civilians. We three were regularly greeted by friendly derisory shouts of 'feather merchants'. We had a comfortable little suite with one saltwater shower of our own, and I got to know and appreciate Senator Pepper of Florida, known as Red Pepper for his radical views, and Edward R. Morrow, the flagship of Columbia Broadcasting Corporation, whose famous broadcasts beginning 'This is London...' won hearts and minds on both sides of the Atlantic. He and I had long and, I think, very fruitful conversations about D-Day and beyond, agreeing at the very least that the US needed British help to prevent something like the Blitz ever reaching America's shores.

The mood in Britain reflected a weary gritting of the teeth to get across the marathon finishing line – which was victory in Europe and the smashing of Hitler's Germany. After that, as I found in conversation with old friends, pub companions and at Oxford high tables, there were no great ambitions of empire or leadership.

Europe was under the heel of an evil emperor and the British did not look forward to any closer association with the Continent after the emperor had been overthrown. Of course there was considerable admiration for what the Russians had done, far more than the gratitude to America which was called for almost daily by the British government. But not many people wanted a more perfect union with either of these giants.

British people in general wanted a warm soothing Beveridge. Indeed, at the rather belated wedding of Sir William Beveridge, author of the report on post-war social services and now Master of University College, Oxford, I heard the perfect summary of the national feeling about the Beveridge promises sung to the tune of 'The Mountains of Mourne' by the *Punch* humorist A.P. Herbert:

> Oh won't it be wonderful after the war
> There won't be no rich, there won't be no poor
> We'll all get a pension about twenty-four
> And we won't have to work if we find it a bore.
>
> Oh won't it be wonderful after the war
> The beer will be better and quicker and more
> And there's only one thing I would like to explore
> Why didn't we have this old war before?

The British people saw two main scourges to be eliminated by all the efforts they had made over five long years of war. The first scourge was involuntary unemployment and its grinding poverty. That must go, never to return; there must be full employment, with a safety net to catch the handicapped and disadvantaged. The second scourge was war itself. That must be prevented at all costs by a world organization in which at least the 'Big Three' powers would remain united to stop any such folly as had landed us in two world wars. Hitler must be smashed, then war must be made impossible by a diminution of national sovereignty, and Britain must be one of the great powers that supervised this, along with Russia and America – but without broken reeds like Western Europe and China. British people felt they must do their duty to America and our Far Eastern empire in the war against Japan, but their heart was not in it – so all the polls conducted by the Ministry of Information told us. Neither was there the least enthusiasm amongst the under-forties for any action to impose imperial bonds

21

on India or any other part of the dependent Empire. It was regarded as a free association of like-minded people, who were lucky to get some of the best brains and athletes in Britain to help with their governance and sport; if they wanted to go, let them. But I noted that this rather flippant point of view did not extend amongst the over-forties.

The great D-Day drama, when it came, was not really a success for the British propaganda service in America. Almost inevitably all our careful background preparations were forgotten in the rush and excitement of the reporting and photography of the invasion. The photographs and newsreels showed the British and American troops as indistinguishable since it had been agreed that the Allied forces would go in with the same single star on their vehicles as identification. Probably most Americans thought that D-Day was carried out by a totally American contingent. But D-Day did more than enhance the apparent Americanization of the European conflict. It also made sure that news about the advancing Red Army in the east was very much downplayed in the American media.

The moods in Britain and America were entirely different. The Americans were convinced that victory in Europe would follow in a matter of weeks, and for them this was (in an earlier Churchill phrase) the end of the beginning. Their real war was against the Japanese and would take full precedence when the European war had ended. For the British, whose government was commendably loyal to the Allied cause and kept stressing their determination to take part in the war against the Japanese, it was the beginning of the end. Popular opinion in Britain was profoundly bored at the prospect of a long Far Eastern war, especially as it was expected that the war in Europe would not be over in a trice, nor would it be over without some further heavy sacrifices on the part of the Russians, and the British.

For the British community in America, official and volunteer, there was this problem of reconciling public protestations of unity with the reality of a divergence of outlook rather than of war aims. It was not easy to do when there were hundreds of thousands of Americans based in Britain and meeting with the ordinary, grumbly, parochial British working man and private soldier. The United States, in the middle of its third year of war, was confident, expansive, nationalist, and felt the vigour of its economy, which had been the marvel of the world, being restored as the arsenal of all the allies. Again, there was very little appreciation or knowledge of

22

the incredible feats of rearmament after defeat performed by Marshal Zhukov on the eastern front. Britain, approaching the fifth anniversary of its declaration of war, was tired, it wanted a better world order, by which was meant primarily a European order, and a quieter world with a fairer deal for the disadvantaged.

The Anglo-American part of the triple alliance was headed by two great leaders, both unrepresentative of the majority of the people they were leading inexorably to a victory they had long planned together. FDR was a liberal aristocrat, planning a world without empires and with a degree of international egalitarianism while free trade acted as the glue that held the structure together. Roosevelt was very conscious of the importance of what we now call the Third World which was then mostly Latin America and the colonial world. It was he who had pressed for liberal development measures in the charters of the Bretton Woods institutions. The great mass of American people shared little of this interest.

Churchill on the other side was an old-fashioned imperialist, who had imperilled his own career by opposition to the Government of India Bill in the 1930s, and in 1942 had proclaimed, in direct confrontation with his friend and major ally Roosevelt, that he had no intention of 'presiding over the dissolution of the British Empire'. He was an old free trader who after the First World War had turned to policies of imperial preference. He was far more aware than most British people of how weak the United Kingdom was, but he was absolutely determined to preserve its status of independence from both its major allies; but ultimately he recognized that everything depended on the Big Three remaining united to crush Hitler, and after that on the Anglo-Saxons remaining united to curb the USSR. It was to preserve the Anglo-Saxon alliance that he was determined to earn a throne at the Japanese peace conference and to use it to reclaim and control the British Empire.

British officials in the Embassy in Washington and in posts across the country could see how absolutely essential these two leaders were to holding the Anglo-Saxon and, indeed, the Big Three alliances together. They did not prevent divergence of view from arising and coming up to the Joint Chiefs of Staff level, but with the acceptance of the need for military secrecy they kept these quarrels from becoming the footballs of politics. Eventually, after a good deal of debate, and a certain amount of fudging of issues if necessary, Roosevelt and Churchill would tell their Joint Chiefs just what they were to do and to get on with it as quickly as possible.

There were only rare instances of the underlying rivalries, particularly Service rather than national rivalries, coming into the open. I do remember one press conference about the situation in the south-west Pacific when a four-star admiral was being questioned about the strength of the American fleet, and replied with some hauteur that the American fleet could easily out-gun the Japanese or the British fleet, or both together if necessary. There was a cracking sound like the breaking of a great sphere, which turned out to be only Jim Forrestal, the Secretary of the Navy, biting right through his pipe stem. Then, while spitting out the pieces, he said, 'The Admiral misspoke and that will be corrected in the record.'

At this time I was spending quite a lot of my working life in Washington, and in particular tried to attend the weekly Reports Conference (which under Isaiah Berlin's brilliant guidance provided the main political report for the Embassy) at least once a month. I attended with particular interest the rather long meeting in which we considered the results of the November 1944 presidential election. Roosevelt had of course been swept to power with a massive majority. The reports to the Embassy from the regions, and the general bias of the political officers in the Embassy, viewed the election as a battle between isolationism and interventionism. The conclusion was that the 1944 election had proved a massive setback for the traditional isolationism of Senator Lodge who kept America out of the League of Nations in 1919/20, and of Colonel McCormick who tried to keep America out of the war in 1940/41. Both Isaiah Berlin and myself protested that this was a rather superficial view of the whole issue and I remember that one of us (probably and properly Isaiah) sought to make the point that the scene was entirely dominated by Roosevelt as a fourth-term president and that the isolationists who had been defeated had not been driven from the field; there was every sign that they were preparing a comeback in what was still expected to be a long war in America's back yard, which was then the Pacific. We did not succeed for the very good reason that what interested the Embassy, and the British government in London, was how were things going to go for the next few critical months. As long as there was no threat to Roosevelt's mastery of Congressional and Washington politics they were content, feeling secure in the double alliance of Churchill and Roosevelt.

But there were threats. In April God took Franklin Roosevelt from the scene and in July the British electorate dismissed Churchill from office. Only Stalin of the Big Three remained. Three enigma variations were to settle the future of the world as the Second World War crumpled to its end: Truman, whom nobody had yet assessed; Attlee, who had never held office higher than that of Postmaster-General before becoming leader of the Labour Party and so gaining a place in the coalition War Cabinet; Stalin, who had engineered the 1939 pact with Hitler and had then torn the guts from the Wehrmacht at an incredible cost in Russian blood and treasure.

I spent the last few days of the war, as it happened, back in the Middle West taking John Miller, Graham Hutton's successor as head of BIS Chicago, round the newspapers of the region. The nuclear age for me began in Des Moines where I saw a handwritten poster outside the *Des Moines Register* newspaper, saying, 'America drops an atomic bomb.' I had little idea what it meant, nor did most other people until the next day when a massive information blitz descended on the puzzled American public. In particular the extremely detailed accounts given in the *New York Times* by a reporter who had been involved with the process for some time told us all that we needed to know about atomic energy and the fission bomb. It omitted to mention that both Canada and the United Kingdom had played a major part, though in the subsequent book somewhat more generous tribute was paid. The trouble was that we in the British Information Services did not really know about the subject and since the new British government, which had only been in power for a week, was equally ill-informed on the issue we received no guidance. It did not matter. Most of us felt an initial shock of horror at the extent of the casualties rumoured to have taken place in Hiroshima and, after a couple of days, in Nagasaki, but for the United States this was turned into a moment of extreme pride in their technical and scientific efficiency, and of muscle-flexing amongst the America First group who felt that it was now America first, the rest nowhere.

For myself I suddenly realized what hidden drama I had been living with during a great deal of my time in Chicago. My home in the university area was very close to the squash courts where the first nuclear reactor had operated; my room-mate in that house, Francis Friedman, had been one of the leading scientists with the Manhattan Project, who had brought Leo Szilard to live in our house for a brief period when the university residential club (the Quadrangle Club) said that there was no room at the inn – for the man who actually persuaded Einstein to come with him to see Roosevelt and explain the possibilities of the bomb and the need for association with the experimentation that had been going on in Britain. Leonard Rieser, whose family had adopted me as a weekend son at their lovely home in the woods on the lakeside north of Chicago, turned out to have been working with Robert Oppenheimer at the testing grounds in Los Alamos, New Mexico. The only Englishman I could find listed, which gave me some nationalist pride, was Nunn May who had more than once been to stay at my house as a guest of Francis Friedman. Subsequently, when he was convicted of passing atomic secrets to Russia, my pride of association with him was somewhat reduced – still, it made a good point to raise with the spooks whenever they were positively vetting me and asked whether I had any acquaintances of fascist or communist affiliation. Finally, looking at the crew list of the plane which dropped the bomb on Nagasaki, I was interested to see a very old friend of mine from the University of Chicago, called Fred Bock. I recalled once taking him to dinner with R.H. Tawney and, finding the conversation rather sticky, asked him what he really valued most in life. His prompt response was, 'Bach and thunderstorms.' He had certainly produced for himself a major example of his favourite form of art.

At the weekend I returned to Chicago and stayed with the Riesers until Leonard returned from Los Alamos and took me on the Sunday evening to a reunion party of those people who had worked in the Manhattan Project at both Chicago and Los Alamos. I found a number of friends present, all of them in a high state of anxiety about what use would be made of the bomb that had now been produced. Almost universally they felt that science was in great danger of being perverted for the worst uses of politics. Even more, they thought that mankind was in great danger of destroying its own life. In particular they were appalled by what many of them considered the unnecessary dropping of a second bomb on Nagasaki, and were afraid that since it exploded higher than intended above the earth it might have spread what we now know as nuclear fallout over a wide section of inhabited land.

Leo Szilard, with whom I had often talked rather philosophically about the future without ever realizing his influence on it, came over to me and said solemnly, 'We have been given the Promethean gift of fire. We now have the capacity to destroy ourselves or to turn this new fire to useful purposes, abolishing the misery of the poor throughout the globe and uniting mankind in protecting themselves against the gift they have been given. Today the clock's hands stand at five minutes to midnight. If we do not act quickly mankind will be condemned to a holocaust of fire. If we do act there are prospects of plenty for all of mankind; we could ensure the removal from the backs of the masses of their burden of poverty and misery. We must all work to ensure that the use of this capacity is for good and not for terror.' By this time I was fully aware that Leo was speaking over my head to a group that had come to listen to him in one of his rare public outbursts of political thought. Later I realized that this meeting had been, in effect, the first meeting of Concerned Atomic Scientists with their symbol of the clock face standing at five minutes to midnight. Today it stands at three minutes to midnight.

I had decided that I should get back to England at once for my postponed summer visit and found it surprisingly easy to get onto the *Queen Elizabeth* (returning for the first time to its home port of Southampton). There was no secrecy about this trip and there was plenty of space, so that I had a cabin to myself though I was sharing a shower room with Gene Black, a bond salesman from the Chase Bank with a pronounced Georgia accent. This also was a precedent, showing that commercial civilians as opposed to military and government officials could be well treated on the ex-troopship.

From this chance meeting there was a long trail of consequences. In a few years' time Gene Black became the American Executive Director of the World Bank and later its President for an unprecedented thirteen-year term. I kept in touch with him and saw something of the World Bank in his day when it was a small happy family working on manageable problems. But Gene always knew that it must try and deal with the unmanageable problems of poverty in the Third World as well. When I started the Overseas Development Institute in 1960 he at once showed interest in it and eventually persuaded an American group to set up a 'son of ODI', to be known as the Overseas Development Council of America. I was an honorary member of its board (it could not quite bring itself to have a non-American as a full member of the board) and had a long and happy connection with it.

Just as we were preparing to sail from New York we learned that the formal Japanese surrender had been received in Washington.

As the announcement was made over the ship's loudspeakers it was almost drowned out by a tornado of ships' whistles and sirens from the city. We had five days on the ocean to think over the consequences of our having won the war. What I was particularly interested in was to find what the consequences of Mr Truman would be for the peace, but though there were a lot of Americans on board no one had any very clear idea of what sort of a man he was. Then, on the evening of the fourth day, as we were within a few hundred miles of the British Isles, Gene Black got the news somehow that Leo Crowley, the US economic administrator, had advised Truman to end lend-lease at midnight. President Truman accepted this advice and lend-lease terminated that night.

This came as a tremendous shock to me but Gene Black sought to comfort me by saying that it was a move in the government's game plan to regularize and privatize international dealings on a peace-time not a wartime basis. He said that one could sell billions of dollars worth of bonds on the strength of the credit of Britain as a victor nation, but America was always allergic to 'foreign give-aways'. What was planned by his bank and most of the financial community in New York was to build a banking and business network that would hold Germany, Japan and Russia in check while putting American credit and finance behind Britain and, to a lesser degree, France and other European nations. This, Gene implied, was far better and more solid a basis for peacetime endeavour than purely inter-governmental links. I thought that Gene Black was an honest, honourable and truthful man with good intentions towards my own country, but I could not help wondering whether this was not the polite face of that scramble for buying up the world that I had heard described by some of my older English friends in banking and commerce. I was to find more of this critical attitude within twenty-four hours when I was truly back on British soil.

With the benefit of hindsight and memoirs we can see today that the sudden ending of lend-lease was a technical legal requirement of the Lend-Lease Act and a total political disaster intended neither by Truman nor by his Administration. It was a sign, as we look back, of the manner in which arrangements had been made by FDR when he could always rely on his subordinates following his intention rather than the letter of the law. But none of this was known at the time and the impact in Great Britain of this totally unexpected cut-off was absolutely devastating.

The day that I arrived in London I had arranged to lunch with Kingsley Martin at the *New Statesman* which had been pressing me for some time to do some writing for them, particularly on America, when I returned to Britain. I found Kingsley and his closest staff (Aylmer Vallance, Richard Crossman and Norman Mackenzie) in an uproar about the event. My own views were not at all emollient. I mentioned what Gene Black had said about this being a more businesslike and private-enterprise approach to the problem of international debt, but that only drove Crossman and Vallance into paroxysms of fury at the prospect of Wall Street taking over Britain and, indeed, Europe. They talked amongst themselves for some time about how they could activate their liberal New Deal friends in the United States and Dick Crossman particularly had hopes that he might get some support out of his old friend Henry Wallace. But in the end, like most newspaper lunch conversations, the matter came round to what they were going to say editorially in the next edition.

Kingsley had been listening more than talking and seemed to me to have fairly clear ideas about a moderate but tough leader (it turned out rather tougher than I had expected) and I at least contributed the title, a quotation from Winston Churchill in 1940, 'For years if necessary, if necessary alone . . .' But I did have to warn that there was a great danger that we could not find the money to restore even our pre-war standards of living, let alone our Beveridge expectations, unless we could obtain substantial capital sums for reconstruction, and the only source for this was North America.

But the *New Statesman* was no more upset or scandalized by the events in Washington than was Whitehall. On these occasions when I visited London I usually saw one or two ministers, but not this time. The new Attlee government was in more or less permanent session in the Cabinet Room. Rather advantageously I called on a number of old friends in the private offices of the ministers, and found out discreetly, for my discreet use, what their masters were thinking. Hugh Dalton, the Chancellor of the Exchequer, for instance, was apparently pressing for much more help from the US, otherwise how could the returning victorious soldiers be satisfied, and would the Americans want to see revolution spreading amongst its allies in Western Europe? I also sensed the tensions that were growing up between Keynes and his new political boss Dalton who seemed unaware of the fact that there had been long and tough negotiations to bring Phase 2 (as the settlement of debts and the arrangements for a grant in aid were called) to the point at which Keynes thought they could be swiftly implemented. Many ministers and newly-elected Labour MPs thought that the cut-off was an act of planned hostility by America against the new socialist government, and perhaps also against a Britain saddled with an empire.

I found to my amusement and delight that I was regarded as the expert on the subject of isolationism, its home the Middle West, and particularly on its manifestations in Kansas, the home state of President Truman. Amongst the numerous new MPs whom I met at this time I found that their greatest fear was not about Britain's bankruptcy (of which they knew little) but that Truman would repeat the disasters of Woodrow Wilson and America would sink back into powerful isolation. There was a very great deal of anti-American feeling in both parties, and a number of proposals in the governing Labour Party for creating a socialist Europe collaborating with the Soviet Union and providing some sort of balance to the power of the United States. This was, for instance, roughly the view of the usually establishment *Times* newspaper.

From the scraps of notes that I made both after conversations with private secretaries and in preparation for explanatory talks with people who sought me out to find out about that *terra incognita* the Midwest of America I think I have a picture now of what were the main outlines of opinion in the metropolis. From ministers downwards there was (with the exception of War Cabinet members) an almost total surprise at the extent to which Britain was bust. Winston Churchill had been determined to keep the public eye on the military victory, and not let it wander to post-war planning. As a result even the coalition Cabinet did not seem to have been very well briefed, while the enormous influx of new MPs, after five years in the forces, and of new civil servants returning to interrupted careers or now beginning them all felt like runners in a marathon who had just made the finishing line only to be told that there were another six laps against a new, fresh runner (America) which had joined the race half way through. They were angered by American power and they were terrified by the thought that the unknown but superhuman power of the atomic bomb was apparently in the sole hands of the Americans.

My response to those who seriously questioned me – as opposed to those who merely wished to abuse the Americans – was roughly as follows. The war had been won on the basis of a firm personal alliance between FDR and Churchill. That relationship was now at an end and there was no particular special relationship between Britain and the United States. There was considerable admiration for the British people for having stood it out alone but there was not a basic popular support for Britain, and particularly not for the British Empire. The United States had been pitchforked into the war, not persuaded that it was right to fight, and had little idea of what burdens had been borne for them by either Russia or the United Kingdom. The American objective in the war was, above all, victory over the Japanese who had humiliated and hurt them. They wanted to protect themselves by a ring of bases in the Caribbean and the Pacific, and to secure a renewal of their commercial hegemony, particularly in Latin America, and then to extend it into the British Empire which they had long felt to have been closed against them.

The danger in America, as I saw it, was not a revival of Colonel McCormick's isolationism, it was rather a new form of expansionism and, if you like, imperialism which would attempt to take over the world economically. We simply did not have the strength to stop them by any form of power, but we could perhaps persuade them that some kind of collaboration with their allies would be preferable to pure competition in which everything was stacked in America's favour, except that America would be exposed around the world to envy, malice and hatred. In a nuclear world this was a dread prospect even for the temporary holder of the nuclear secrets. It was easy for me to demonstrate, even to Russophiles, that there was no other source of reconstruction funds than the United States. But though we would have to argue, bargain and compete to get them, rather than receiving them as due to the only continuous fighter against Nazism since 1939, that was a possible way which could bring us into a respected friendship with the United States, and where we could play a leading role in bringing the countries of Europe, and perhaps of the Commonwealth, into a not very special but useful and profitable relationship with the United States.

I gathered from ministerial assistants and hangers-on that this line was not unacceptable to those making government policy, and I even received a word of thanks from Downing Street via the Press Secretary, Francis Williams, who was an old friend. I also gathered from him that Attlee was making his prime concern the problem of controlling the dread power of nuclear weapons. He was convinced that it must be done on a broad international basis and therefore he was expecting to go and see President Truman as the other partner in their manufacture as soon as possible. But already I had a secret dread that the new post-Roosevelt US would use its sole control of the A-bomb to impose its competitive economic system, and to ensure that it won all the hands in the economic game by using its total dominance in this field as the only belligerent not wholly exhausted.

I spent my last weekend before sailing back to America at my family home in Northumberland, where I was able to see my eldest brother and, even more excitingly, my brother Ken who had returned after five years in a German prisoner-of-war camp – somewhat disconcerted to find that the park in front of Feather-stone Castle had been turned into a large German POW camp. In the evening the commandant of the camp paid a social call. I told him casually about my new job in the Washington Embassy which would involve persuading the top opinion-makers that Britain was America's loyal ally in peace as in war. I added that this was not going to be easy, and the commandant agreed, saying that he had had some 'American security blokes' nosing around to enquire about this POW camp, which was none of their bloody business. He then went on to confirm that there was in fact something unusual about the camp in that the prisoners were selected recruits who had volunteered after selection to be trained as civil adminis-trators in the British zone of occupation. They were mostly young men in their twenties and had accepted that they would receive some de-Nazification courses during their training. It was dubious whether this could be altogether fitted into the Geneva Convention on prisoners of war, but the need for such administrators was too urgent for delay after the unconditional surrender had been put into effect. I can only add that thirty-five years later, travelling in what had been the British Zone in Germany and lecturing to groups of the Anglo-German Society, I had only to mention that I had been brought up in Featherstone to have the local mayor or municipal chief clerk come up and say that was where he was trained.

A few days later I left for America and was back in the thick of a crisis-ridden Embassy.

The Transition from War to Peace Washington 1945–6

The reason for the Embassy's sense of crisis was quite simple to see: a totally new set of problems was now at the top of the agenda. Not how to win the war, but how to settle the world after it and how to settle inter-Allied relations in a growingly competitive rather than collaborative setting. The whole personnel structure into which the Embassy had fitted under the aegis of the Roosevelt-Churchill personal alliance had been broken up and all of us from the highest to the lowest found ourselves constantly being met by new American faces who had virtually no personal knowledge of nor files relating to the agreements which had been outlined in the last year of the war.

Within a few days of my return there was a senior staff meeting which demonstrated how fast the changes were taking place on our side too. The senior staff in question were the top twenty or so of the Commonwealth figures in Washington. I had in the past occasionally been asked to attend, in order to bring some news from the Midwestern front line; but this time it was indicated to me by the Head of Chancery Sir Michael Wright that I might as well always take an unobtrusive seat – at the very back since I was by far the most junior person present. I would not have missed those meetings for anything; they were really informative because people let their hair down in the presence of a genuinely friendly and non-competitive group of people, and because they showed how the instructions from home governments were changing as fast as the international scene.

At this meeting at the beginning of September 1945 I could detect that though diplomacy is war carried on by other means, the weight and importance of the characters had changed enormously. Lord Halifax remained the dominant figure as a member of Churchill's War Cabinet and therefore as a past colleague of Attlee, Bevin and Morrison, but a lot else had changed. For instance the military headed by Field Marshal Jumbo Wilson no longer seemed the dukes in this particular upper chamber. On the other hand, some of the Commonwealth ambassadors appeared much more significant, as they deserved to do from their personal ability and the new international status their countries enjoyed as major independent participants in victory. There was Lester Pearson, the Ambassador of Canada, later to be its Prime Minister; there was Owen Dixon of Australia, later to be its Chief Justice and a considerable international figure. And there was Maynard Keynes, a rare attender of such meetings but, when he did, dominating the international economic scene as a world leader of thought. On this occasion he was asked to speak first since he had arrived only a few days earlier and was to hold his first meetings on the post-war economic settlements the following Monday.

Keynes was surprisingly cheerful and self-confident. He felt he had dealt with all the difficulties eight months ago in his talks with Henry Morgenthau, FDR's Secretary of the Treasury, and other people even closer to Roosevelt though not part of the formal Congressional and presidential hierarchy. He told us that he expected between $6 and $8 billion as a grant in aid to enable Britain quickly to assume a leading role in rebuilding free world trade and spreading it throughout the worldwide Empire. This was to be outside the arrangements made for the Bretton Woods institutions and was in fact to be a special reward for the longest battling ally, and a sign of the special relationship between Britain and America. So was to be the total forgiveness of all the long-running lend-lease accounts which were technically owed by Britain to the United States. There was some question as to whether this had not all been put at risk by the sudden cancellation of the lend-lease services, but Keynes seemed convinced that this was a legalistic approach towards the matter of the transition from war to peace and he had no doubts that all would go smoothly, as in fact it did.

Halifax intervened with a word of caution about the number of changes that had taken place in Washington since Keynes was last here, and gave some account of the surprising difficulties that he had had dealing at the top levels of the new Administration. Lester

Pearson supported this. The military voice trumpeted that every-thing seemed to be as good as ever on their side of the fence ('No wonder, when there's no war to quarrel about,' someone whispered rather loudly) except, said the Field Marshal with a frown, that there was still no sign of any Anglo-American liaison on atomic matters, but then there did not seem to be much liaison between the Administration and the American military on this subject.

Sir George Sampson, the Far Eastern expert and a man held in very deep respect by most senior members of the Embassy, was vitriolic about the relationship of General MacArthur to the Allied Control Commission for Japan, saying that he seemed to have assumed the title and role of an old-fashioned Emperor of Japan and that there was very little room left for us to make any interventions. So all we could do appeared to be to try and hang on to our own parts of the Empire and trust that they were not given away by the American President or the United Nations.

To mollify the debate Lord Halifax warned that the real test of the alliance lay just ahead: there were new men facing new challenges, and we must ensure that in America's hour of victory we were not simply forgotten. But in victory, he said, most nations do not indulge in flowery tributes of gratitude to those who have come through to the end with them. 'It might even be said that this was true of Britain and France.' But if we should not expect gratitude we should certainly not indulge in envy, malice, or any uncharitableness. With this little sermon we were sent off to get on with our work.

In the next few weeks I had the opportunity of getting to know my colleagues, particularly in the middle ranks of the Embassy, and found them an extraordinarily brilliant lot with, as it turned out, great careers before them. Perhaps my closest friend was Paul Gore Booth who like myself was a First Secretary looking after United Nations affairs; he was to become head of the Foreign Office in spite of having been earlier the leader of a revolt amongst the counsellors in the Foreign Office against the Suez escapade. In the room next to me was Peter Masefield the Civil Aviation Attaché who had come from a career in the *Sunday Times* and was to go on to become head of British European Airways and eventually of London Transport. Frank Lee, who was part of the Keynes entourage and a brilliant economic negotiator, was to become Permanent Secretary at the Board of Trade and later Master of St Catherine's College, Cambridge. Roger Stevens, the attic of whose house in N Street, Georgetown, was to be my home for more than half the time that I was in Washington, was the Secretary to the Economic Missions and later became head of the Economic Department in the Foreign Office, and Ambassador in Iran when Britain renewed relations after the fall of Mossadegh. Subsequently, on being offered the Embassy in South Africa, he quickly found himself an outside post as Chancellor of the University of Leeds. And of course there was always the warm companionship of Isaiah Berlin who then as now was the most brilliant and witty conversationalist and political observer of any community where he had been for a couple of weeks.

Amongst the senior staff – and there were at this time no less than six Ministers Plenipotentiary and Envoys Extraordinary under the Ambassador – I came to know Roger Makins (now Lord Sherfield) who was a very firm believer in a special and lasting relationship with the United States. He later returned in the mid-fifties as Ambassador to Washington and then took an odd jump – not wholly to his liking – becoming Permanent Secretary of the Treasury rather than the head of the Foreign Office which had always been his ambition. He also found his amazingly versatile brain being used to try and solve Britain's atomic energy problems with its partners in the US.

I probably learned more from Sir George Sampson than from any of the other ministers, if only because he was an expert on Japan and the Far East about which I knew all too little. I shall not forget that he was the first man ever to warn me against the perils for any country of intervening in Vietnam, especially if it was to be against Ho Chi Minh. I also heard from him of the amazingly imperialist doings of General MacArthur representing the United States government and its armed forces in the Pacific arena.

Finally there was the number two in the Embassy (and therefore the Chargé d'Affaires whenever the Ambassador was absent), Jock Balfour whom I discovered had married a rather distant cousin of mine from a Far East trading company. He was the most entertaining raconteur, particularly of Moscow where he had spent two years in the war, with the quaintest habits such as squatting in the lotus position on his desk when conducting meetings or, if he had a new secretary with whom he was not at ease, dictating from inside his coat cupboard. But he also had a serious message, which had a good deal of influence, that there was no such thing as One World; as long as there was a Soviet regime in Russia, that area would always be separate from the rest of the world. This was in contrast with Isaiah Berlin's approach towards Russia. Jock had been Minister and Chargé d'Affaires in Moscow before he came to Washington and he had seen the Stalin regime at its most brutal. Isaiah had been born in Russia and knew the people well and could describe in amusing terms the oddities of Soviet Russian life, for instance his well-circulated description of the Russian press in comparison with English public school magazines: 'There's a lot about the matches we won, not very much about the matches we lost and of course no criticism of the masters.' This seemed to make it, at least for British public schoolboys in the Foreign Office, a manageable proposition that we might be able to reach some sort of terms with the Russians.

The middle-level staff of the Embassy discussed Britain's strategic hopes and fears regularly but never formally. We used to find ourselves choosing a table with friends in the Embassy canteen and carrying on the discussion from where we last left it. My impression of the time, and it is still a vivid recollection, is how much we were influenced by the feeling that the atom bomb had made old-fashioned power politics quite obsolete. We were determined to carry out our own little bits of bargaining at the diplomatic tables, but we all felt that there must be a change in the international lifestyle. There must be less pure competition and more collaboration. There must be less imposed rule (of the imperial type whether Russian, British, French, American or whatever). There must be a more collaborative Commonwealth, including countries of very different origins and styles of government. In other words, our more cynical seniors would say, we wished for a brave new world, but how were we to achieve it faced with the Russian drive for mastery in Europe? How even were we to do it in the economic field in the face of apparent American determination to break up the British Empire and penetrate its economically worthwhile portions? How, we asked ourselves, could we in any way justify the sacrifices of the war if the victors were to bring back in their baggage train the old curse of unemployment, the old menace of unstable balances of power and, above all, the new cataclysmic threat of atomic warfare?

While we were all agreed about the threat of Soviet imperialism in Europe, we were increasingly aware of the danger of an economic hegemony by the United States in the West, Latin America, and the Far East. So much of what we had hoped for and planned for in the last years of the war – a greater collaborativeness through a reduction in sovereignty, a further global working together through the United Nations within which all major powers would operate – all of this now seemed to be being lost and we were returning to a more frightening world than that which we fought to prevent in 1939.

What was in fact happening was that within the Embassy and around the world there was a debate going on as to what the Soviet Union and America were beginning to reveal as their post-war aims. A group of us in the Embassy decided that from a British point of view there were three things to watch carefully: one, the financial settlement which was to be worked out by Keynes; two, the control of atomic power which we expected to be worked out in October by President Truman, Prime Minister Attlee and Prime Minister Mackenzie King; three, the global settlement on political spheres of influence to be enshrined in a series of peace treaties. These treaties would be drafted under the Potsdam agreements by a series of meetings of the Council of Foreign Ministers to which France and China had been added.

The returns began to come in first from the Keynes mission. At the very first meeting it was agreed, to our delight, to separate off the whole issue of the lend-lease settlement and other debts incurred during the war from the one-time special grant in aid to the UK. Frank Lee was assigned to the lend-lease settlement and the Americans proved so generous that in the eyes of officials they almost atoned for the manner of its cutting off. The grant in aid was left to be organized and negotiated by Keynes. After a few days it was clearly apparent from Keynes's comments in his telegrams back to the Treasury that he was far from happy and in fact deeply disappointed by the American attitude. 'I have been speaking poetry to them for the past few days telling of our magnificent feats when we stood alone during the war and thereafter, but they are not interested in poetry, they are only interested in balance sheets.'

Right up until the end of 1944 Keynes had always negotiated with chosen representatives of President Roosevelt on this tricky issue of the golden handshake for the bravest and most constant of the Allies. But now all that was gone and he found himself facing once again an essentially Congressional team such as had made the final negotiations of the Bretton Woods agreements so difficult. Indeed, at one of the later meetings to settle the Bretton Woods charter Keynes had allowed his sense of wit to wound the Secretary of the Treasury Fred Vinson by telling one of the delightful Russian stories which he had learned from his Russian ballerina wife, in which a christening party is ruined because someone forgot to invite the bad fairy. Vinson was convinced that this was aimed at him and for months afterwards kept on saying, 'He need not have called me a fairy. That's the last thing I am.' Once again on finding himself facing Vinson, Keynes made a damaging private joke in choosing as the code-names for the exchanges of telegrams on the negotiations Nabob/Baboon. Inevitably this leaked and Vinson was of course convinced that the baboon was himself. He was probably right.

What was becoming increasingly clear to us in the Embassy was that with the death of Roosevelt the US war aims were less for a brave new world than they were the view held by a Congressional/business team that there must never be another 1929 crash in the United States, and that meant that there must be no barriers to American exports. So the United States war aims had become free trade, free access to markets to buy or sell, and a free right to invest and repatriate profits, with most of which Keynes was in agreement, for he was a dedicated free trader. But there was to be no tempering of the wind to shorn lambs like the United Kingdom. Indeed, the US Congress's objection to the British Empire, especially the imperial preference closed system, was very, very deep. There was to be no real collaborative economic society, only a pure competition between partners in which one partner already held all the counters. This Keynes and Dalton knew to be a wholly unacceptable, unworkable proposal, so recognized by FDR and his Administration.

Keynes continued with this impossible task, not made any easier by the fact that he had very little confidence in the instructions he received from Dalton's Treasury. At one particularly low moment in the negotiations I was sent for by the Treasury delegation on some quite minor point and found Maynard Keynes reading the print-out on a continuous roll of paper as it came in from the cipher machine. One end of the roll was firmly put into one of the vast wastepaper baskets that existed in all American offices while he fed the other end through his fingers making comments such as, 'I sometimes think that late at night, when the Chancellor has gone home to his well-deserved rest, the cleaning women come in and take over the machine. It must be they who have produced this series of instructions for us, and I wonder whether I should let the Chancellor know just what is happening in his office.'

Gradually the amount of aid that Keynes had been promised in December 1944 based on an original request for between $6 and $8 billion as an interest-free grant in aid was reduced to $2.5 billion, repayable with interest over a fairly short period.

One November day I was alerted to the fact that the afternoon meeting was going to be a make or break affair and I should find myself a chair in the British delegation's serried ranks. It was left to Lord Halifax to make a very gracious speech which concluded with the statement that as the terms now being offered were unacceptable to Britain because they did not deal with the realities of the problems that six years of war had brought to Britain, His Majesty's Government must reluctantly make a break in the friendliest way possible and in full recognition of the enormous assistance given to Britain in wartime both before America joined the war and afterwards. 'We must now go it alone.'

I did not receive any instructions, though a careful enquiry by Security could have revealed that there were some nods and winks, but I went back to my office and after thinking it over carefully decided to leak that particular phrase 'Go it alone' to one print organ and one radio commentator. I chose Raymond Gram Swing for the radio commentator partly because he would be listened to nationwide by an audience largely sympathetic to Britain who might be outraged by this turn of affairs. Secondly, I gave it to someone young and infinitely less prestigious than Raymond Swing, who was a newcomer to the *New York Times* business pages. As I expected, his superiors did not believe that he had a firm and reliable source, and he was forced to ring up the British Embassy, asked for the duty press officer and was of course put through to me. There may have been half a dozen ears glued to the telephone at this point and I said, 'We are not making any statements about our joint meetings with the Americans, but I am not prepared to deny that story.' Presumably they then rang back to the Treasury Department and got some reluctant confirmation. Anyway, it was a front-page story in the next day's *New York Times* and within a short time was known around the world. It would be nice to say that this turned the tide, but it was not so, though it did result in recognition outside the perennially isolationist US Treasury, for instance in the State Department and the Department of Commerce then headed by Henry Wallace, a pro-British and particularly pro-Labour Party character.

The US Treasury was told by the White House that it must not kill these negotiations, but they were not told officiously to strive to make them satisfactory. As a result, after a few days the Permanent Secretary of the UK Treasury, Sir Edward Bridges, came out to tie up the negotiations in a decent shroud and a final settlement was agreed. Keynes was almost visibly wounded by his replacement.

The wartime debt part of the settlement was good, the loan was made as attractive-sounding as it could be by our united Anglo-American efforts. 'The real problem now,' Lord Halifax told me, 'is to get this wretched piece of baggage through the British Parliament and through the American Congress without too much damage being done to the vital alliance.'

We worked very hard with the new US Administration and I really got to like for the first time the information and Congressional relations side of the Treasury. But we were singularly unsuccessful in getting anyone to show any enthusiasm for this wretched orphan child. In Congress, which we observed closely from ringside seats in the Embassy, there was a field day for wholly irresponsible anti-British statements. One representative demanded that we should put the Crown Jewels in hock to pay our debts to America; returning Northern Ireland to Southern Ireland, or Palestine to the Jews, or India to the Indians were all part of the rich political pageantry of the Hill. But, as so often, the speeches were really intended for home consumption in Nebraska or North Dakota, so the Administration, which was largely drawn from Congress, was able to whip the bill through in fairly short order.

We were able to observe the debate in Parliament with much less care; there was curiously little attempt to keep the Embassy informed about what was going on in the parliamentary wing of the government. Eventually we got our newspapers and our copies of *Hansard* and could see that it had been a very tough battle for the Labour government to get the Bretton Woods agreements plus the loan agreement through either party or either House. The Labour Party thought that this was a takeover by Wall Street. The Conservative Party thought it was the *nouveaux riches* of America buying up a Britain which had bankrupted itself in the course of saving the world from tyranny. At any rate, there was a lot of cross-voting and I remember how furious Lord Halifax was with his Conservative Party – particularly in the Lords where he belonged – for their irresponsible attitude towards both the alliance with America and the future global trading arrangements on which he still placed a great deal of hope. What we only gradually came to

41

realize was how deep the split had been within the Cabinet: Bevin found the settlement very difficult to swallow since he thought that reconstruction was by far the most important part of the peace-making process and for him this began with reconstruction in Britain. Dalton simply saw that there was going to be no chance of carrying out the terms of the loan – we could neither pay it back on time, nor could it give us the capacity to fulfil the obligations we had undertaken, for instance to go for convertibility of the pound sterling in 1947, under the Bretton Woods agreements which were tied up with the loan.

The only effective defence of both agreements was in one of the last speeches of his life given in the House of Lords by Lord Keynes, as he had become. The vision he had of the future was indeed a vision of a better ordering of humanity's affairs, but the instruments with which he had been presented by a commercially-minded Congress were not adequate for the purpose.

Many of my colleagues, and I myself, thought that the loan agreement was really the nadir of Anglo-American relations, and marked the rise of a beggar-my-neighbour policy in international trade.

It was a very gloomy beginning to the year 1946 and I was delighted to be sent off early in January to Bermuda to act as the press secretary for the conference which drew up the first worldwide civil aviation agreements, the so-called Bermuda 1. It was a delightful place to have a holiday, and the conference was not in fact very hard work, but we were soon reminded of the dreadful albatross round our necks created by this loan now proceeding through Congress. As we were forced to concede point after point, both on international civil aviation and on the American bases in the Caribbean, I realized for the first time – something which was to dog me for the next forty years – the tremendous braking force of Congressional debate on making a helpful gesture towards a country in need but not in the desperate need of a wartime ally. Time after time we had to yield on points which we felt were really important to a decent organization of the civil aviation industry because our chairman, Sir Henry Self, who had been part of the negotiating team with Keynes, reminded us that we could not afford to offend Congress.

The regular American excuse, particularly from our old friends who were hold-overs from the Roosevelt Administration, was that it was essential to produce post-war policies that could be got through Congress, for to be defeated in Congress was to tread the path of Woodrow Wilson. We nodded our heads at what they said and learned the great all-purpose phrase, 'I hear what you say.' The fact of the matter was that the new Administration was headed by a group of men who had risen through many terms in Congress: the President himself, the Secretary of State Jimmy Byrnes, and Fred Vinson the Secretary of the Treasury and our main negotiating partner during this economic period. This was the new ruling class, and they ruled by a series of deals with their old Congressional colleagues. Truman had to learn that no president can ever be a real friend of Congress, but is rather its Chief Whip, driving this motley herd in the directions which he chooses for national or even global reasons. It was only then that the President could put on the front of his desk the slogan 'The buck stops here'.

We suffered another very minor humiliation with our first ministerial visit which was paid us by Philip Noel Baker, in the rather unlikely guise of Secretary of State for the Royal Air Force. His purpose in coming was to try and persuade the Americans not to put the United Nations in New York City, nor even in San Francisco, but to let it grow where the League was planted – in Europe and specifically Geneva. It was not a very powerful argument but it was made with great courtesy and sincerity, and was simply swept aside as being incompatible with the demands of Congress and therefore not to be considered seriously.

Noel Baker did rather a good job at a lunch I gave for him with the premier columnist in the United States, Walter Lippmann, and a few other rather more liberal columnists or radio commentators. I included Raymond Gram Swing and it was an extraordinary pleasure and an eye-opener to his fellow Americans to find out what a powerful impact his regular broadcasts from America on the BBC had made in Britain. Noel Baker seemed much more pleased at meeting Raymond than he was perturbed at missing the President. This was a period when we were thought to be trapping the United States into an anti-Russian posture so as to be able to carry on our perennial policy of divide and rule and thus save the British Empire. The liberals at my lunch party particularly were impressed by the obvious sincerity of Noel Baker as a member of the socialist administration in Britain in pressing all ways for some method of coming to an accommodation with Russia. His particular remedy for all ills was to get the Russians to participate in the 1948

Olympics – since he himself was both an Olympic runner as well as a winner of the Nobel Peace Prize.

Shortly afterwards Lippmann devoted his immensely powerful column to a story under the title of 'The Silken Curtain', describing how Britain was building up a revanchist German army in the West to fight against the Russians. The article created a sensation, in Washington at least, and I sought out the information with which to deny it. I realized almost at once that there was something to the story, because people were so reluctant to talk about it either in the higher reaches of the diplomats, or in the higher ranks of the military. Eventually I discovered that the real problem was the isolation and concealing of some prisoners of war whom we had taken over from the Germans – I now know better than I did at the time that these were Russian 'Cossak' deserters imprisoned by the Germans whom we were trying to avoid repatriating to a virtually certain death. In general we failed in this endeavour, but I believe that some on this occasion were in fact held back and absorbed into the miserable hordes in the centre of Europe.

I asked Lippmann if he would mind if I came and saw him to talk about his 'silken curtain' article; he was somewhat reluctant but perhaps because he had recently been my guest agreed that I should come round. We had a fairly frank conversation (and I do not mean by that a battle of words). It emerged that Lippmann had indeed received some information about our fiddling statistics on prisoners of war (I admitted that this was almost certainly true). He would not say where the information came from but it had been given him with a clear indication that this was an anti-Russian move. I then came clean, said that I thought that this was probably true but the circumstances were different and it was an attempt to avoid returning minorities which had already been transplanted by Stalin in Russia to death or what could literally be called a fate worse than death. With a sly appeal to Lippmann's Jewishness (though he was not a Zionist) I said that I felt sure that he would not wish to pursue this line. He gave no answer but went on to a second complaint, which came straight out of the blue to me. It was that the British were also setting up a special camp in Britain to train officer material for a revanchist war against Russia. He did not know the name of the camp, but he understood it was in a very remote part of the north of England. I then very simply told him of the conversation that I had had with the commandant of the camp at Featherstone, adding that the house in question was my family home. I could see that the coincidence surprised him mightily, and he made some notes, which doubtless he checked, and sent me away, warmly thanking me for being so frank with him. There was never any further reference to the silken curtain, and from then onwards Lippmann was one of my most regular telephone callers. We did not always agree, and we sometimes had fights, but there was never any bitterness and I regarded him till his death as a close and trusted friend, a true liberal in his view of the future of the world, and because he was not partisan one of the most powerful influences on the public and the establishment of the United States.

One of the results of the extreme shortage of dollars which was hamstringing Britain after the sudden cutting off of lend-lease and the clear indications that a large grant would not be forthcoming was that Britain's supplies of food became more and more difficult to pay for. There were two ministerial visits in 1946 to deal with this problem by getting a concessionary and long-term deal on cereals, such as we already had with Canada.

The first ministerial visitor was John Strachey who found himself unable to make almost any dent on the American party line which was that food should be bought and sold in an open market and paid for in dollars. The second was Herbert Morrison who did manage to get some promises of long-term access to American cereal supplies, but at no concessionary rate. The result was that Britain had to introduce bread rationing, and the British people found themselves on even shorter commons than they had been during the war. I remember that we received from the Foreign Office a detailed analysis of British food supplies, their sources and destination. What the paper wished to make clear to us and for us to make clear to others was that Britain had no intention of reneging on its promises of food to the British sector in Germany or to India where the Bengal famine was slowly drawing to a close. In a private note from some high official to the Ambassador it was stressed that there had been a good deal of debate, including in Cabinet, whether we should continue the supply to overseas countries, and both the Prime Minister and the Foreign Secretary had been absolutely firm in saying that economic interdependence must be recognized as the foundation of the post-war world.

How far this ideal was from the American popular mind was demonstrated by the two press conferences held by the two ministers. They were not successful and as the person who arranged them I must take a good deal of the blame, but I had not really expected from a group of well-informed but regular run-of-the-mill journalists used to covering various departments in Washington quite such ignorance or uncaringness about the state of the world. The questions at Strachey's press conference turned entirely on how it felt to be received as a prominent member of the British government when the last time he had attempted to enter the United States he had been turned away and denied entry on the grounds that he was a communist. With an opportunity of asking far more wide-ranging questions of a very senior minister such as Herbert Morrison, most of the talk at his press conference was about the meaning of his title Lord President of the Council when, as he explained, he was neither a lord nor a president, nor did he operate in a council; he added that his colleague Mr Greenwood was not a lord or a privy or a seal (laughter). It reminded me of an earlier occasion at the United Nations when, after long pressure, Molotov agreed to give a press conference to a packed theatre in the San Francisco opera building where the UN founding conference was being held. He made a reasonable statement, and then to everyone's surprise said he would accept questions. There was a long pause and a somewhat bibulous journalist asked, 'How do you pronounce vodka?' To which Mr Molotov replied, 'Wodka. Thank you, if there are no other questions. . .' and got up and left.

But there was one part of the Administration which showed interest in the world food problem. Henry Wallace, who was Secretary of Commerce and had been from 1933 to 1944 Roosevelt's Secretary of Agriculture and then his Vice-President, was not part of the Congressional mafia which was now running the government. He intervened with some friends of his (in the Agricultural Attaché's department of the Embassy) to try and find out just how serious this situation was for Britain and the Empire. I went along with some higher ranking British officials and found him a breath of the old New Deal globalism aimed at the eradication of poverty; a policy which was now derided as foolish idealism (globaloney and milk for Hottentots, as Clare Boothe Luce described it) and contrasted with the new, hard-nosed, pragmatic businesslike policies which were to dominate the post-war world if businessmen and Congress had their way. Shortly afterwards, for questioning the government's policies towards Russia, he was removed by the Secretary of State Jimmy Byrnes and soon afterwards was invited, with my great good will, by the *New Statesman and Nation* to address groups in Britain. But even there he was only accepted by the hard left and then for the reasons that he was supposed to be very moderate in his views of Russia, which was not the real basis of his approach. The ordinarily fair and pro-American (or at least explanatory of America) *Economist* magazine published an article entitled 'The New Statesman' about Henry Wallace describing him as someone who saw the world while standing on his head.

We were beginning to realize how totally the mood in Washington had changed, though not necessarily irrevocably. In Canning's famous phrase about breaking Britain's alliances in Europe, 'So it is each for himself and God for us all; for the time of Areopagus and the like is past.' America was anxious to run the world in its own particular way, ending empires wherever it could, establishing American zones of influence wherever it seemed possible.

The old 'special relationship' seemed to be withering and public interest in the post-war government of Britain, and indeed in the post-war future of Britain, seemed to be at a very low ebb. But still we had great hopes that a visit in November 1945 by the Prime Minister, though Attlee's presence could not be expected to rouse the enthusiasm of a Churchill visit, would be a significant and trend-setting advance, and I for one set about the preparations for a Prime Ministerial press conference with high hopes.

Attlee was clearly not accustomed to the arrival ceremonies for heads of government as they are arranged in Washington. After driving from the airport to the Embassy accompanied by a blaring twenty police sirens and motorcycles he said to the Ambassador, 'What a very odd way to welcome one, so that one can't even talk to one's friends in the car. Well, perhaps we can have a private conversation now.'

Early in the evening the PM turned up for a briefing meeting, very small and select, to which I, along with Francis Williams, the Prime Minister's Press Secretary, had been invited because we had a need to know. The meeting was held in an extraordinary cave which had been built for the Prime Minister in the annexe to the Embassy. By modern standards of security it belonged to the pre-musket era. It was largely built of wood and had some thin electric wires running along most of the planks. We were warned that the meeting would have to be short because the Prime Minister had to attend a state dinner in the White House. I noticed that he was accompanied by the slightly sinister Sir John Anderson who had been a member of the immediately preceding Conservative government and remained seated on the Opposition Front Bench though he had continued his job as the guardian of Britain's atomic effort.

Attlee was very brief and to the point. He said that he thought the most important issue in the world today was whether the coming of atomic power would serve or destroy civilization. Then, with a rather special dignity, he said, 'The President and I as heads of the governments which have control of this great force need to give the world a lead on how it can be controlled internationally for the benefit of all mankind.'

He went on to say that a secondary part of his mission was to maintain the Quebec agreement of 1943 which explicitly gave Britain rights to share in all the scientific work that followed the placing in American hands of our considerable scientific knowledge in the nuclear sphere for speedier wartime development of weapons which were to be used in the common cause.

The Ambassador was the only other person who spoke and he warned that President Truman was not yet in charge of the ship; Congress was in charge and felt that Truman was an old colleague no wiser or better than one of them. The same applied to their views of the Secretary of State Jimmy Byrnes and the Secretary of the Treasury Fred Vinson, as well as many senior members of the new Administration. None of these Congressional leaders – including President Truman – had known about the mid-war atomic agreements between Britain, Canada and America ('Nor did I,' interjected Attlee) and they still had no realization of the amount of the effort that had been contributed by Britain. They would instinctively be opposed to any sharing of what they thought to be their own peculiar invention, and especially after the Gouzenko affair (which revealed that there had been Soviet espionage on atomic matters in Canada) they would be very reluctant indeed to share anything with the Russians. Halifax thought it would be best to try and stick to the letter of our agreement which demanded British sharing with America, and could hardly be set aside. He also issued the regulation warning that we must try and avoid any sharp offence to Congress because it held the keys to the success or failure of the Keynes mission. The Prime Minister looked surprised but said nothing and gathered up his papers. Halifax added one word:

'I think we should be very careful about giving any publicity to these negotiations; it is bound to cause more friction than agreement.' Again Attlee was sphinx-like.

For the next day and a half, while private discussions took place on the Secretary of the Navy's yacht on the Potomac, there was a total news black-out, even extending into the lower reaches of the Embassy. Then, to all our surprise, on the evening of the second day there was a background briefing by Francis Williams for British journalists only. It took place outside the Embassy but inside the British Information Services' downtown office. The briefing was a very carefully phrased indication that Britain had called on its wartime agreement for a full sharing of atomic knowledge with the original partners. It did not say directly that this had been refused but it certainly suggested it to the numerous British journalists who rang me to get further explanations which I would not because I could not give. But in the course of the evening I was able to find out that the Prime Minister felt he had been hardly done by and had run up against a brick wall on the matter of our participation in the scientific progress that had been made since we handed over our share of the secrets.

This briefing had never been discussed with anyone in the Embassy, nor the White House entourage, and it came as a complete surprise to Leslie Rowan, the principal private secretary to Attlee. However, I was never quite sure that Francis Williams had not in fact acted on some laconic orders of Attlee, who was certainly determined to go on pressing for an international solution to the overarching problem of global control of nuclear weapons. Many years later, when he was widowed and living in King's Bench Walk and I had started the Overseas Development Institute, I had a conversation with the old man about those early days in Washington. He said that it was one of the deepest regrets of his whole premiership and particularly of his first year that he had failed to bring the United States along the path which would lead to world government. 'And it may yet destroy us all.'

The Prime Minister was asked to speak to a joint session of Congress which he did with his customary brevity and incisiveness. It was nothing like as good a show as Churchill had put up in the past when he was Prime Minister, but most of us felt that its description of what socialism meant in Britain did much to educate Congressmen and Senators who believed that we were now run by the Kremlin. And he had one little phrase which pleased me very much and was a sly, inoffensive dig at the isolationists: 'We in Britain have learned that we cannot make a heaven in our own country and leave a hell outside.' I soon had that in the hands of my internationalist friends in the commentators' ranks.

A few days later, in the House of Commons debate on Attlee's report on his Washington visit, Anthony Eden referred to this phrase with favour and went on to say that the only way of creating a safe world in the light of the bomb was for men to modify their ideas of national sovereignty. This remark was greeted with stony silence by his own Conservative benches and warm applause from all parts of the Labour government benches. Ernie Bevin, never slow to take a good parliamentary opportunity, later in winding up the debate remarked that he felt the only important thing about the creation of peace in the world and particularly in Europe was to concentrate on the international aspects of reconstruction and gave a warming account of the future of the working man in Britain and Europe if only we could concentrate our attention on these matters. Again I found ways of getting some of this debate, including some of the criticism of America, into the hands of internationalist commentators who could use it to indicate to Americans that their actions were not always received with unmitigated respect, and also perhaps revise their views that Britain was still the same divide and rule, hard ball, balance of power nation that it had been under George III and his successors.

On his last full day in Washington the Prime Minister spoke to the Overseas Writers Group. He said very little about the aspects of atomic energy and turned aside the questions on this, implying that he had no doubt about the US fulfilling its pledges. In fact, he clearly did not very much enjoy the company of a large group of critical journalists and as a result spoke more tersely even than usual. This would have been all right if we had not had three-quarters of an hour to fill. The speech lasted barely twenty minutes, whereas Churchill's similar wartime performances had usually lasted the full half-hour leaving time for one or two questions to be answered in his usual orotund manner. The first question came from General Sarnoff, the chairman of the RCA broadcasting companies. He asked somewhat lengthily – for which I blessed him – whether in the light of the splendid performance of American broadcasting during nearly four years of war the Prime Minister might see his way to allowing the BBC a little more freedom to accept advertising and thus expand its worthy services. Attlee

50

popped up from his chair and said, 'Not as long as I'm Prime Minister it won't,' and sat down again. I realized we were in trouble and started smuggling suggested questions from my seat at the high table to my friends in the audience. We got through nearly twenty questions and still called a halt slightly before the forty-five to fifty-five minutes were over. It was not a great success, but some commentators felt they had taken the measure of a determined character with the welfare of the poor masses worldwide at heart.

As we came to pick over the bones in the Embassy in the next few weeks and months we realized, and the Prime Minister realized, that on the matter of atomic sharing we had been duped. There were of course explanations for it. President Truman was anxious to fulfil the pledges that had been made in 1943 but he could only do that by giving way on what mattered to him much more, which was civilian rather than military control of atomic energy. He wished to be just to Great Britain and to the Prime Minister, whom he liked, respected and admired, but he was not yet the master of Congress by any manner of means. Congress had reacted most violently to a suggestion by the American Secretary of State for War, Henry Stimson, that there should be some sharing of atomic scientific knowledge with at least all the major allies in the war and probably with the United Nations. Any suggestion that the secret of atomic energy, which was held by the United States in sole possession, should be shared would never get through Congress. And Congress was too ill-informed to realize that while it was very difficult and expensive to manufacture an atom bomb, it was not a very complex scientific feat to find out how to and, if the resources were there, to do so. As a final result, the McMahon Act passed by Congress declared that the genie was to be put back into an American lamp and there was to be no sharing of its powers or secrets with anyone other than Americans.

Within a couple of years Russia exploded its first atomic weapon, and it was not primarily as a result of traitors giving away the secrets. The last best hope of what Attlee once called a re-ordering of the arrangements of humanity's relations with its fellow men had been lost. Of course it was not easy to assign blame. The extreme Russian intransigence in Eastern Europe and in the Far East made it very difficult for Congress to agree to any concessions there. The breaking of the atomic agreements by the Americans was explicable in the political circumstances of the time. But it did destroy the possibility of building some sort of alliance of weapon-holders

51

which might have eventually included other nuclear powers and would have been able to give to those who did not produce weapons a speedy and easy way of using 'atoms for peace', a phrase that President Eisenhower was to popularize. By August 1946, in any case, the McMahon Act finally brought down the clamps on this hopeful endeavour.

However much the government in London was depressed by the new face America was presenting in the sudden cut-off of lend-lease, in the failure to recognize or approve the agreements made, however informally, between Keynes and the Roosevelt regime, and finally in what was felt to be a denial of a perfectly formal agreement on the sharing of the responsibilities and benefits of nuclear energy, the British Embassy in Washington still tried to explain the difficulties facing a new and untried President and emphasized how essential it was that we did not drive Americans into isolation nor destroy any of the links that we were making with the new Administration. Above all, we sought to explain why public criticism by members or associates of the new British government, and the old Churchill government, would be far more damaging than useful. In all of this Ernest Bevin was a tower of strength. He was very loath to support the Bretton Woods agreements and the American loan of 1945, but he was persuaded that it was essential to the larger purposes of keeping America in the great game of settling the world after the world war.

Britain had not the strength or the economic capacity to make much of a dent in these negotiations (it was a very humiliating discovery for us all to make) but it could guide the negotiations into paths that were more likely to have fruitful results. This was generally known around the Embassy as our playing the role of the Greeks to the Romans, a phrase that had more probably been invented by Harold Macmillan in his Algiers days than by Ernest Bevin who would have been more earthy. But the fact was that we Greeks, with all our experience and wisdom, did not have much clout in moving the United States or (even less so) the Russians. The settlement of Europe which derived from the Potsdam agreements and was being carried out by the Council of Foreign Ministers at a series of meetings held in the capitals of the Big Three seemed to be running roughshod over the views of Great Britain as well as, of course, the attempt of the French and the Chinese to play a real role in these meetings.

In Washington we received all the relevant telegrams about these negotiations and the comments of the local British ambassadors, as well as sometimes the messages of Commonwealth ambassadors in the area under question. From these we learned a great deal about how things appeared to the people on the spot, and it was not very good.

In the Far East the United States, or rather MacArthur, was acting as the new Mikado. The United States was utterly irresistible in this sphere except where Russia had claimed territory and instantly put it behind their iron bars. Whenever we or the French or the Dutch attempted to do anything outside our imperial positions we had our fingers stamped on by the US and soon learned that the better part of valour was to get on with organizing the empire that we possessed rather than attempting to intervene in the new American lake of the Pacific. The Americans claimed as of right a virtually imperial tutelage over all sorts of small islands on the far side of the Pacific and we did not make any protest, nor even compare it with their attitude towards British or French strategic imperialism.

It seemed to us that in his last days Roosevelt had really designed the United Nations as a means of ending empires and bringing them into the same sort of relationship with their metropolitan countries that America had towards the southern hemisphere of the Americas. The local ambassadors or colonial governors or military governors fumed about this. The younger amongst us in the Embassy wondered whether Roosevelt had been naïve or immensely far-sighted. I think Lord Halifax had a feeling that it might have been very far-sighted of Rossevelt, but it was certainly not well thought out. For instance we discovered that he had been dangling Hong Kong before Chiang Kai-shek's eyes as a reward for being loyal to America, and the State Department always showed a bias towards 'liberating' India, on the grounds that it was in the common interests of India and the United States towards which India was expected to gravitate as its liberator.

Under Truman the doctrine was changed somewhat; the political needs of particularly the Far Eastern countries were relatively downgraded, but the importance of breaking up British imperial preference and allowing America to penetrate economically the supposedly vast markets of India, Malaya, etc. was considered supreme.

This was too much even for the leading advocates of self-government for India, which included Lord Halifax as well as some people in the Indian High Commission such as Humphrey Trevelyan, a political officer in India who had come to Washington as the Secretary to the Indian High Commission (and was to go on to become Ambassador in Cairo during the Suez episode, Ambassador to Moscow in the 1960s, and the troubleshooter who sorted out the Aden imbroglio, finally finishing up as a peer and a Knight of the Garter). Humphrey, who was one of my best friends and teachers on the periphery of the Embassy, used to explain that he was indeed in favour of passing the government of India to the Indian people; he was not in favour of slicing up the place to please American tycoons and enable them to take over the enormous markets that were supposed to be there. But it was the doctrine of the early Truman years that one of the objectives of the war had been to end overseas imperialism, and this was even elevated by Henry Luce, the proprietor of *Time*, into America's main moral war aim.

We heard rumours coming out of the office of Will Clayton, who was in charge of the day-to-day negotiations with Keynes, that he was waiting to see the British Empire and the sterling area collapse into bankruptcy – when the dollar zone could swallow and nurture its component parts. Mr Clayton, who was the world's biggest cotton dealer, could not be uninterested in his business life in such an outcome.

The war settlement in Europe, where the Big Three all had conflicting interests, was certainly the most difficult task to be undertaken by the Council of Foreign Ministers. It had begun badly in the autumn of 1944 when Churchill had met Stalin and discussed the division of the European countries under German occupation in crude arithmetic terms of a percentage proportion of spheres of interest. Thus somewhere like Bulgaria was to be assigned to almost ninety per cent of Russian influence compared to ten per cent of Western concern. Greece, on the other hand, was some eighty per cent assigned to Western influence and less than twenty per cent to Russian influence. Stalin never accepted these figures but he certainly read them with interest and it was not very surprising when in late 1944 a 'popular' revolt against the monarchy occurred in Athens and spread to the country.

Churchill reacted strongly because he saw this as an attempt by Russia to upset the broad agreements for the post-war world which he had discussed with Stalin. He therefore acted unilaterally to give his support to the monarchy and to the Regent, Archbishop Damaskinos. Within a week this was involving Britain in a civil war fought in Greece and drawing away British troops from the main objectives of defeating the Nazis. America reacted very coolly to any movement which was led by a king, especially a king called George. They gave very little help, and the liberal commentators in America began to criticize almost violently Churchill's reactionary policies.

In the midst of the civil war came the meeting at Yalta and a further attempt to make the settlement in Europe a reasonable and agreed affair between the Big Three. But the American public always believed that attempts to arrive at agreements in secret were morally wrong, and ineffective. From this period on, for a year or more, there sprang a belief that Churchill had been making secret treaties dividing up Europe, and attempting to sow discord between Russia and the US. (As one of the wittier American liberal commentators said, 'What this country needs is open disagreements openly arrived at.') It soon became clear to me from talking to American liberal commentators that this version of events was being sedulously spread around by James Byrnes who had attended the Yalta conference at the request of Roosevelt (though he held no foreign affairs portfolio whatsoever at this time). Byrnes put it about that he was the only person who had had training as a stenographer and had kept a careful note of all the Yalta discussions which should ensure his credibility against any of the rumour-mongers from particularly Britain. It was rather disturbing to us when in June 1945 President Truman appointed James F. Byrnes his Secretary of State. He continued to maintain that the British were the real villains of the peace.

Jimmy Byrnes was a conventional southern intriguing politician but he had been employed in senior positions by Roosevelt during the war and he had been within a few votes of being chosen as the vice-presidential candidate to run with Roosevelt. If he had been chosen I suspect we would have had a very much rougher ride after the end of the war in 1945. As it was, Truman could hardly ignore him and once he had made him Secretary of State Byrnes was a very important influence on the European settlement. He continued to intrigue – not very skilfully if only because I always learned about it within a few days – against Ernest Bevin whom he had met at Potsdam and thought dangerously belligerent against the Russians and a simple advocate of British imperial divide and rule. Byrnes shared these thoughts with his particular choice of columnist or radio commentator, and in a suitably ineffective form of concealment they came back from them to me. I discussed them with Michael Wright, the Head of Chancery and a very strict moralistic Wykhamist with long training in the Middle East for the Foreign Office, and it was decided not to pass them on to Ernest Bevin on the grounds that it would only exacerbate the conflict. I do not think we were successful in concealing them from him and the dislike for each other of the two men was a running sore throughout 1945/6. But we decided to try and stop the rot by making the columnists recognize that Britain was not quite the raging lion against its ex-ally Russia that it was represented as being.

I have mentioned the story of Walter Lippmann and the silken curtain, but there was another successful effort to stop an adverse rumour before it became an accepted truth. This concerned what had gone on at Yalta. On this theme I took a considerable risk but one in which I felt quite safe. I wanted to choose not a prominent national columnist, but a respected provincial journalist whose word would be trusted by his fellow editors. I had made close friends in my Chicago period with Lindsay Hoben, the well-established editor of the *Milwaukee Journal* which was a liberal, highly informed newspaper owned by its staff and published in Milwaukee which was the centre of the German colonies in the United States. On one occasion when Lindsay was in Washington for quite other purposes I asked him to save a couple of hours in the late afternoon to come to my office so that we could have a talk and I could show him some things. What in fact I showed him was the printed record of the Yalta conference as it emerged from the British Foreign Office. Lindsay, having heard the scurrying rumours that only Byrnes knew what took place at that meeting, was absolutely amazed to find 100 pages of *oratio obliqua* summarizing the debates that took place. Of course he knew that things must have taken place outside the conference chamber, but because he saw an actual formal record which contained at least one secret that had not yet been revealed (the fact that America had originally requested multiple seating in the United Nations to balance the three seats that Russia had demanded in order to balance the five seats of the British Empire) he was quite prepared to believe that there had not been formal agreements dividing up Europe. He kept the secret of having seen the document till his dying day (but quite properly not beyond that and made a record which was published after his death about twenty years later), but he was not at all loath to say that he had special knowledge which proved to him that much of what was said about Yalta was false and nonsense. He said this at lunches in the Midwest with the Inland Daily Press editors, and at the meetings of editors of major newspapers in New York or Washington; it did quite a lot of good.

In a more permanent way we boosted the circulation of the BBC daily press survey, even getting it rebroadcast on several local radio stations. The great advantage of the BBC press survey in peacetime, as we had discovered in Chicago in wartime, was that it gave a non-government-controlled account of the public debate in Britain. As a result listeners were treated to the passionate outpourings of *The Times* which at that particular moment had swung as far to the left as it had been to the right in the 1930s. It was constantly appealing for an understanding of the Soviet position, and it had good left-wing correspondents in many of the East European countries which were shortly to be swallowed up by Russia. With such an establishment organ speaking out in this way, who could really suppose that a government of the left was behaving in a totally anti-Russian manner?

But the British reaction to Byrnes's supposition that Russia and Britain were two equally guilty fighting cocks on a single dunghill rankled very greatly with the Foreign Secretary and the Foreign Office. It seemed to them that there was a clear attempt by Russia to divide the US and the UK and thus enable the Soviets to thrust forward. For instance, the American dislike of British bases in Egypt (a long-held dislike on which John Foster Dulles was reared) enabled Russia to make a demand for their own base in the Mediterranean so as to give them equality with the United Kingdom. We in the Embassy, and I think this applied to the Foreign Office as well as the Foreign Secretary, believed that if Russia was kept within bounds we could be friendly, but we could not accept an ally which was being encouraged to press ahead extending the bounds of its empire across Europe. This view was of course very strongly held by the US military, who were not, however, at this time in a very strong political position.

Then came the climactic visit of Winston Churchill in early 1946. His speech at Fulton, Missouri, where he had been invited by President Truman, made all our efforts seem rather small and, to be frank, rather misguided. The first I heard about the contents of his speech was at a senior staff meeting when Lord Halifax mentioned that he had had a telephone call from Winston who was staying in Bernard Baruch's mansion in Florida. The Ambassador said that Churchill had told him that he was going to say something pretty rough and we had better be prepared for some ructions. But that was all that Halifax was prepared to say.

I had a long-standing engagement to give a talk to an English-speaking Union meeting in Florida during the last week of January, and was not wholly surprised when Miss Randall, the Ambassador's secretary, asked me if I could possibly divert from my speaking point to Baruch's plantation and give Churchill a very private letter from the Ambassador. I said of course I was willing and would take it to the plantation by leaving a day or two earlier on my trip. I was not sorry during the Washington winter to get a few days extra in the sunshine. I never asked what was in the letter and I have never learned, but I was courteously received by Mr Churchill and handed it to him personally as I had been told to do. He read it and put it into his pocket and asked me if I would like a drink. I said I would.

There was a certain amount of paraphernalia about getting the drink ready and Churchill asked me about what I did at the Embassy. I told him about my work in informing the American press and radio and then, greatly daring, spoke about my unhappiness that there had been so little modification of sovereignty since the war and I mentioned Anthony Eden's speech in the Commons on this topic. Churchill listened rather moodily and then said, 'I have always thought it was a great mistake for the English-speaking peoples not to have a common citizenship.' He did not seem anxious to continue this line of conversation, and was clearly thinking about something else. Suddenly, after a long silence, he looked at me intently and said, 'There are some who say that communism and Nazism are poles apart. So they may be. But how different are those two poles? On one perhaps a few more penguins, on the other perhaps a few more polar bears, but over both blows a bitter wind which freezes free speech on the lips of man.' Clearly I was not meant to comment on this and after a minute or two I got up and took my leave and drove about 100 miles to where I was to give my lecture next day.

But that was not the end of that interesting phrase. After the speech at Fulton I was invited by Jock Balfour to a dinner for Churchill to meet some of his old wartime comrades in arms, as he always referred to them. It was a thrilling occasion and I saw many four-star generals with whom I had never hoped to sit down to dinner. In the middle, Winston suddenly began what I had come to think of as the 'penguins on the poles' speech. He went on a little further about the generally horrid situation that came to people who lived on poles and there was a murmur of applause from those seated around the table as they expressed their agreement with the old man about his views, especially as they were expressed the previous week at Fulton. But even that was not the end, for some years later, in his famous speech at Amsterdam calling for a European union, the whole phrase, by now considerably polished, appeared again. I was then a journalist and in the press bar I ran into Randolph Churchill and asked him how it was that his father had repeated himself on three occasions in my hearing. 'Oh,' said Randolph, 'he never likes to let go of a really good phrase. In fact he's used it dozens of times in the years since he polished it up for a rally in the Albert Hall which happened to coincide with the night on which King Edward VIII abdicated. The speech got absolutely no publicity and my father has kept it as a little item to introduce on suitable occasions.' I was later to learn that public men, generally speaking, have what we might call linotype minds which recall whole paragraphs which are useful for all occasions.

I did not go to Fulton though Charlie Campbell of the downtown British press office went to look after the hordes of British journalists. I felt that it was the American President's occasion and was his tribute to the man he probably most admired in the whole world. But I was touched and flattered to receive by special messenger a carbon copy of the speech in its authentic Psalm style – i.e. with the breath pauses indicated by lines, as in poetry. It was indeed an exercise in the art of poetry and rhetoric, but its impact on the world, where it exploded like a bombshell, was very diverse. On Truman it was a flash of vision such as he had not had during his presidency. In a way it was the beginning of the end for Jimmy Byrnes though he had another eleven months to run as Secretary of State, but increasingly Truman held him to a tough anti-Soviet line, and prevented him from slithering around as if he were playing American domestic politics. The speech intensely irritated Halifax, who felt it was a great waste of Churchill's commanding position simply to cut off any progress towards an accommodation with Russia. The Ambassador sent a note to Winston (which has since been published but was kept very secret at the time) urging him after Stalin's vitriolic response to reply by saying he was quite prepared to come to Moscow to talk over these issues. Churchill refused on the simple grounds that he could not be seen to be crawling back. Bevin also was irritated by the speech, partly I suspect because he felt it would make life much more difficult for him with his own party and introduced a measure of rigidity into the situation which was the last thing he wanted at this stage. But the Fulton speech was to some extent the passing of the torch in Europe to America; and it culminated in the Truman Doctrine of 1948 when the United States virtually took over the British positions containing the Soviet Union in Greece and Turkey.

Yet the immediate reaction of most Americans to Churchill's words was shock at the idea of an actual alliance between the British Empire and the United States which were seen to be permanent rivals or even enemies, though they could respond to an external threat in the strength of unity.

Stalin's reply was aimed entirely at the US public and especially at the Zionists. Stalin berated the speech for its British imperialist racialism and was not altogether unsuccessful in making the proposed military alliance seem a plot by the wicked British Empire to drag America once more into a war in Europe.

All in all, I think the Fulton speech brought forward the time at which the intransigence of Russia was recognized, but it is possible that it crushed in the bud some overtures to a European settlement which might have been worked out by Byrnes – under firmer supervision – and Bevin, with slightly less anxiety that he was being betrayed by his American opposite number.

The Fulton speech certainly changed the course of history, and at the time, with varying hopes and fears, we in the Embassy recognized this. What we were not immediately aware of, though quite soon the British Embassy in Moscow clarified the issue in its telegrams, was that Russia had been badly shaken by this rallying of the English-speaking peoples. It therefore decided on less direct confrontation in Europe and on rather gentler tactics in penetrating the soft flanks of the Anglo-American alliance. Almost immediately after Fulton Russia began its movements into the Middle East, particularly by refusing to withdraw its troops occupying northern Iran. Britain took a strong line against this, and the Americans with their oil interests in Saudi Arabia had to come in on our side.

I remember how well managed this Anglo-Iranian crisis was, owing to the simple fact that Ambassador Ala of Iran had only to walk a few hundred yards up Massachusetts Avenue from his Embassy to reach a private gate, to which he was given the key, and enter the British Embassy garden where he could inform and consult with Lord Halifax.

What we first noticed with extreme pleasure and a certain feeling of triumph was that Soviet troops in Azerbaijan in northern Iran, who had long outstayed their welcome and by 2 March 1945 had outstayed their legal right to remain in occupation, were quite openly withdrawn. Reports from the British Embassy in Tehran, and verbal reports from the diminutive figure of Ambassador Ala, told us that the uniformed troops had been replaced by political agitators, so that there was a real fear that there might even be a communist government at the centre and a dismemberment of Iran starting from the ex-Soviet zone in the north.

This was the beginning of the Russian attempt to break up the Anglo-American alliance at one of its weakest links – the Middle East – where UK and US rivalry over oil, their disagreement over the future of Palestine where Britain was the Mandatory Power, and their permanent contest over imperialism provided a wonderful opportunity. For the next ten years it can now be seen how the Russians succeeded in their efforts to divide the allies outside what became the NATO area, with the ultimate triumph at Suez when the USA and the USSR were in 'alliance' against Britain, France and the new anti-Arab State of Israel.

The USSR in 1947 began a very powerful programme of radio propaganda (supported of course by communist cells and Soviet Embassy press attachés) which told each audience what they were prepared to believe: the Arabs were told they were being sacrificed to United States Zionism; the Jews were told they were being oppressed by British imperialism; the rather limited number of British listeners to Soviet radio were told that the UK was being tricked and blackmailed by US oil imperialism, and by US-backed Zionist terrorism. The US itself simply had the golden oldies played back to them on the iniquities of the British Empire from which they had cut themselves off in achieving nationhood. The Irish and Caribbeans and others had it pointed out to them *ad nauseam* that Britain was a racialist nation which was always oppressive against minorities – such as the Jews, where they were rapidly replacing Hitler.

61

All of this was duly made available by Jack Rennie in his transcripts of foreign broadcasts from the BBC listening post at Caversham in Britain. It was an extraordinarily good coverage, though I believed that not enough attention was paid to it in government circles on the grounds that this was journalistic gossip rather than solid diplomatic information. But Lord Halifax, whose bent for appeasement might in retrospect at this time be called a realistic appraisal of what was possible, before the Second World War had quite ended advocated abandoning the British Mandate in Palestine and placing it squarely in the hands of the United Nations. His main private reason was that he did not believe that Britain could afford the deep quarrel with the United States which he saw ahead.

In the Embassy there was a great deal of opposition to this idea of handing the Mandate to the UN, and in the Foreign Office and Colonial Office in London even stronger opposition which certainly came early to the ears of the new Foreign Secretary Ernest Bevin. It was also quite apparent that the US government and particularly the State Department were opposed to such a radical idea, while the Jewish establishment in Palestine much preferred the devil they knew to a new incarnation wearing stars and stripes. But American Zionists were quite naturally hysterical about the holocaust in Europe and the destruction of six to eight million Jews in the gas chambers. The intense glare of publicity which was played on the relief of the concentration camps with their skeletal figures and piteous appealing faces quite obscured the fact that the Germans had killed some twenty million Russians whose bodies lay in the fields of western Russia and eastern Europe. The American Zionists used this propaganda to press for unlimited entry into Palestine, the Jewish homeland, for all Jewish refugees around the world. They then went further and demanded that there should be a Jewish state of its own, occupying the whole or most of Palestine. This proved to be the time bomb that the USSR had planted at the heart of the special relationship between Britain and America.

These demands, in their less extreme form, found a lot of popular support in the United States and Britain, where there was immense sympathy for the Jewish people in their sufferings at the hands of Hitler. I know that this was very much so in the broad mass of the British Embassy in Washington, though the regular foreign service and colonial service officers were constantly drawing attention to the dangers of taking precipitate action. I personally felt that the need to act quickly and decisively on behalf of the refugees who were attempting to flee their prison once the gates were open was very strong. However, Britain and its Foreign Secretary, and his advisers, were well aware of the fact that they had been given a Mandate from the old League of Nations to try and reconcile the demands of Jew and Arab in what was often called the twice-promised land. Intelligent and thoughtful experts on Palestine to whom I spoke (e.g. Malcolm Macdonald who had been Colonial Secretary and therefore in charge of Palestine just before the war, and Hugh Foot (Lord Caradon) who had been a senior serving officer in Palestine) argued that it was really no kindness to force the Jews on the Arabs without some prior consent from the Arab authorities, and thus condemn Israel to an Ishmaelite existence with every man's hand against her and her hand against every neighbour. In the light of forty years' experience I would think this judgment has proved true.

But something must be done and something must be done quickly. Judging from the telegrams we saw, a great deal of effort was put into persuading the Arabs that they would still have a share of Palestine but they would need to allow a larger number of Jews from Europe into Palestine. The Arabs proved fairly intransigent. They pointed out on all occasions that it was not the Arab states which had persecuted the Jews, it was a European state, the Jews were citizens of Europe which should take responsibility for the resettlement of the bulk of them. The history of the negotiations has been written in many accounts fair and unfair, but what I experienced at the time was the very great efforts that were made to get the Arabs to accept a larger number of Jewish refugees, on condition that we did not overwhelm them with a sudden entry of a million Jews who would certainly try to take over the whole of Palestine. In proof, the Arabs pointed out the reign of terror against Britons and Arabs within Palestine by the Irgun Zwei Leumi headed by Menachem Begin and by Haganah, the Jewish defence force.

What we were faced with in America was the extremely powerful force of organized Zionism which had decided that the new Hitler and the new enemy was Britain and particularly Bevin. What was surprising was how far this almost fanatical hate transfer was carried, both in terms of policy and in terms of recruitment of moderate liberal Jews. I went one evening to a fairly regular event which was dinner with Supreme Court Justice Felix Frankfurter, and found that there were only four of us present, Felix and Marion his wife, and Joseph Alsop, the elder of the two Alsop columnists. Almost immediately Felix, who had spent a year at Balliol College, Oxford, and had received an honorary degree from the university, and whom I regarded as a very firm friend of Britain indeed, launched into a bitter attack on Ernest Bevin whom he described as the true successor of Hitler, determined to produce a final solution by the elimination of the Jewish race. I could hardly believe my ears, but he persisted in this attack and it was only his wife's glances at me that made me realize that any real response would only make for a worse situation. I left early and in future meetings we managed to keep off this terrible topic, but it had taught me how treacherous the ground ahead would be. I never reported this formally to anyone, but I did have a word with Lord Halifax about the issue and that was when he told me that he had strongly advised dropping the Mandate before the war ended, on the grounds that the capacity of the Jewish lobby to whip up anti-British feeling was not only a real peril for the Anglo-American partnership, but was quite impervious to reason.

The organizing genius behind American Zionism was Rabbi Silver, and he worked from a base in New York City where the Jewish vote was absolutely crucial to the election of the Mayor and even to the state's Senators and Representatives. But he extended his influence throughout the country by uniting all those who for whatever reason were opposed to the British Empire. This gave him a rich harvest of supporters. At the time, he was able to exert very considerable influence by threatening to withdraw Jewish contributions, which went mainly to the Democratic Party and were a critical part of the money that was needed. The Rabbi was soon able with this hammerlock on the majority party to bring it to heel on a number of topics not strictly related to Zionism. For instance, he organized in Congress with Representative Emanuel Cellar a very strong but somewhat motley opposition in Congress to the American loan to Britain. This was indeed one of the greatest dangers that we faced and provided a very weak spot in our armour.

On another occasion, when Ernest Bevin was spending some time at the United Nations, we had seen fit to give him an afternoon off at an American football game so he could see something of the national sports, and be seen as a human being, recognizable as such to the majority of American people. But the game was in New York City and the Zionists had got in there first. As soon as Bevin

64

appeared in the box reserved for him and his party of British and American *prominenti* the crowd began to chant, 'Hitler, Hitler, Hitler. Who is going to kill the Jews whom Hitler missed? Bevin, Bevin, Bevin.' It was not a pretty event, and it deeply offended a large number of Americans. Reflecting on this particular incident I began to understand the basic anti-Semitism that had so shocked me when I first came to America and found myself having to sign a lease for a flat which contained a clause saying that I should not sub-let to Jews or blacks. This is all part of a forgotten past today.

In the Embassy we received many expressions of sympathy from officials who, however, warned us of the very real dangers of defying the Jewish lobby, just because these officials knew quite well that the leadership by ex-Congressmen in the new Administration could not and would not stand up to these pressures.

Bevin had been deeply hurt by the demonstrations against him and made a number of attempts to arrive at an accommodation with the Truman Administration, but never felt that he got onto firm ground. His main effort was to set up jointly with the Americans a commission under Mr Justice Singleton, a Lord in Appeal, to examine the problem, in particular the American requirements and the British constraints as Mandatory Power, and to make recommendations for future action. Mr Justice Singleton came to my office at the end of his first day in the Embassy and asked if he could have a few minutes of my time. I was very flattered that he should wish it, but somewhat embarrassed by his request. He said he had been told that I was probably the person who might be able to answer his questions with least official glosses. The Justice told me that he had tried to see the Foreign Secretary several times before he left London, but had failed until the very last moment when he had a completely unclear impression of what Ernest Bevin was aiming at. Could I enlighten him in any way about this? I really could not, but I tried to put him in the picture of the Anglo-American squabble and explained to him how important it seemed to us to try and defuse a quite unnecessary threat to the whole Anglo-American partnership. I do not think I did a very good job because he went away looking very troubled, as indeed he would have done if he had thoroughly understood the import of my answers. I had felt embarrassed lest I should seem to be trying to influence the judicial chairman of a bi-national independent committee.

The final report of the Singleton Committee was a grave document, trying to strike a balance between Jewish and Arab aspirations by rather complicated methods. What stood out was the suggestion of an additional 100,000 Jewish entries, which we all knew would upset the apple cart amongst the Arab residents of Palestine and their neighbours irreparably.

As soon as the document was made public, indeed actually at the moment at which it was made public, President Truman (we understood against all the State Department advice but with all the Zionist and Democratic Party advice) accepted the idea of the 100,000 extra entries, and totally ignored the rest of the report. It was this I think that finally disillusioned Bevin with the President, though he argued against Attlee in favour of getting the report signed by the US and the UK. This was done in April.

Some time later in 1946, after Bevin had painstakingly agreed a partition agreement with the Jewish Agency, which represented the Jewish community actually in Palestine, and after it had been publicly accepted with qualifications by the head of the Agency, Chaim Weizmann, Rabbi Silver dropped his final blockbuster. He addressed the Jewish Agency and persuaded them to overthrow the agreement in return for his promise that America would finance an all-out war to give the whole of Palestine to the Jewish people. Truman, faced by the mid-term elections, gave his support openly to the Zionists of America. This rendered Britain's position as Mandatory Power quite impossible.

Truman's blatant bid for votes deeply upset Ernest Bevin, as he showed in some of his private messages to Lord Halifax, and the Ambassador reiterated his personal belief that an Anglo-American alliance could not survive a quarrel over the British Mandate in Palestine. From then on there was contingency planning – much opposed in the Foreign Office – for giving up the Mandate to the UN. This period was also the nadir of Harry Truman's reputation at home and abroad and his party was heavily defeated in the November 1946 Congressional elections.

The eventual climax over Palestine came two years later (when I had left Washington, but kept in close touch with some of my friends at the UN and the Embassy). After Britain had surrendered the Mandate in May 1948 there was the usual UN quarrel about how to replace or restructure the situation. The US State Department argued first for partition, then switched to trusteeship and finally to a truce under a UN mediator; and at the climax of the US representative's speech to the UN in favour of a truce he was handed a bit of tape from the Associated Press ticker saying that there had been within the last half hour a unilateral declaration of an independent State of Israel, followed in fifteen minutes by President Truman's recognition of the new state. The State Department had not been informed, and the then Secretary of State General Marshall seriously considered resignation. Bevin was really furious, but, I heard reliably, he talked to Marshall on the phone and the two men both decided to carry on in spite of what Bevin always referred to as 'little Truman'.

The worst was still to come. Two or three days later as I was coming out of the Foreign Office where I had just attended the regular Friday evening briefing of the 'trusties' (i.e. the 'quality press' diplomatic correspondents, as opposed to the tabloids' lot, known as the Circus and usually entertained by Guy Burgess of the Foreign Office News Department), I was hailed by an old Washington Embassy friend who was now fairly near the top of the British delegation to the UN. He carried me off to his club (The Travellers of course) and told me his tale of woe. Everything had gone as badly as Ernie expected; the war in Palestine had already broken out, and now the Americans were trying to lay all the blame on the Arabs and especially on Jordan, Britain's ally. Finally, the US had proposed a resolution charging the Arabs with aggression under Article 39 of the Charter (all this I already knew in my capacity as 'trustie' representing the *Observer*). But what I heard next was real news and I was asked to keep it secret in detail though not in broad outline. The Foreign Secretary, I was told, had decided to use the British power of veto against the American resolution and would not yield to the anguished pleas of the Foreign Office that this was in real danger of smothering NATO at birth and destroying the Anglo-American alliance. Had I any suggestions about how to persuade Bevin or the Americans?

I replied that I would not try to persuade the unpersuadable. 'Leak your concern as much as possible diplomatically, not journalistically, but explain that the Foreign Secretary is absolutely determined, so our veto *will be cast*. With that knowledge most of the Security Council will be relieved to hear the voice of sanity from a great power and will kill the resolution.'

I have no idea whether my advice was followed, but the resolution did not get sufficient votes to be put before the Security Council. Britain abstained, but did not have to cast a veto. I strongly suspect that Bevin was calling America's bluff, which

67

rather too readily at this time assumed that it could manipulate the Security Council and even the General Assembly. That period was passing and with it the United States respect for the UN as the foundation of the post-war settlement. At the same time, the minor powers were beginning to unite against the great powers. Thus there was beginning to appear the break-up of the UN. The industrialized world was already divided into the Eastern (Soviet-led) bloc, and the Western (American-led) bloc. But a third force of the poorer countries was beginning to emerge, led by India (also a full member of the League of Nations long before it became independent) and the larger and more stable nations of South America. A whole new world order with a possible North/South, rich/poor rivalry was establishing itself as the pattern of the future. Realistic but not exactly a force for stability.

I had planned to leave the United States on my thirtieth birthday at the end of July (1946) but as I woke up that morning with a disfiguring case of chickenpox my departure had to be delayed for about six weeks until another 'fast opportunity' had space for me. I was not altogether sorry because it gave me an opportunity to go to Chicago and say goodbye at some length to my old friends there and to put in order some of my reflections on the job I had been doing for the past five years in Chicago and Washington.

It had been a most unbelievable opportunity for a young man in his twenties; and though I was only a First Secretary substantively, the departure of my superiors soon after the end of the war had left me with a counsellor's office and a minister's car and driver (for the only time in my life I was provided with a large black car with the capacity for flying a flag). I felt, too, that I had learned more in this past year at the Embassy than I could have done in a five-year course in diplomacy at the best of universities on either side of the Atlantic. I had, however, in 1945 agreed with the *Encyclopaedia Britannica*, based in Chicago, to return and take over their office in London as the European editor. I fear that my motivation in going to the *Encyclopaedia* was not wholly unconnected with salary. I was paid £2,000 a year which compared very favourably with the £300-£500 offered by two Oxford colleges. I also believed that being the titular editor of the *Encyclopaedia Britannica* would give me a better jumping-off place and more opportunities for entering journalism at the sort of level that I had become used to dealing with. On the whole I think this estimate was reasonably correct. In fact, before I left Washington I had an offer from David Astor passed on through Isaiah Berlin, to whom the first refusal was given, to become the Washington correspondent of the *Observer* – an absolutely first-class job. I refused it with very great regret but I explained to a sympathetic David Astor that I really was at that moment sick of the United States and very disillusioned about its position and policies, and even more I longed to be home amongst my own people, the extended family, the old school and university friends, and, to some real extent, the establishment which put choices before government and people in Britain. This was probably an overweening ambition, but I did in fact find that being part of a country where one could say, 'Well, I think the government is wrong,' without receiving the reply, 'If you don't like it here, why don't you go back where you came from,' was the real meaning of living in a free democracy.

My chosen successor at the Embassy was Philip Jordan, the distinguished war correspondent of the *News Chronicle*, and I felt sure that he would know how to get on with the press much better than I had. But in my jottings about my job, which were put onto a file for my successor, I pointed out that I had never been a journalist, did not feel really at home in that world, and saw that the newsmen were very adequately handled by the British Information Services downtown in Washington. What I had concentrated on was a limited number of prominent and influential columnists and radio commentators based in the capital. At the time they were a crucial part of the American scene because the tradition of American reporting was to separate news from comment and even interpretation very strictly, so that the casual reader of even the excellent papers spread around the country – like the *New York Times, St Louis Post Dispatch* and *Chicago Sun* – did not receive much guidance as to the full meaning of the events that were reported. Men like Lippmann and the Alsop brothers in newspapers, radio commentators like Raymond Swing, Elmer Davis (who had been head of the Office of War Information), and Joseph Harsch of NBC were an essential part of the public understanding and since they did not have news from the ticker tape to fill their columns or commentaries they were glad to discuss issues with informed people, not necessarily to repeat their views but to add them to the mixture which would otherwise have been almost entirely Washington official leaks and comments.

69

I used to give these people as we established a mutual trust a great deal of information derived from reading our secret diplomatic telegrams. This needed to be done with care and I only very rarely showed telegrams to people, but with the catch-all phrase, 'Seen from our point of view . . .' I could try and express carefully reasoned British points of view on events. How else were these commentators to get this material? It would not come in the normal course of reporting by radio or cable from London. Because the news items had to have some hard attribution I thought it well worthwhile to have what Stewart Alsop used to call 'the best warm leak in Washington' flowing into the curious and not always friendly commentators. So did the most senior members of the Embassy, and I was a more or less licensed leak. One day, however, it was discovered that I had never 'had the Official Secrets Act drawn to my attention'. This, it was felt by some administrator, must be done at once and the following account is a record of this curious event, written at the time but touched up in the light of events in 1955.

I was summoned to the Head of Chancery's room for the purpose (as his secretary put it) of having my security talk. I had not been so excited since a dozen years earlier my housemaster had given me (similarly belatedly) my obligatory talk on sex.

I was kept waiting only a very short time and then ushered in.

'Good morning, William.'

'Good morning, Donald.' (Though we knew each other only slightly we of course observed the proper Foreign Office familiarity.)

'I find you've never done the Official Secrets thing, and so I thought we ought to clear it up. Could you just sign this.'

I was handed a slip of paper on which I was asked to acknowledge that the terms of the Official Secrets Act had been drawn to my attention. I asked if I could see a copy of the famous Act whose terms had been drawn to my attention, but was told a trifle testily that this was quite unnecessary, though if I insisted there was probably a copy in the British Information Services library in New York.

I must have looked crestfallen because the Head of Chancery unbent and said: 'Look, honestly, it's just a formality saying you must never pass information gained in the course of your work to unauthorized persons.'

'Are journalists unauthorized persons? Because if they are, I seem to have taken a Trappist vow of silence which would not suit my temperament.'

'Don't be frivolous, William. Of course you should talk to *good* journalists. It's not them we're after, it's people who might make use of the information. For instance . . .' and he carefully disconnected his phone by pulling out the jack on his desk, 'I would always disconnect the phone when talking to businessmen, because of course our phones are tapped by the US government, and we don't want them to get all our trade plans. And one last thing, William, don't ever tell secrets to the French, they leak like sieves. Goodbye now, and be discreet.'

'Goodbye and many thanks, Donald.'

I went away pensive and a little puzzled, but I always feel I was lucky to have had my security talk from one so well qualified as Donald Maclean.

The group of commentators with whom I dealt were mostly based in Washington; a few were editors or editorial-page writers for the best and most influential papers in the Middle West. They did not include the best known of the radio commentators, men such as H.V. Kaltenborn, who were based in New York and dealt primarily with scoops, because they were handled superbly by Major 'Bill' Ormerod of the head office of the BIS in New York. He is alleged to have provided so touching a story of valour and hardship about Britain for one of the favourite popular commentators that he actually broke down and sobbed on the radio till he was hastily replaced by a message on haircream from his sponsor. Dealing with the more popular and highly-spiced commentators was a special art that Ormerod did with extra-special sensitivity.

But the flock that I looked after was of very considerable importance to the thinking class which tended – at that time – to congregate on the East Coast and was in danger of becoming a rather cut-off, old-fashioned elite. The importance of making them rethink some of their basic assumptions was that there was so little real thinking about global affairs in America at the time. The war had galvanized opinion into action, and after the action had proved brilliantly successful there was a tendency to relax into unconsidered supremacy and uncalculated hostility towards Russia.

American politics are indeed extremely local. Senators represent a state which may be an entity with a population not much larger than 200,000 and with very little involvement with the outside world. The House of Representatives, which is re-elected *in toto* every second year, is made up of members who have managed to win the good will of their district, probably about 100,000 people who are particularly interested in the affairs of their locality. They are more like British county councillors or borough councillors than Members of Parliament. The system only works when these very disparate but individual interests can be marshalled by a strong, secure president. This had been FDR's greatest asset. He had been President for three full terms and was beginning his fourth; he knew instinctively how to manage little local difficulties, even though his methods of management often led to corkscrew-like chains of command and a good deal of overlap. Truman, in spite of many years in Congress and the Senate, had virtually no knowledge of the outside world, and very little experience in the management of independent politicians except within the committee system of the Senate. But it was his misfortune to be catapulted into the position of supreme power for the supremely powerful United States before he had had any training in the tasks of the presidency. Even Franklin Roosevelt, who had been in the First World War Secretary of the Navy – a fairly international job – in his first three months as President managed to scupper the London Economic Conference of 1933 which was the main European hope of getting out of the disastrous economic collapse that had begun with the failure of the credit *Anstalt* in Austria. This act was at least as bad as Harry Truman's in cutting off lend-lease so abruptly. And one should remember that the glamorous internationalist John F. Kennedy, who had lived as a boy in the American Embassy in London, began his presidential career with the calamitous Bay of Pigs adventure, admittedly planned by his predecessors, but authorized by him.

Clearly the first year of an American president's term of office must be a very shaky period for the whole world, and there is probably nothing to be done about it. But it is at this time that the position of the independent non-partisan expert and public commentator can be very useful. Columnists should not imagine that they are entitled to lay down and execute policies for their country; but they should realize that they can point out to a new and hardly trained Administration, and to a public which voted on primarily domestic and local issues, what are the consequences of carrying out certain policies. If President Truman had given notice that he would be cutting off lend-lease in two months' time there would have been an opportunity for the public to consider just what the consequences would be. Maybe they would have been in favour of such action, but at least it would not have been possible for Truman in later life to say that it was one of the acts he most regretted in his Administration and that he had simply not known what he was doing.

I then considered how far the American scene had changed since Pearl Harbor and particularly since the death of Roosevelt. It was not a very encouraging review. First of all, as I was constantly trying to point out without a great deal of success, America First had changed from being the isolationist party to being the war party and now the victory party, with America's interests in the peace settlement always being put first, last and everywhere. The extreme unpopularity of Truman at the time that I was writing and the expectation that his Democratic Party would suffer sweeping losses in the mid-term elections of 1946 made this seem a *fait accompli*. The prospect of a Republican landslide in 1948 by either Thomas Dewey or Robert Taft further increased the fears that America would be not isolationist but more simply anti-Russian, and anti anyone's imperialism other than America's.

Looking back on Truman's first year in office it was difficult to see any hope that the United States would remain a good, close ally of Britain as it had been under Roosevelt. There had been no real gesture of support for the United Kingdom and its new government by Truman in that period. The only gesture that might be so interpreted was the forgiveness of lend-lease up to almost exactly the point at which the Churchill government fell; for all lend-lease after 1 August 1945 payment was to be exacted. The President's welcome to Churchill in his own state of Missouri, which was the occasion of the Fulton speech, was a tribute to Churchill rather than Britain. On the positive proposals put forward by Britain, the Keynes loan, which had been programmed during the Roosevelt period, was a bust. The refusal of any subsidized grain shipments to Britain's empty granaries, though perfectly logical in strict legal and commercial terms, was a cruel blow at an ally who had fought to the last penny of its reserves and now had to put its people onto tighter rationing than they had suffered during the actual hostilities. The very indecisive support given by the Secretary of State James Byrnes to Bevin in his attempts to agree with Russia and America some world settlement of the war issues at the Council of Foreign Ministers meetings made some of us wonder whether in fact the Congress of the United States had decided to settle its ancient grudge against the British Empire before it turned to deal with Russia. What rankled most with the British government but not with the general public which was not fully informed was the betrayal of the 1943 promises in the Quebec agreement about the sharing of atomic secrets with Britain and Canada.

All of this fed anti-American feeling at all levels in Britain, and I certainly got an earful of it on my return at the *New Statesman and Nation*. I shared a great deal of the feeling but I still believed that only the United States could defend us from a continuance of the drive across the Continent by Russia. Nor could I see any other source of funds for British or European reconstruction. I deeply feared that support for defence and reconstruction would lapse under a Taft or Dewey presidency, or would be made conditional on a partnership in anti-Russian policy beginning with the use of nuclear threats or weapons against the Soviet Union. As I was to learn later, this was being urged on the Americans at this time by Winston Churchill. Like many of my erstwhile colleagues in the Embassy and Whitehall I felt great relief in January 1947 when Byrnes was replaced by General Marshall as Secretary of State. No one that I knew had anything but the deepest admiration for Marshall's principles and practice. But President Truman's behaviour over Palestine (which very nearly led to Marshall's resignation in protest) made us feel that Truman was a small-time politician pushed into prominence by a mischievous Providence.

---4---

The Rescue of Europe
1946–9

I got back to England after an uneventful voyage on one of the Queens at the beginning of September, and decided that as the youngest in a family of six I should really spend a month trying to make contact with them all again. It was an education because they had led such different lives in the war, yet were all picking up the threads of peacetime existence roughly where they had left them in 1939. At least I was broken into the post-war rationing system (far more extreme than in the height of the war) in a quite comfortable manner. Nearly all my family lived in the fairly rich farming country around the Roman wall and along the south Tyne. Ration goods from the shops were as skimpy as ever, but even through the war people had been able to keep their own chickens, eat their own eggs, and occasionally even share one of their own sheep with family or friends.

I went to stay first with Ken, the brother who had been a prisoner of war virtually throughout the hostilities; he was in fact captured on about 12 or 13 May in the beginning of the Dunkirk debacle, and only released in mid-May of 1945 after a full five years in duress. Not unnaturally he felt quite strongly that the best part of his youth (he was now thirty-four) had been taken away from him, and he blamed both the enemy and most of his allies. He quite simply hated the Germans, not on a personal basis but on the grounds that their government started the war and put him in prison unjustly; he despised the French whose broken lines had left him without support and gave the Germans their breakthrough in which he was knocked out and then made a prisoner. He also had a good deal of ill will towards the Low Countries which had not, he felt, been very supportive of the British effort, while the Americans had come into the war too late and were how hogging all the credit while they were refusing to lend us money or sell us their abundant food on concessionary terms. I was to find as I went around the country that this attitude was not untypical. It seemed to very many English people that we had won the war and received very little thanks for it; more sophisticated appraisals only said that we had held the line while others came in, and were given very little credit for that too.

My eldest brother John had moved back into the home where I was born (called Bellister Castle), surrendering Featherstone Castle to the prep school evacuated from Rugby where all us boys had been educated before the Second World War. The headmaster there was my godfather – he had been a junior master at the same prep school when it was evacuated in the First World War to Featherstone from the north-east coast of Northumberland where I was born – and Ken's 'elder' twin had married the headmaster's daughter and was about to take over the school. John had never been abroad before that day when he commanded his battalion of the Northumberland Fusiliers on their march through France towards the Belgian border, and within a few weeks of arriving there he was a gallant leader of the retreat through Dunkirk. On arrival back in England, without any sleep in a bed or even a recumbent posture, he was efficiently transported with the remnants of his battalion to the railway station nearest to our various fortified farmhouses which were what our castles really were. John dropped into bed at about eleven at night absolutely exhausted and was still sleeping soundly at 8.30 in the morning when his wife awoke him to say that the whole parish council had assembled below stairs to congratulate him on his safe return. He should have known better than to go down in his dressing gown, but maybe the war had put such things out of his mind. After a very brief word of congratulations on his safe return the chairman of the parish council turned to him with a glowering look and said, 'Colonel John, there is one more serious matter that we have to raise with you. The new vicar whom you helped to bring here has started to use candles on the altar. We can't stand much more of this.' My brother tried to still the waves of emotion but, as I remember, the vicar was transferred to a rather Higher Church in the diocese. The parish was not going to have its faith subverted by enemies domestic or foreign.

John too shared a lot of the isolationist views of that area of the north of England. His particular hatred was more directed against the Russians and the socialists, which of course included the government of the day which it was thought (correctly) was about to bring in an act for town and country planning that seemed tantamount to nationalization of the land to my brothers. Though a trifle extreme, my eldest brother was not untypical of most of the landowners and officer class of the district. They felt betrayed by the throwing out of the Conservative Party and the coming in to government of the socialists. There was, however, no attempt that I ever heard discussed of trying in any way to reverse the electoral process. Some of the Conservatives of my acquaintance simply blamed it all on the Army Bureau of Current Affairs which had been teaching socialism in their courses throughout the war; others who took a rather more desperate view decided to leave for the sunnier climes of Africa (officers to Kenya, NCOs to Rhodesia) or if it were possible they tried to go to Canada or the United States. The US was not popular, but it was known to be rich, and Canada was quite popular but it was known to be cold.

We were joined at Bellister Castle by my sister Elizabeth and her husband Dennis Herbert who had spent the years since they crossed Europe in June 1940 teaching at the best educational establishment in Uganda, King's College, Budo. They were soon to return to their first love in Africa which was the Gold Coast where Dennis had been one of the founding fathers of Achimota College and had a special charge of someone of whom he often spoke but of whom none of us knew anything, Kwame Nkrumah. They added a quite new element to our conversation which was a consideration of what the black African (as opposed to settler-dominated) states saw as their future. I remember my sister insisting that no Africans who had fought in British contingents during the war, particularly in Asia, would be quite the same again after having seen as their enemies but equals such relatively unsophisticated peoples as the Burmese who were claiming that with Japanese help they were fighting for their own freedom. Dennis agreed that this had had a profound effect on the thinking particularly of Ghanaians who had made up a large contingent in the war in Burma and in confidence to me dared to predict that many of these African states would be self-governing and probably even independent by the year 2000.

In fact Northumberland was very isolated and mostly isolationist. The other ranks who were pouring back after demobilization,

77

and their families who were still known as the working class, had a
very poor opinion of most of the rest of the world. They had been
abroad and saw that it did not work – i.e. it could not defend itself,
nor rescue itself from the German tyranny. Many European
countries tried desperately to arrive at some sort of political
connection with Britain (Norway had private conversations about
becoming part of the Commonwealth, and the Netherlands was also
making enquiries in the same direction), but the British people
were not at all welcoming. They regarded the French as having let
them down, they regarded the neutrals as yellow-bellied, they
regarded the defeated Axis with real hatred, even if there was a
slight exception in favour of the Italian prisoners of war who were
such cheerful blokes and were very helpful in staying on after they
might have been released and lending a hand with our harvests.
The attitude towards the United States was somewhat ambivalent.
Friendship and respect had grown up for Americans billeted in
Britain before D-Day but they were very much a race apart and
living at a considerably higher standard than the British around
them though always prepared to do some sharing. The United
States as a nation was not very highly regarded at this time: the
breaking off of lend-lease and the refusal to provide concessionary
food supplies led to a feeling that the Americans were unfairly
throwing their weight around. In fact the majority of British people
probably simply wanted a quick demob, the full benefits of
Beveridge and, above all, a steady job with no prospects of
long-term unemployment. There was, it seemed to me, a surprisingly dim realization of the economic position that Britain was in
and the need to get fairly massive sources of funds to reconstruct
and push ahead with a new modern Britain.

I reassured myself that this was the ignorance of the British rural
population and as I set off in October 1946 for London and a
working life I fully expected to find a different, more sophisticated
attitude. But in London I was to find how desperately damaged the
whole fabric of society had been by the Blitz, by the constant
anxiety and difficulties put in the way of leading any normal life,
and the far greater impact of rationing in the cities than in the
countryside. In writing, not without a lively expectation of favours
to come, to my American friends I find such remarks as 'We all had
an egg for Christmas but we won't get another one till February
. . . You can't get replacements for such things as radios, and it is
really very difficult to get any consumer goods such as one could

find so easily in any Chicago drugstore when I was last there.'

There was indeed a dreadful shortage of almost everything and the ease with which one could see how much better people lived in America in their glossy magazines or their films did make for a certain amount of bitterness. Who was really to blame for this sad state of affairs after the victory? Of course some people blamed the Labour government, particularly Mr Shinwell who was in the unlucky position of being Minister of Fuel during that winter of 1946/7, but on the whole there was no real revolt against the Labour Party or Attlee. It was much easier to find outside, foreign devils to blame. Some people would do this by complaining of the fact that we did not have a proper peace yet because of the way the Russians were behaving in Eastern Europe, but sadly it was the Americans who came in for most of the muttered comment about why we were deprived of food and fuel, and money to buy food where it was plentiful.

All of these Anglo-American problems struck me with their full force as soon as I settled down to doing some work. The first task before me (which did after all pay me my living wage) was to come to grips with the problems of the *Encyclopaedia Britannica*. It had been bought by Americans during the First World War (when they had failed to buy *The Times* newspaper in which the *Britannica* had been lodged during the production of the eleventh edition) but its editorial offices remained under the control of the British and finally under the control of J.L. Garvin. In the course of time the copyright had been transferred to Sears Roebuck (the largest of the American merchandising mail order firms) and for long sales in America had greatly outstripped the sales in Britain, so eventually the printing went over to America. The copyright of the *Britannica* was subsequently bought by Bill Benton (later Senator Benton of Connecticut). Having made his fortune by inventing singing commercials on radio and establishing one of the biggest American advertising organizations, called Benton and Bowls (Bowls was later Ambassador to India after the Second World War), Benton decided to turn from good words to good works, which he did with an admirable devotion to duty. He attached his flag to Robert Hutchins, the young president of the University of Chicago, and amongst many other generous deeds gave the copyright of the *Britannica* to the university whose seal appeared on the fly leaf of each volume. But Benton did not at first make much change in the editing of the *Britannica*, though instead of having massive revisions about every fifteen years he continuously updated the volumes by inserting new or revised articles into the old mass of print (an idea, I am told, which he borrowed from the way that the US telephone directories were kept up to date).

When I first went to a board meeting of the *Britannica* in Chicago in September 1946 I was shaken to find how dominant the American and the sales side was in the production of the encyclo-paedia. After the meeting I went off with the three university people on the board and asked them whether there was really going to be any opportunity for me to act as any sort of an editor in London. Bob Hutchins, who was the dominant character in this group, at once replied, 'Not really. You see it's the salesmen who really edit the *Britannica* today and that is because they get all the complaints from customers and try to get the encyclopaedia altered to meet their complaints. Now when Mortimer Adler [a professor at the University of Chicago and a brilliant popularizer of academic ideas, therefore much disapproved of by many of his academic colleagues], with Bill Benton's help, can take control we will try and make it a real world encyclopaedia with a global point of view.' He was as good as his word but it was the mid-1960s before Mortimer really obtained control of it and planned a massive new edition, but by that time he had to find a wholly new editor-in-chief, and chose another, much more distinguished, Englishman in William John Haley who was leaving the editorial chair of *The Times* shortly after the Thomson family from Canada had bought it.

I had some further serious talks with Bob Hutchins who promised me support in trying to make the *Britannica* somewhat less provincial than it had become. It struck me as I got to know it that it was a combination of eighteenth-century rationalist Scots parochialism plus Victorian moralism based on the manufacturing ethics of successful imperialism, with an increasingly thick veneer of the new American science and salesmanship. It was not an unattractive mixture, but I did feel that at the end of the Second World War we needed to take a fresh global view of the planet which was now facing a wholly new series of power balances with the awful threat of total destruction from our ultimate scientific endeavour, the atom bomb. Bob Hutchins, Bill Benton and Mortimer Adler were in agreement but they did caution me about the need for making a commercial success of the sales side of the *Britannica*, and to avoid it being too American we needed to get readers and buyers in other countries of the world, particularly

Britain. Now in London I was finding the impossibility of doing this form of sales promotion in the post-war world when the British government limited the amount of imports of books very drastically, and the very real poverty that extended to the ordinary middle-class buyers of the *Britannica* made sales droop even below the attenuated supply.

We did have some successes in my short period at the *Britannica*. First of all with the essential help of Bob Hutchins and the prestige of the University of Chicago we managed to persuade the universities of Oxford, Cambridge and London to lend their names to the editorial process of revision of the *Britannica*. Secondly I managed to get agreement that Sir Maurice Powick, the Regius Professor of History at Oxford, should undertake the editorial supervision of the *Britannica*'s whole section on history which consituted about one-twelfth of the encyclopaedia. Being a modest mediaevalist (with whom I had a fairly close friendship when I was an undergraduate and he was resident in Oriel) Powick was able to be slightly above the battle of prestige which began in 1776; he therefore was able to use many of the very able historians to be found in America while not always preferring them because of their propinquity to the head office in Chicago and this stimulated competition from young and upcoming British and European historians who did not want to let the Americans dominate historical thinking, but now at least saw an opportunity of meeting them on fair terms. Thirdly I was able to have the *Britannica* printed in Britain where it had the largest single print run of any book or series at that time. Needless to say there were the usual old school connections because we used Hazell, Watson and Viney, the last of whom had been at Oundle with me. But I did sadly see that our attempts to maintain a monopoly of the English book trade in the Commonwealth was failing fast and that our real competitiveness in publishing was threatened by more modern printing methods used in America and some few other countries in the world.

It was not only the encyclopaedia that we produced, there was also a supplement to cover the war years, called *Ten Eventful Years*. This had already been half prepared by the time I came on the scene, but I was able to give a number of articles specifically about Britain to reasonably distinguished British writers who had experience of wartime Britain and even of wartime British foreign policy. It was in this manner that I substituted a good English journalist to write about London's wartime experiences in the Blitz, etc. rather than having it done somewhat exotically by a Midwestern professor of history who had not the advantage of having been in Britain during the war. I must confess also that being able to describe myself as editor of the *Encyclopaedia Britannica* (however exaggerated the claim was, as the Chicago office kept on pointing out to me) gave me a certain *entrée* into literary circles. With the help of the reigning London hostess of the time, Sibyl Colefax, I was introduced to a fairly glittering set of famous people whom I could make use of in giving some British prestige to the *Britannica*. Such men as Basil Liddell Hart, the military historian, Harold Nicolson, the diarist and littérateur, and even Field Marshal Wavell gave me help in keeping our British end up in that most ferocious of battles which follows all wars, the struggle between historians.

Another series of prestigious books to come out from the *Britannica* in these early post-war years was 'The Great Books of the World'. I had comparatively little to do with this except in clearing copyright of such people as Dr Freud (which proved very difficult indeed) but it brought me into touch with the book publishing world and also by a happy chance with Unesco where I got to know Ritchie Calder, the scientific popular writer, and Julian Huxley who was then Director-General of Unesco. Through the Unesco link I tried to see if we could not make a real European contribution both to the *Britannica* and to the learned debates on the present situation of mankind. My main difficulty in getting anywhere with this was that the Germans were of course totally absent, and the French were highly critical of anyone but themselves taking a lead in cultural matters. I remember at one dinner in Paris, where I had been expounding and indeed enlarging on my concepts and the range of activities in which I was involved, a Frenchman of about my age turned fiercely on me and said in perfect English, 'I suppose that you believe that because you have written the *Encyclopaedia Britannica* and "The Great Books of the World" that you are capable of restoring the seamless web of European culture!' I responded, 'If I have a fault, Monsieur, it is modesty.' After a moment the laughter ran right round the table and I felt that I had established myself as someone who could defend his honour by a witty repartee; no one round the table knew that I had stolen it entire from my mediaeval history tutor at Oriel, Billy Pantin. But it must be confessed that the idea of getting a real European round table of the younger future eminent thinkers came to nothing largely because of the refusal of the major societies in Europe to come together in some merging of sovereignty at intellectual and other levels. My own next attempt in this direction was to be with the notable absentee – Germany.

Finally, the London office of the *Britannica* did have one publication of its own. This was the yearbook which summed up in encyclopaedic fashion the events of the previous year. The first we produced was for 1948 covering 1947. Since it was the size of an ordinary *Britannica* volume it was a considerable effort to produce with all its illustrations and a staff of only about four in the course of a year but I think we did it quite well. It was intended as a gimmick for the salesmen who would thus have a chance to show to prospective customers that the encyclopaedia was not all ancient history and far-off countries of which they had never heard. I tried to turn it into a really useful work of reference for those potential customers, the newspapers, and some of their senior personnel. To do this I used very extensively young aspiring journalists who did not mind being paid a penny halfpenny a word for their writing (in fact were rather glad to get any writing to do). Since there were a lot of them coming back into civil life from various parts of the world and seeking a place where they might rest their feet before launching into Fleet Street I had the advantage of getting to know many of the new crop of journalists and quite a number of those who were already established but were still pretty junior and ill-paid. They gave a liveliness to the yearbook which was commented on by quite a number of people, particularly in the journalistic world. The yearbook also contained a great deal of western hemisphere articles written by Americans and shipped across to us in galley proof form. This provided the average European or Commonwealth newspaper office with a fair amount of information about affairs and prominent people in the United States. I noticed with pleasure that we were able to get copies also into the American press offices to do the same for their knowledge of British leaders of government and opposition as well as the literary and scientific world of Great Britain and the Commonwealth.

I thoroughly enjoyed my time as an encyclopaedist if only because it gave me an opportunity for looking into the most diverse and exotic branches of history, science and the arts. I became quite an expert on what other encyclopaedias were like and about, including reviewing a Dutch encyclopaedia for the *Times Literary Supplement* at the express request of its editor. Also I think the first

bit of real freelance journalism that I ever did concerned encyclopaedias and was for the highly popular humorous magazine *Lilliput*
in August 1947. It was a very brief account of what the origins of
encyclopaedias had been and how they had become more and more
popular. These brief excerpts from the article give some impression
of the trivial pursuits that I was able to follow in what was really my
leisure time though it was described as research: 'The first English
encyclopaedist Bartholemew de Glanville, in a fascinating work
divided into nineteen books called "The Properties of Things",
began with the latest information on God, then the angels (the
number of angels who could dance on the point of a pin was not yet
settled, and Bartholemew left it an open question), worked on
through colours, flavours, scents, liquors, concluding with a list of
thirty-six kinds of egg. This handy compendium of useful knowledge remained a bestseller amongst the monks for many years after
its first appearance in 1360 and was one of the earliest books to be
printed in England, 135 years after it was written . . .

'Earlier encyclopaedists had never been above putting in some
helpful hints to housewives. For instance Michael Psellus, writing
about the middle of the eleventh century, gave full details of how to
make a tough steak tender by hanging it on a fig tree . . .

'The earliest encyclopaedia of which there are still copies in
existence is by Pliny, and runs to 2,493 chapters. It is packed with
useful ideas for almost all occasions, though its medical remedies
sometimes seem impractical. They had a tendency to begin, "Take
a long black hair from a virgin . . ." His cure for chilblains is "to
lay on them the cooling bellies of live frogs".'

Then in a final reference to the problems of the present day
Britannica I wrote: 'The great difficulty for editors lies in keeping
their editions up to date. Knowledge progresses and interests
change very quickly. New events and new discoveries demand that
something old be omitted. Luckily there are many entries still
carried that are no longer of great significance. An historic event
replaces a minor nineteenth-century watercolourist. I reckon that
amongst other things the atom bomb will get rid of ten eighteenth-
century Scottish divines.'

The salesmen and their representatives on the board of the
Britannica were not much amused by this article and enquired of
me what it was doing to sell the encyclopaedia.

Every Thursday morning I used to play truant about midday from the *Encyclopaedia Britannica* and go to a very different, more volatile situation in an old Dickensian building at the edge of Lincoln's Inn Fields called Great Turnstile. It was here that the *New Statesman and Nation* was edited, and I had just become their American correspondent or editor – I was called both at various times. I had been a long time in coming to these offices since I had been urged to do so by the editor since 1944, and had indeed very much wished to take up this post because of the prestige of the *New Statesman* as a magazine of thought. It was of course to the left of centre, but then so was the government in power. It was suspected of and charged with leaning to communism, or more simply of being fellow travellers or pro-Russian. Nonetheless at this time it was a magazine of very considerable power. When a few years later Kingsley Martin saw that he must retire soon, two eminent Labour politicians were prepared to give up politics to get into line for the editorship. One of them, John Freeman, had been a junior minister in the government until he resigned with Aneurin Bevan in 1950; the other, Dick Crossman, was a rebel within the party who had organized the Keep Left movement to the intense fury of Ernest Bevin, but though he promised faithfully that he would cease to be a politician if he were given the deputy editorship and a chance for the appointment by the *New Statesman* board as editor he was firmly turned down by Kingsley on the grounds that he was really a politician and though he might be an excellent journalist he was not an editor.

It was perfectly clear to anyone who regularly attended editorial meetings that the person in charge was Kingsley Martin himself. He was a man who was very open to persuasion, but to say that he was often persuaded wrongly and that he had a reputation for being weak in his editorial decisions is only partly true; he was not dogmatic in thinking that he knew everything there was to know about the policies that should be followed but he was determined that those policies should be for the benefit of the majority of mankind and not just for some faction, however attached he was to it, such as the Labour Party in Britain or the new socialist world or, for that matter, the West where most of his cultural values lay. But he had little ability for pursuing a really consistent policy, which anyway he regarded as the necessary compromises of party politicians and not the careful conclusions of thinking men with experience of the world. The editorial conferences were really great fun.

There was a very interesting and powerful set of minds firmly determined to take over Kingsley's thinking and set the editorial policy of the paper for the next week. They did not often succeed though they very often set the general tone of the editorial – I even think I succeeded in doing this myself on a number of occasions.

The most regular attender at these meetings was Aylmer Vallance who had come to the *New Statesman* before the war from editing the *News Chronicle* and was indeed still Kingsley's *chef de cabinet* for actually getting the paper out. They were however not on very good terms in the period that I knew them both and though Aylmer was extremely helpful to a cub journalist like myself – he taught me a very great deal about the simple means of being effective as a writer – I was always somewhat suspicious of his motivation towards the *New Statesman and Nation*. Since he had been in British army intelligence in both world wars he was naturally a suspect for being either a double agent or a full-blown communist. I do not believe he was either but I think he had a sense of mischief which left him with the ability to insert items at the last moment in the magazine so that they could not be removed but were regarded with considerable ill will by both Kingsley and a good number of the board of the paper. His method at the editorial meetings was to raise unanswerable queries about anyone's suggestions which made them seem slightly absurd. This was disconcerting but not altogether useless since it exposed some pretty wild ideas – which on occasion Aylmer used to insert as his own while the magazine was actually going to press.

The most powerful debater at these meetings was Dick Crossman, whom I had known and liked for some years. But I did find, as Kingsley had too, that his real interest was in the party political aspect of affairs. He founded Keep Left as a pressure group of the left wing – but not the extreme fellow-travelling left wing – of the Labour Party and made it a gadfly of the broad centre of the party, especially of Bevin and Attlee. Keep Left was not an order to grow left; it was neither pro-communist, nor notably anti-American, but its aims were to avoid being taken over by either the US or the USSR. Dick's most regular comment was to say that 'we in the Labour Party have only two enemies, communism and anti-communism'.

The third quite regular attender was Norman Mackenzie whom I met during the war wearing an RAF uniform. He had been invalided out of the RAF and a quite long period in hospital seemed to have cured him of communism also, though out of a sense of decent loyalty he remained a member of the party and Kingsley was very much criticized by his colleagues for permitting such a Trojan horse into their midst. I do not believe Norman ever did any subversive work within the paper or outside, but I must say I have been fooled by so many subversives that I do not think I am the best of character witnesses.

There were also a certain number of rather eminent irregular attenders such as the Oxford economist G.D.H. Cole, H.N. Brailsford, J.B. Priestley the novelist and playwright and a member of the *New Statesman* board, and in my earliest days of going to the magazine one occasionally had a fleeting glimpse of Maynard Keynes who was also on the board. These *prominenti* more usually joined us at lunch after the editorial meeting and frequently the editors of the more or less autonomous literary section (always known as the back end of the book) used to join us. Such people as Raymond Mortimer, V.S. Pritchett and Leonard Woolf appeared to be the Boat People of Bloomsbury, but they were extraordinarily good conversationalists and made the lunches less intense, more enjoyable and perhaps more stimulating than the strictly political editorial meetings.

At all these meetings one thing was absolutely apparent. The people working for and around the *New Statesman*, whether literary, political, managerial or anything else, were all in favour of socialism in various forms and thought the recent victory of Labour gave an opportunity to Britain to take a lead in Europe as it had not done since perhaps just after the Napoleonic wars. But the question which divided the group was whether this pro-socialist point of view involved enmity with the United States which was the temple of capitalism (under Truman though hardly under Roosevelt) and whether in fact there was any possibility of bringing power to bear so that America might revert more to the liberal idealism of the New Deal and less to what seemed to be a distinctively anti-Labour government attitude in Washington.

The persuasive arguments of Dick Crossman in favour of the Keep Left policies were really the outcome of the breakdown of a certain cross-bench consensus that existed in the very earliest days of the peace which was that Britain should try to build a new post-war alliance that would stop Russia or the US from dominating Europe, and indeed the world. What Dick particularly feared was that the Europeans in their present state of economic collapse would be totally dependent on the US and Wall Street, and dragged into an anti-communist line of policy. Kingsley's attitude was rather less extreme, and I must say that I learned more about it from some long talks at his delightful converted pub in Essex than I did from the meetings with the *New Statesman* staff. Kingsley did indeed believe that Wall Street and America's businessmen were determined to make this the American century and firmly to exclude Russia from contact with the West, while the US got on with dominating the Western economies. Kingsley saw Britain's main duty as being a third force between the distrustful but admittedly despotic Russia and an expansive, imperialist but admittedly democratic United States. Britain itself must ally with liberal Europe – the name that always came first was M. Spaak of Belgium – but firmly excluding Germany, though it was showing early signs of revival in a democratic socialist manner. Finally, Kingsley believed that America owed Britain aid to get started again, and we should not accept any political strings from the business-dominated Truman government, particularly no strings that would divide us permanently from Russia. It was indeed the breakdown of any genuine relationship with Russia at the end of the Council of Foreign Ministers meeting in Moscow during March and April of 1947 that brought a lot of the *New Statesman* group, and even more of the Keep Left movement, to believe that we were in danger of being made over-dependent on the US and Wall Street in an anti-communist alliance.

My own views, which I tried quite hard to put across both in the paper and in the editorial meetings, was not radically different. I too believed that we should not sacrifice everything in order to get money from the United States, and I felt that the willingness of Halifax and Keynes to break with the Treasury negotiators over their attempts to produce a wholly unsatisfactory and unacceptable loan proved that this point of view was held across the board in Britain. Equally I was aware that there was really no alternative to American finance for the devastated countries of Europe, and I also believed that Europe would have to act jointly if it was going to be any sort of an equal partner of the United States. (Kingsley Martin on the whole agreed with me on this point, though with the exception of the horrid Germans.) Secondly I believed that we were really dependent on the United States for stopping Russia, if it so wished, from subverting the whole of Europe, possibly up to the Rhine. With these considerations in mind I thought that what we should be doing is trying to play to the best of our possibilities the role of the Greeks to the Romans, i.e. we should be trying to get closer to the Americans and persuade them of the folly of any forcible action to drive Western Europe into an alliance directed primarily against Russia. Later, by the time that NATO was being created, I began to feel that it was necessary to have a military alliance to stop Russia's advances, for instance in Berlin; but I always had hopes that the NATO treaty would have clauses in it which attempted to make Western Europe more determined to join forces, socially as well as militarily, and that it should have a Clause 2 (much pushed by Lester Pearson of Canada) which attempted to look after social and economic problems within the NATO area and within the neighbouring countries as far afield as Africa. I believe my views were listened to quite seriously but the majority of those who were vocal felt that the establishment of an anti-Russian military alliance would give America too much power over us and would give Russia a cause for believing that we were their everlasting enemies in an alliance with a revanchist Germany.

The problem from my point of view was that to plead for some greater degree of tolerance towards America was difficult when the new government had shown so little real friendship to the new socialist government of Britain and the people who had elected it by an overwhelming majority.

It was at one of these lunches that Norman Mackenzie took up an old suggestion that I had made in the week that I returned to the *New Statesman* offices which was that we ought to try and find what links we had with America and how far they could be utilized to produce the friendship and co-operation which did seem to have existed during the Churchill-Roosevelt era. He suggested that the paper should approach Henry Wallace who had been Roosevelt's Vice-President and who was Truman's Secretary of Commerce until his resignation in a row with Jimmy Byrnes at the end of September 1946. After some discussion it was decided that Kingsley and Dick Crossman should write to Wallace and ask him if he would come across and make a series of appearances, press conferences, etc. in Great Britain to try and show (as I put it) that there was more than one line of policy current in the United States. Henry duly came across and performed all the functions that he was requested to. I thought he did it pretty well and that his central message, which was that the world was going to be facing a severe food shortage in the next few years and for decades to come, was well put and should have had more impact than in fact it did. I fear that we all were rather too anxious to keep Henry Wallace for that small group of intellectual democratic socialists who disapproved of the swing to the right taking place at that time in America. There were also probably too many genuine fellow travellers in the audience, and because Henry Wallace was a rather bland and casual speaker it was easy for the right-wing press (and even the *Economist*) to take pot shots at him. But it was apparent that Wallace was representative of the old New Deal which Keynes and the Labour Party of Attlee had been close to in the thirties. That was probably worthwhile but the rapidly darkening clouds of pure anti-communism in the United States engulfed Henry Wallace when he returned; he was not truly a politician, he was really a scientific agriculturist, and he fell into the hands of some foolish if not maleficent characters of the extreme left in America and when he ran for President on the Progressive ticket in 1948 he was demolished as third parties usually are in America.

From the days of the heavy Congressional defeat of Truman and the Democrats in 1946 I had also been increasingly depressed by the evidence of America's more and more chauvinist policies. It seemed almost inevitable at that period that the Democrats would be defeated in the 1948 elections (after all, they had been in power for fifteen years) and that there would be a Republican succession which would be either Dewey who was an old East Coast domineering character or Senator Taft who was an old-fashioned American isolationist from Ohio. It did seem to me that the political prospects for America and for America's allies particularly were pretty gloomy, though I did not share the universal beliefs of the left that America was about to enter into a depression and export it worldwide by dumping goods just when we were trying to rebuild our industries in Western Europe. My reason for this small crumb of hope was that I had been told this was not so by many of the Midwestern businessmen and bankers I had kept in fairly close touch with, who were now beginning to come back to Europe on business trips. A number of them were old liberal Republicans or even real Democrats and they assured me that the present very bad administration of America's affairs would not necessarily last for ever and might change, with or without a change of party, in a quite progressive or liberal way. I was also encouraged by the fact that Jimmy Byrnes was sacked by Truman and replaced by General Marshall early in 1947, according to rumour because Truman did not like the way that Byrnes was treating him as a junior partner in making foreign policy. As a result of all this I wrote a fairly long article in the *New Statesman* of which the theme was from Belloc's *Cautionary Tales*: 'Keep a hold of nurse/For fear of finding something worse'.

There were also messages from Dean Acheson, now General Marshall's number two, saying roughly, do not despair, help is on the way. These did not come directly from the great man but from a group of extremely bright assistants who surrounded him and were quite largely responsible for the building of a new policy. In May there was even a speech by Dean Acheson in some out-of-the-way place proposing a plan for the economic recovery of Europe. It was not carried by news agencies at all thoroughly, and I think that Donald Tyerman of *The Times* and myself at the *New Statesman* were the only people to get a full text in advance of publication from Ned Kenworthy, an old friend of mine who had worked in the press in Washington during my time at the Embassy. Donald Tyerman ran the Acheson speech as a rather isolated little piece, fairly thorough but without any explanation about it because their correspondent had not sent any. The story petered out completely.

And then on the evening of Wednesday 4 June I had a call from Ned Kenworthy who came round to my house, which I had just moved into with the American Amassador's private secretary, who had quite properly kept his counsel. Ned was excited and told me that there had been a further move on the Acheson front and it was hoped that the Secretary of State, General Marshall, would at his degree ceremony at Harvard on the next day speak about the plan for helping Europe to recover. I asked if this was going to be very general news, and he said that the Department had rather given up on the British press after the earlier fiasco, but they were going to try and do something with the BBC.

I then as now had the habit of listening to the BBC World Service (then called the BBC Overseas Service) at various times in the day and night, and I think I actually heard the news of the Marshall offer on the Thursday evening when it was given at the degree-conferring ceremony in Harvard. As I pointed out to Ned Kenworthy, it was all rather academic for me since the *New Statesman* used to go to press on a Wednesday evening. Still, on Friday morning I went round to the *New Statesman* offices and bearded Kingsley who was almost alone in the office. I said that this was a magnificent opportunity for us, that there should be a real offer for us to make a plan for Western Europe and that if we could not do this we would really have failed in our leadership role on this side of the Atlantic. Kingsley nodded and asked some questions. Would it include Russia? I said I thought it had. Would it attempt to include a revanchist Germany? I said that that seemed likely to be negotiable but it would certainly be offered to Germany. I then did all I could to persuade Kingsley to have a special long article, both welcoming this offer and stating what we ought to do about it, in the next week's issue. He said he thought this was a very good idea and would consider it carefully and I should be present at the next editorial meeting to put my case.

There was very little mention of the plan in the British press, though Leonard Miall of the BBC had carried the news to a very wide audience; Sunday's *Observer* had a lyrical piece on the editorial page welcoming the offer and saying that we must seize this opportunity. I gathered from friends in Bevin's private office that he had sent for the full text and wondered why the hell the Embassy had not sent it already and was going to try and do something about it. On Monday morning therefore I was quite hopeful that it would be the major article of the next week's *New Statesman*. I argued my case at the editorial meeting but was fairly quickly cut off by Kingsley who said that he had discussed it with his colleagues earlier in the morning and they felt we needed to know a lot more before we could issue any welcome to the proposal from General Marshall. Kingsley thought that he should get an article from a good economist after he had studied the text (which he still did not have) and I was apparently not to be allowed any major part in this operation, which was not what I had been after, I had hoped that it would be a full editorial group product.

I did not stay for the lunch that day (I am not certain that I had been invited) and I walked through Lincoln Inn's Fields down through the law courts directly to the editorial offices of the *Observer* in Tudor Street and asked to speak to David Astor. I was told that he was never in on Mondays but it happened that he was going to be in for a little in the afternoon and did I want to see him urgently. I said yes, and was asked to come back an hour or so later. I put it to David, whom I had met several times by now, that we ought to take a leaf out of the *New Yorker* which recently had secretly set up a complete issue on the tragedy of Hiroshima by John Hersey, and see if we could not in that way make a real impact. David said that he would like to see if that was possible though he doubted it for administrative and other reasons, but he was keen on doing something and asked me then and there whether I would help. I said I would. Eventually it turned out that our article did not appear until 22 June. In those days the paper alternated between six pages and eight, and the immediate Sunday following was going to be a six-page paper whereas with some pre-planning not the whole but almost half of the subsequent paper could be given up to the Marshall Plan. There followed ten days of intensive discussion.

My particular task at the beginning of the research into the basis for the article on the Marshall Plan was to try and go round those embassies which I knew well – including particularly the American Embassy and one or two of the Western European embassies. I also talked about this to Kingsley and some other members of the *New Statesman* editorial staff, to try and find out what their anxieties really were. As was to be expected, the main problem was fear of American domination, and the second problem was a fear that we would break up the alliance which seemed to be sustained by the United Nations, and build up an anti-Russian grouping.

In the American Embassy, where I was given extremely good access and briefing, I discovered that General Marshall's speech had been so studiously vague about what was wanted or planned because the State Department felt that any attempt to impose plans on Europe on the grounds that such plans were acceptable to the US Congress would have a very deleterious effect on public thinking. There were in fact limitations to what this Administration could do to get a massive aid programme through Congress, but there was no reason to put that up front as a target for opponents of the American leadership role. They were also very aware of the harmful effects if Russia were to accept the offer but with a number of very difficult conditions. One of the counsellors at the Embassy who looked after Eastern European affairs said that he was fairly sure the Russians did not want to see this plan succeed because they did not want to see a strengthened Western Europe; he therefore thought that they would ultimately refuse to participate, but they might do a great deal of harm in the meanwhile.

I was then asked just what point of view the *Observer* was going to take. I said that the paper had written very favourably about the Marshall Plan, and they should judge from that. I added that having lived for a long time until very recently in America my ambition was to see a great reduction in the divisions of sovereignty that existed in Europe. I said that I would like to see first of all a customs union in Europe, followed by at least an economic federal union, though there would probably be a good deal of divergence in, for instance, educational, religious and social affairs. There followed a very sharp question from the Chief of Mission (the Ambassador being absent at that moment): 'Would you see that federal arrangement extending beyond Europe?' I replied that personally I would hope that it would include the whole Atlantic community and would eventually be able to make the United Nations work as the basis for a world federal government. 'Idealistic,' came the reply, 'but none the worse for that.'

I had further conversations with my old friends in the Foreign Office where I found a great deal of support for the Marshall Plan, and a great deal of gratitude for the support that the *Observer* had already publicly given. But they were insisting on the old British policy of keeping a special relationship with the United States and they hoped that the Marshall Plan could work between the US, Britain and perhaps the Commonwealth without letting the awkward and unreliable smaller states of Europe make for trouble. In particular it was clear that they feared the political and diplomatic consequences of any attempt to bring Germany into the recovery plan. What little I could find out from the European embassies convinced me that France, which was being wooed by Britain on this issue, would go along, and that the Scandinavian countries and the Low Countries were certainly prepared to move as closely with Britain as was possible. The problem about finding out anything about Germany was that there was no such entity and no representation in London. Germany was governed by the Allied Control Commission and that had begun to degenerate into a divided sovereignty.

But I need not have worried about hearing the voice of Germany, for when I arrived at the *Observer* for my first ever editorial meeting there I found that more than half of the editorial group was German or central European. This was a cause of some complaint amongst the highly respectable trustees of the *Observer*; indeed at this time one of the bankers who was on the board complained rather bitterly to David Astor after seeing some draft notes on the article that was eventually to appear, 'Oh well, I had hoped to see rather more of a British point of view, but I suppose you have been over-persuaded by all your German refugees.' David replied very quietly, 'Well, you see we Astors are only German-American refugees from a little peasant holding at Waldorf in southern Germany.'

The most striking and significant of this editorial group was Sebastian Hafner who had adopted these two pseudonyms as a tribute to his two favourite musicians, Sebastian Bach and Mozart's Hafner symphony, when he fled Nazi Germany in the mid-thirties. David Astor had picked him up on a recruiting mission in the Isle of Man where all 'enemy aliens' were relegated in 1940; he also found quite a large number of other 'enemy aliens' who became pillars of the *Observer* throughout the forties and fifties. Raimund, which was Sebastian's given name by which he was always known in the office, dominated the foreign policy writing of the paper during the early post-war years, though always in close consultation with David Astor who was technically the foreign editor while Ivor Brown reigned as editor, and was on the side the best drama critic in London. Isaac Deutscher was a Polish Jew who originally took refuge in France and later came to Britain. He was a Marxist who had broken with the Polish Communist Party because they were prepared to make a compromise with the Nazis. He was an historian and wrote classic lives of both Trotsky and Stalin, and he advised us particularly on Russian affairs. Jon Kimche, a Swiss Jew, was the *Observer*'s military correspondent after the war. He became the editor of the Labour left's magazine *Tribune* towards the end of the 1940s. Another German Jewish refugee, who was not on the editorial side, was Willie Guttman who was both responsible for that extremely entertaining and at the time novel collection of sayings of the week, but perhaps more important checked all of our copy against the files of the paper and the 'morgue' where we had clippings from a wide variety of papers. I know for myself just how much correction he gave to my always hastily written pieces, and how much very modest advice he gave to me about the European scene, particularly at this time when I had not been in touch with it since I was an undergraduate.

As this editorial group got together over several days, preparing the basis for the article, I began to realize what a remarkable and unusual set of critical journalists they were. They had a great deal of self-confidence, and they had experienced in their lives the dire results of extreme nationalism, race prejudice and chauvinism. They all wanted to find a better way than had been found in the past, but they were not a well-knitted group. On the whole, Sebastian Hafner was the most brilliant and perceptive of the group. He saw through to the end of his propositions, and he managed to express his point of view in a remarkably lucid and powerful English prose. But if we had tried to produce major articles or the regular weekly editorials on the basis of a committee consensus, or equally if Hafner or Deutscher had run away with the policy formulation, we would have been in a very poor state as a newspaper of thought. It was always David Astor who intervened in the discussions to settle a point with quiet authority and, as I saw it, with correct judgment.

David had learned his way in political journalism chiefly by talking unassertively but as an equal to the many eminent people whom he had had the good fortune to know and to make friends with. He lived in a highly political family, which might not have shared his left or liberal points of view, but who were always willing to discuss them with him and bring in their partisans from various parts of the political world. I think at this time David was very much influenced by a long friendship with two people who had tried to avoid leading Europe into its present predicament by an unconditional surrender imposed on Germany. The first was Stafford Cripps who had been Ambassador to Moscow during the Churchill years. He returned to lead the House and then to become the economic guru of the Attlee government and eventually its Chancellor of the Exchequer. The second was a very different sort of character, the Bishop of Chichester, George Bell, who had probably missed his chance of becoming Archbishop of Canterbury because he had spoken out against all the attempts to destroy Germany as a nation. But whatever David learned from his mentors he always digested and thought through for himself, never having any real doubts about the competence of his mind – without particular expert learning – to see the way to solutions.

It was certainly so on this occasion when we had meetings both of the editorial staff and expanded to include quite a large collection of eminent persons. For instance we saw Lord Beveridge, Oliver Franks, subsequently to be the chairman of the Organization for European Economic Co-operation, the operative engine of the Marshall Plan, Sir George Schuster, Barbara Ward, a fellow journalist from the *Economist* who also brought in her colleague Paul Bareau (of Belgian origin) who was a trained economist, and many others of both the staff and acquaintances of the staff who added a lot to our information. But it was the small nucleus of editorial staff and in particular David Astor himself who produced the hard core of the *Observer*'s Marshall Plan doctrine. I remember very clearly how the strain and tension mounted as we neared the deadline. Eventually, about eight o'clock on the Friday evening, 20 June, Hafner bustled into the editor's office carrying a bundle of typescript pages sufficient to fill about half that issue of the *Observer*. David thanked him warmly, and when I came in early on the Saturday morning I found him still at work on this text and only ready to send it to the printers by nine o'clock – when he went home to bed and did not return till the late afternoon.

The article itself had the clear flavour of the *Observer*'s editorial staff, including the strong European element, the brilliant rhetoric of Hafner, and finally the moderating but still radical rationalism of David Astor. It was a unique flavour but it was not a very popular flavour. Neither Germany nor Europe were what the people of Britain at that time wanted to be associated with, and the suspicions about America's motives were still in the forefront of most British minds. I thought at the time that the greatest contribution of David Astor was that he felt on level terms with Americans, neither suspecting them of all evil motives, nor supposing that they were without a powerful band of pirates who wished to extend American influence and trade as far as they possibly could. Sebastian Hafner's capacity was to recognize that while Germany had certainly produced the most evil regime in modern history, it was not necessarily a permanently diabolical people who must be suppressed for all time, rather its immense productive capacity must be used to buy their way back into the European community, and at the same time to help that community to be economically successful.

The article, which was entitled 'The Rescue of Europe', seemed at the time to be extremely revolutionary (but not left wing) and demanded a change of mind that was really not being considered by any part of political Britain in the immediate post-war years. Today it seems above all to be a survey of the tragically lost opportunities which lay before us at that time, and which we have not been able to seize fully in the subsequent four decades.

It began by saying rather shockingly that the economic survival of Europe depended entirely on a United States loan. For instance, Britain or France could not possibly purchase the food or the consumer goods or the capital goods which were necessary to a full recovery. The Anglo-American loan had proved completely insufficient and had by now virtually been used up. The World Bank, which had been for reconstruction first and development afterwards, had found that its funds were completely inadequate for the needs of Europe.

Europe, which had led the whole world in the nineteenth century, had destroyed itself by the conflict between a series of separate, independent and rival sovereignties and the consequent wars, of which the last and greatest had just recently ended, leaving Europe broken on its own battlefields. To try and make each country viable economically and capable of standing on its own feet was an impossibility, and must be accepted as such. The Marshall Plan offered help to create a Continental economy for the long haul which was essential to any revival of Europe's power and prosperity in the world today. It was essential to create a genuinely united Europe for any real recovery to take place. There therefore must be at least a customs union amongst the Western democratic European countries and in some relationship with the Eastern countries of Europe. There had to be an acceptance of giving 'hostages' to prevent any future war, i.e. there could be no specially protected strategic interests. (This was looking forward to the Coal and Steel Community of Monnet which within three or four years had come into being with the recognition that it made a Franco-German war virtually impossible for the foreseeable future.)

Russia should, if possible, be brought into this scheme of things. Its presence in the centre of Europe was not solely the result of aggressive Russian impulses towards the West; Russia was also there because it had been thought to be necessary in 1944 and 1945 to have its full weight to topple the Nazi tyranny and to counterbalance the power of an almost certainly revived Germany. Furthermore, it was our belief that a reconstruction race between the East and the West would lead also to an arms race and eventually to a nuclear conflict. This was clearly not in Russia's or America's or Europe's interest.

The second half of the article was entitled 'Ways and Means for Action Now'. It was an urgent plea for an immediate response to the Marshall offer, and a fully manned stategic group to carry the plans into action more boldly than most government officials could have done. We pointed out that 1948 was a presidential election year and we must keep this brilliant and generous offer out of a series of Congressional nitpickings which would intensify as the election came closer.

The article contained proposals for the actual working out of a co-operative Euro-American plan. First of all, the objective was stated clearly that the plan must make the group of participating states in Europe 'viable, not self-sufficient'. Europe should in fact be an active partner once again in world trade, not a closed economy.

This should be achieved by setting up a central agency for the planning of European recovery. Again boldly, it was suggested that this should be placed under the aegis of the United Nations. There was one institution in Europe which included both East and West in its discussions on economic progress – that was the United Nations Economic Commission for Europe with its headquarters in Geneva. Its first act should be symbolic and appealing to the United States, a declaration of interdependence amongst all the divided sovereignties of Europe. Then the experts, under loose ministerial control, should produce priorities for investment in a united Europe. Eventually of course this would have to be approved by ministers at the highest level, but it was necessary to have some new and well worked out ideas to present to ministers.

The *Observer* offered a number of fairly startling ideas about in which directions this planning should go. It insisted that European productivity had fallen so low in both manufacturing and food that we must not, for political reasons, abandon any advantages that we had once had. For instance, the Ruhr which was the 'most important single industrial region in Europe' was getting the lowest food priority, which was economically indefensible. The Ruhr needed to be once again the centre of European heavy industry, spreading its knowhow and wealth-creating capacity across the boundaries which were to begin fading away, even between ex-enemies. Since all investment must be for the speediest recovery of Europe, and since it was food that was taking up four-fifths of the dollar debts that Europe was incurring with the United States, investment in agriculture must have a very high priority. At first it should be concentrated on France and Eastern Europe as the agricultural areas which could most quickly be made super-productive. If by any chance Eastern Europe stayed out of the plan then we must invest in an agricultural revolution in Africa which would provide both a better diet for Africans and extensive imports for Western Europe.

Thirdly, the enormous cost of all these investment projects, which were, however, essential to the recovery of Europe, must be estimated at this time and put before the Americans. It would be fatal to the success of the plan if we had not 'counted the cost thereof' when we set out to build our European structure, and it would be necessary to get the Americans to accept that they had undertaken a commitment in this area.

Finally, looking to the future, we saw the function of the Central Development Agency as growing larger for a long time. Europe should be made into an expanding market and should provide outlets for North American food exports, tropical products, and consumer specialized goods. Thus, planning a new Europe in the devastation of the old rather than patching up the old to try and make it work again within the awful limitations of divided markets and divisive sovereignties, the Central Development Agency should eventually form the embryo of a European federal government with possibly the prospect of a confederation with the other half of the industrialized world in North America.

The article concluded with a chord from the *Dies Irae*: 'All this, undoubtedly, sounds a little like a dream. But the present European reality looks more than a little like a nightmare . . . Only one thing is certain: if the nations of Europe do not take this unprecedented opportunity their punishment will be swift, terrible – and deserved.'

I was lucky at this time to have very good contacts in both the Foreign Office and the American Embassy. Immediately after the *Observer* article appeared I was asked by David Astor to keep a careful eye on what reactions were in those official circles as well as to a lesser extent in the Labour and Conservative Parties.

At the American Embassy I found I was received with more or less open arms, but was asked whether I really thought the present British government would go along with the suggestions we had made about a unity of Europe, an involvement of Germany, and an elimination of imperial preference. I first of all pointed out that we had not said anything about the elimination of imperial preference, though it would obviously have to be modified very considerably if there was to be a European customs union. But we wished to maintain a role of close trading and economic assistance in relation to the emergence as politically independent nations of both India and Pakistan. I realized from the downcast expressions that at least at this level of economic minister and commercial counsellor there was no real change from the old belief that the object of American foreign economic policy was to break up the imperial preference system and substitute the totally free trade system of the International Trade Organization. They were still very much under the influence of the Congressional briefings that they had been given both by visiting Congressmen and by visiting commercial people who had listened with some pleasure to what Congress was saying, and the new Administration did not seem to be speaking against.

In the Foreign Office I learned how strongly Roger Makins, the head of the economic side, felt that Britain should have a direct undivided relationship with the US, and that we ought not to be dragged into a European system which would lessen our liberty of individual national action, and would incidentally divide the money between far more, and less worthy, applicants, so reducing the funds which were available to Britain. Amongst the older Foreign Office hands there was an almost universal feeling that we must maintain the special relationship with the United States, for it was really our only lifeline. Amongst the younger officers, particularly those who had joined during and just after the war, there was much more feeling that we needed to find some relationship with the powers, small as they might be, nearer to us and less dominant than the United States was bound to be. This opinion was also reflected very strongly in the Keep Left movement of the Labour Party, and in a talk with Dick Crossman at the *New Statesman* I gathered that it was the Keep Left movement which had pulled him over from a pro-Marshall Plan line into a mood of fear about the dominance of the United States business interests. He hinted to me that some members of the Cabinet (I gathered it was Dalton) were very disillusioned by the American attitude over the Anglo-American loan and did not want to go that way again. I was rather surprised to find how strong the Conservative feeling against becoming too dependent on America was, and assumed that this was because they thought they were wrongly cast in the role of an Opposition and they did not much care about what was possible for a socialist government.

Public, as opposed to official and parliamentary, opinion was also in a state of considerable confusion and suffered from an almost total lack of real knowledge about what was the intention of the Marshall Plan, and what its real terms were meant to be. It certainly struck me and my young friends in the American Embassy that something was lacking in the American presentation of this issue. But it may have been, with the wisdom of hindsight, that the Americans and in particular General Marshall, a new Secretary of

State, were biding their time before endorsing or even proposing ideas which had not been subjected to scrutiny and negotiation by both Congress and the European governments.

The first meeting about the Marshall Plan was held in London on the three days of 24-26 June. This was in the same week that our *Observer* article had been published, and the Foreign Office was considerably disgruntled that we had dismissed some of the more important points of action that they had intended to put forward.

I soon gathered that the Anglo-American meeting was very far from smooth. Will Clayton, who had been so tough a negotiator of the Anglo-American loan, was in charge of the American side and brought with him the new Ambassador to Britain, Lew Douglas, who was going to be the main intermediary between the British government and Washington on these issues. Ernest Bevin opened with a strong attack on the idea of treating Britain as 'just another European country'. It was, he said, really part of the Big Three and should be treated as such, and indeed he suggested that the aid should be filtered through British hands to the European countries which were unstable, relatively isolationist, and quite incapable of dealing with a worldwide or even European-wide problem. Britain on the other hand was a world power close to America and he emphasized that 'Britain with an empire is on a quite different basis from the small, somewhat irresponsible European nations and governments' which were not true partners of the United States in the sense that Britain was. Will Clayton replied very strongly that one of the war aims of the United States had been the elimination of barriers to trade by such things as imperial preference. No aid programme which attempted to maintain imperial preference would have a chance of getting through Congress. He reiterated this several times, and when questioned as to whether it was the view of the United States government he said that he had not had time to have a full discussion with George Marshall but he knew enough about Congress to know what the limiting factors were. There must be some limits put on the Commonwealth preferences and there must be a real economic integration in Europe, a united states of Europe, which inevitably must include Germany as a partner.

The meeting broke up on the second day with real fears on both sides that there was going to be a breakdown in the negotiations. But the next morning Ernest Bevin changed his tack almost completely. Nobody knows whether he had been pursuing his usual trade union negotiating tactic or whether he was sounding out the real opinions of the Americans. He may simply have wanted to place on the record his strong desire to keep Britain in a special relationship with the United States and not be treated as 'just another European country', but equally he may have wished to demonstrate the American position to the Keep Lefters in his own party, which included a wide swathe of backbenchers who would particularly object to anything that seemed to be bringing Germany back into play, and Hugh Dalton, the Chancellor of the Exchequer, and Aneurin Bevan, the Minister of Health and a titan of the left. But Bevin did not give way entirely. He tried to get some improvement in the Anglo-American loan since, as he put it, the Marshall Plan was going to be the short-term aid which Britain had expected under the Anglo-American loan but had not got and was now being asked to face the convertibility of sterling long before it was possible. But again he got smiles and sympathy but not much change out of the guardians of Congressional puritanism such as Will Clayton.

Britain had not done very well in the first round of negotiations. But those of us who knew about it in any detail felt that it would be very counterproductive to publicize such a fight between the parliamentary isolationists and the Congressional isolationists. It would be a damn near-run battle in either case as to whether the $25 billion over five years could be obtained and accepted by Europe, and without that sum a total collapse seemed possible. There was a good deal of discussion in the Keep Left group which originated from Dalton about an austerity plan that would amalgamate the smaller powers of Europe and France, but excluding Germany and Spain, which could form with the sterling area an economically viable grouping. But this would involve the ending of convertibility which had been insisted on by the Americans as a condition of their loan to Britain.

In the negotiations in Paris the threat of British bankruptcy was always waved by Will Clayton whenever there was a threat by Bevin to break out of the encirclement that the United States had built round their offer of extensive aid. But though the negotiations in Paris were very, very tough and sometimes very nasty we at the *Observer* had to recognize that this was the way in which democracy run by rather provincial parliaments or congresses would inevitably conduct its business. We also had some inkling (which has been fully confirmed as documents have come to light) that the Secretary of State, Marshall, was keeping a careful eye both on his negotiating team and on President Truman to ensure that there was no possibility of an actual economic breakdown in Britain or the rest of Western Europe, including Germany. Yet it was by threats from Britain of jumping into the chasm that Germany was kept out of the negotiations, and it was by threats of similar dire action on the part of the United States that Britain was forced to continue the almost impossible task of achieving convertibility on the relatively meagre resources of the Anglo-American loan.

What was cheering was that the big men at the top did not lose their tempers with each other and did not attempt to close the negotiations, perhaps out of desperation and perhaps out of a sense of America's need for a viable Western Europe. When the negotiations were all over, the Americans had a package which they could reasonably expect Congress to accept, and Britain and Europe had a bundle of assistance which should and did enable them to make a recovery as a partnership of nations and not as a beggar's cure.

The long-drawn struggle in Congress was extremely agonizing for us the potential recipients (I remember that Congressional votes on Friday nights used to make the main headlines in the *Observer* for approximately three weeks in the month), but the miracle eventually happened and Congress voted by a substantial majority to appropriate roughly the $25 billion which we in the *Observer* had suggested was necessary – and which seems to have been accepted eventually by both sides in the negotiations. Thus the most generous and successful plan for recovery was brought to fruition in spite of very rough bargaining which had taken place over nearly a year.

A few days after the *Observer* article on the Marshall Plan I received an invitation from the new minister for the British Zone of Germany – Frank Pakenham, an old friend of David Astor to whom he had introduced me. Frank asked me to lunch with him and we arranged to meet at the Athenaeum in a few days' time. I was particularly glad of this opportunity of talking to him because I did really believe that quarrels between all three of the major allies over the future of Germany could break up the alliance and leave Europe in a terrible mess. This was clearly Frank's view also, though he was inhibited by his loyalties to the government from saying so very openly. I therefore took the burden of this and found that he did not disagree. He then rather tentatively asked whether I would possibly give up some time in my holiday period in August to visit Germany and perhaps give some lectures.

In the end I found myself agreeing to go at British government expense to Münster University where they were going to hold a seminar lasting two weeks from 8 to 21 August 1947. Frank also hoped that I would take advantage of government facilities to see something of the state of Nord Rhein-Westfalen which constituted the majority of the British Zone. He promised me introductions to Robert Birley, the head of the Education Department, and to the commandant of the British sector. Later I was told that I should talk on Anglo-American relations, with the object of displaying to Germans that there could be quite close alliances with a considerable amount of disagreement and even quarrels. This sounded just the sort of thing that I would thoroughly enjoy as I was now quite a long way into my book *Less Than Kin* about Anglo-American relations over the long years since 1776.

Near the beginning of August I set off on a cross-Channel steamer which was carrying troops for the occupying forces. It was quite a jolly occasion, even though it was overnight without proper accommodation for most people. I made a long-time friend on board in John Althorp who was commanding a company, or even a battalion, of rather unwilling soldiers carrying on after the end of the war.

At the Dutch disembarkment point we were delighted to read a notice in English offering 'A typical English breakfast, two fried eggs, bacon and a glass of port'; there did not seem to be quite the same shortages on the Continent. But soon we noticed as we reached the German border that there were very ragged and malnourished children standing all along the railway line, holding out little bags in the hope that the troops would throw in things that were edible – and so they did. Facing Lord Althorp and myself in the other two seats of the compartment were my two academic colleagues on the University of Münster seminar, Brian Reddaway, a professor of economics at Cambridge, and Asa Briggs, a young and brilliant post-graduate student at Oxford. As we chugged slowly along in the rather elegant first-class surroundings of this German train they began to talk about the future of these little waifs standing by the railside, and wonder just what was going to be the state of Germany in post-war Europe. Rather to my surprise and

105

pleasure I discovered that all of us wanted to see Germany firmly lodged in a democratic Western Europe and not about to launch a war of revenge on Russia.

At Münster we were swept away in a British military commission car with the Union Jack flying and within minutes were being introduced to a modest, obviously intellectually able man who was described as His Magnificence the Rector of Münster University. We were told that we were very welcome, that we now had time to ourselves to settle into our modest quarters and would be expected for dinner with the whole student body (with whom we would eat all our meals on equal terms) in the Great Hall. The students when we assembled looked comparatively well dressed but also quite thin, even to the point of emaciation. The meal consisted, as it seems to have done to the best of my recollection for the rest of the fortnight, of mashed potatoes with an occasional addition of mashed turnips and with various forms of gravy poured over the pile of food. Sometimes the gravy had lumps which were generally considered to be a special treat of solid meat; I doubted this. There was also with each meal a regulation mug of cocoa clearly made with Red Cross dried milk.

But if the food was dreary beyond belief, the conversation with the students was, without being brilliant, extraordinarily informative. These students were not nasty Hitler Jugend types; they were inhabitants mostly of the worst blitzed city in the British Zone, and they all firmly believed because no one worried to contradict this that parts of the Ruhr, for instance the relatively nearby Buna rubber works, were spared from the worst of the bombing because 'they had a valuable new technique for making chemical rubber, while poor old Münster only had an ancient cathedral and a large university'. The students had been at most teenagers during the rise and reign of Hitler and had some considerable doubt about why they in particular were being punished, what they were being punished for, and what right the victors had to inflict punishment on a people now perfectly prepared to stand up to Russia, and therefore no longer old enemies but new allies. They attributed all their present troubles not to Hitler (who was nonetheless something of a devil figure) but to the occupying powers who did not seem to be aware of quite what they were doing.

After very many hours of conversation with the students, we all on the British side came to the opinion that German youth knew almost nothing of what was going on in the immediate post-

106

Potsdam period and had rather a faint knowledge of what had gone on in the rest of the world outside Germany during the past five years. Worst of all, as I felt it, they were being gravely alienated from the Western democracies by what they did not know and were not likely to be rescued unless they were given a lot more information and education. Their newspapers were authorized by the occupying powers, and consequently seemed unreliable. The BBC was believed and trusted by a generation which had probably learned a lot of truth through secretly listening to the BBC German Service during the last year or so of the war but there lay another trouble: the BBC was genuinely unbiased in its Overseas Service, which was easily heard mostly in English in Germany, and it broadcast reports of the criticism of the new socialist government by the old Conservative government. These critical reports were believed implicitly because how otherwise could they have been 'authorized' to appear on the official national service.

I talked to a number of journalists both in Münster and in my travels after the seminar had ended. The British Control Commission was extremely glad to make arrangements for this since making some alliance with the new journalistic generation seemed to them to be very important. I thought so too and everything that the journalists said to me (though much of it was self-serving) confirmed my belief that we must allow people in the occupied territories to test their suspicions or beliefs against some form of reality which was outside the control of the British, French and American governments. Otherwise the people of Germany, without government, without a national press, without correspondents abroad, without the capacity to travel abroad, would continue to blame everything (including the advance of Russia into and beyond Berlin) on the victorious powers and would dream of revenge or at least of the possibility of hostile relations with Britain for instance until the end of their lives. I felt it absolutely imperative that there should be some proper information service that was not simply a litany of Nazi crimes flowing into Germany from the outside world. As one student whom I got to know quite well and who stayed with me in England many times in the 1950s said to me rather poignantly, 'What I personally resent most is that we are forced to live in this form of solitary confinement while we know that our future is being decided in some far-off judicial tribunal of which we know nothing and about which we shall only be informed of its decisions. It is that,' he said to me late one evening, 'that is beginning to make many of us feel that, looking back over the years, *früher war besser* (earlier it was better).'

These young people who had never borne any real measure of responsibility enquired plaintively of us: why should anyone be afraid of us who are so weak? How can anyone fail to see that Europe and not just Germany is in danger of being destroyed by the Russians? How does anyone expect to make a respectable, productive nation again out of Germany by starving the industrial workers and carrying away the most useful modern machinery on the grounds that it might possibly be used for war?

Finally, more in private than at the plain board tables where we ate, people used to come up to me and ask whether this was the way we had always run the British Empire. When on one occasion I lifted an eyebrow and asked, 'What do you mean?' the student simply pointed to a group of outdoor lavatories over two of which was the inscription 'For British gents only'. I could not help laughing and as my interlocutor began to chuckle too I said perhaps in the coming decline of the British Empire (India and Pakistan had become independent while we were at the seminar) Germany would become known as the prickliest thorn in Britain's imperial crown.

These younger Germans had heard on the BBC and other radio sources all about the Marshall Plan and were sure that it meant that there would be a European union with a proper place for Germany within its capacious bounds. They naturally deeply resented what was common knowledge, that it was the British and the French, and not the Americans, who had excluded them from the conference table in Paris which was to set up the machinery for implementing the Marshall Plan. Germany was to be represented by members of the Control Commission, not its own nationals. It seemed certain to me that there would be a split between Germany and Britain before very long and fairly finally.

On the last day of the seminar I asked if I could see His Magnificence once again to have a chat before we left. He ushered me with warmth into his bare-boned study, where General Bishop, the commandant for the British sector, was also present. I was a little embarrassed by this because I wanted to say some things a little critical of the British, but I went ahead anyway since I was not under the command of the British army; all they could do was expel me and I anyway wished to get back to Britain. I said that I was worried by the amount of ill will that was building up amongst even the good English speakers and those who seemed to be both non-Nazi and slightly pro-British. I wondered what we could do to bring some information to these young people about why the situation was as it was, what possible future there was for them all with their life before them, what we intended to do, and how far we intended them to become partners in Europe, and indeed the world, again before too long.

I glanced at the kindly face of General Bishop and he said, 'If you can diagnose the problem as clearly as that, and find a solution for it, you will be doing more for Europe, Britain, and the German people than any of us have been able to do so far. What would you suggest as a first step?' I replied that I thought it was the blank ignorance of young Germany that was really at the root of the trouble; the Allies were doing lots of things to teach the Germans why they were being punished for what particularly horrendous deeds. This proved quite popular with those allies who had suffered direct attack by Germany, but was it in fact making it less likely that after a twenty-year interval Germany would not start up again? I repeated what I had often said before in the seminar to other British participants, that Germany was going to be a major force in Europe within ten years and it was a question whether we wanted to see them exerting their power as friends or enemies of Britain. I was convinced that the most important thing to do was to give the Germans, and particularly young Germans, information about what was going on in the world, why the British and French, for instance, were behaving as they did, and allow the Germans somehow or other to test these opinions against non-governmental sources of information. That was the advantage of the Münster seminar, that three British delegates were either academic or journalistic. I proposed that we held either at Münster or some-where else in the British Zone a seminar composed primarily of the new German journalists, and secondarily of leading British journal-ists who might be hostile to Germany or only mildly friendly.

The Rector absolutely agreed that German youth was puzzled and becoming increasingly hostile to the Western allies, especially Britain and France. Something should be done soon to enlighten them more about what was being said about Germany and why. He suggested perhaps a very much enlarged seminar at Münster University. General Bishop responded by saying that we really must not repeat what he was going to say in official quarters in Germany or London, but he did agree and would give any help and facilities he could to such a conference. I said that I thought it would be best if we tried to have already working journalists, mostly young Germans, with a smattering of academics from both British and German universities. In a few years it would be right to bring in German and British politicians, but until a German government was in existence this was hardly practicable.

Within a few months Lilo Milchsach from Düsseldorf in the British Zone came to see me and told me about the plans that she had been discussing with the Rector of Münster University, which were more or less along the same lines that I had been suggesting. I put forward some names, including Kingsley Martin, and she told me about some German journalists who might take part. There was a planning committee meeting in 1948, and a fairly full-scale journalistic meeting in 1949. But it was at this point that a sharp change took place. With the advent of German national government (at least of the three Western Zones) politicians needed to be invited and indeed to be the majority of the participants.

We held the first conference in about Easter of 1950 in the village of Königswinter on the Rhine, in the rather forbidding building of a large German trade union. Almost every year since that period the meetings have been held in the same fairly cramped (and therefore, like the House of Commons, rather intimate) halls of the Steger-waldhaus.

There was quite a lot of bristling between the British and the Germans initially as we met in the conference centre. As soon as the British, who had come across by chartered plane, were settled in, there was a party for everyone to get to know each other. This was always for more than thirty years dominated by the emollient influences of Lilo Milchsach, a constant flow of Rhine wine, and Lilo's shy and retiring husband who was also a very shrewd businessman. He had a virtual monopoly of the Rhine barges from the mid-thirties onwards; during the war he made use of this to evacuate hundreds of British escapees either up to the port towns of the Netherlands or at least into the relatively friendly area of Holland. Without Lilo's magnetic and warm charm Königswinter would never have succeeded, and the consequences might have been that there was a permanent hatred between the two peoples. As it was, in 1982 a poll revealed that amongst the British people the Germans were by far the most popular Europeans.

In those early days of the fifties much of the discussion, either in groups or in the plenaries, was about differences of opinion between Britain and Germany. There were plenty, and they were

110

expressed with a fair amount of vigour. But one of the things that Lilo and I had prevented (with a good deal of tacit support from Lord Pakenham and General Bishop) was allowing a large amount of officialdom on either side. I was particularly anxious myself to try and keep the British representation almost unsullied by the Foreign Office, and Germany did not allow the emerging party politics to mean that anyone who spoke, spoke for his party. As a result one usually discovered that the disagreements were milder and not as nationalist as would at first appear. Over the years it became in fact quite easy to have strong arguments which were definitely not nationalist in tone, though they might be quite ideological and even geographical.

For instance, West Germans from the borderline of the Eastern Zone were usually, but not always, passionate against their Russian neighbours. Quite a number of British people agreed with this point of view though the Labour Party which was then in government was on the whole quite opposed to being dragged into any sort of revanchism by Germany. But there were milder questions such as what degree of destruction of German industry should be allowed to take place and for what purpose. I do not think that anywhere in Britain was there any real knowledge of the feelings of hatred that were created by this particular method of preventing German industrial recovery so that the country could feed and employ its still rather miserable people. The Germans learned (if only from me) just why and how much distrust there was in Britain of German industry and the barons of the Ruhr. Had we been surrounded by Foreign Office officials from either side we would have found it impossible to have such candid conversations.

In later years the Germans were keen advocates of bringing Britain into Europe, and that showed up the deep divisions in Britain about this subject, but it did nothing but good that they should be known. As the years rolled on, the official level of representation did rise, and in 1983 we had the advantage at a meeting in Cambridge (which now alternated with Königswinter) of hearing Chancellor Schmidt and Prime Minister Thatcher making up after one of their more quarrelsome summits.

For myself I got onto friendly terms at Königswinter with President Weizsäcker, Chancellors Adenauer, Brandt and Schmidt, as well as many politicians and journalists. Spokesmen such as Egon Bahr were of great help to me later on in putting together the Brandt Commission and, indeed, in persuading Willy Brandt to head it. Generally speaking, government people in office on either side of the Channel did not attend the informal meetings of Königwinter; as a result one saw great men at a time when not everyone was seeking their advice and opinion, and consequently it was possible to catch their ear and have a long walk and talk with them up the Siebengebirge. I was of course by no means the only one to take advantage of these chances. An invitation to Königswinter was much sought-after. I attended every Königswinter meeting during my time at the World Bank, and I can remember one rather junior and unhapppy minister saying to me in London, 'I hope we manage to get out of office before Königswinter next April, and I will probably have a chance to go.' In fact that was the one year when the government chose to go to the country in the sacred week of the Königswinter conference and it had to be cancelled.

It is my belief that Königswinter played a real part in bringing Britain into close and friendly relations with Germany and so Europe. I shall never cease to admire the spirit of Lilo Milchsach and her indefatigable efforts to keep the attendance at Königswinter meetings up to the high and current standards which were her constant requirement.

I came back from the seminar in Münster elated. This meeting and my participation in the Marshall Plan article in the *Observer* were just the sort of journalism that I wanted to do. It was constructive, had political impact (or was hoped to have both these effects) and it began to give me a certain status in the journalistic world. I received requests for articles from *Punch*, *Picture Post*, the *Economist* (for whom I wrote anonymously), the *Spectator*, and a continuing series of notes in the *New Statesman*, where I used a pseudonym because in 1947 I had been too recently very close to being an official spokesman. Above all, I was used on the overseas programme of the BBC and found myself thus gaining something of an international recognition.

By mid-1948 I had become the diplomatic correspondent of the *Observer*, and at the beginning of 1949 I also undertook the Pendennis column. But how was I to become, as Lord Halifax had urged me to do, the best informed person in town? It was not easy because I had not been in town for any length of time for some years. But even that absence had its advantages. I knew a lot of people in the Foreign Office who, coming out of the hothouse of the Washington Embassy, were sent to difficult or important posts around the world, and I was well known in America. But getting to know new faces and power points in post-war London was not so easy. I cultivated my American friends when they came on visits to London, friends such as Walter Lippmann or Joseph Harsch or the Alsop brothers, and they were all very kind in including me in some of their parties to meet great men who are always prepared to meet American columnists, but rarely deign to meet the humbler fry of junior British journalists.

I even managed to climb into high society during this early post-war period when in 1948 my old boss from Chicago Robert Hutchins, the president of the university and the chairman of the *Encyclopaedia Britannica*, came across to Britain to try and complete the arrangements for bringing the *Britannica* under the aegis of the universities of Oxford, Cambridge and London. He was picked up by Sybil Colefax who had revived her famous salons and, after a number of refusals, finally agreed that he would come back from Oxford via Thame where Sybil was staying. There we met Laurence Olivier with his hair bleached so that he could play the blond Hamlet. We had an amusing tea party, just the four of us, and I kept up some connection with Olivier for the next few years and have had his son Tarquin as a close friend since that time. But what was most remarkable was that Sybil really thought me a master of the conversational art. Through all my life I have been a fairly combative conversationalist, and that I think is what she particularly liked. Invited to lunches at her house, and to her 'ordinaries' at the Dorchester (where you paid for your own meal via her), I met a very wide selection of people of considerable interest to me in various parts of my career. It was with Sybil Colefax that I met Harold Nicolson, whom I got to know much better when we found ourselves living opposite each other in Albany, Piccadilly, T.S. Eliot, and Lord Wavell, with whom I had a passionate conversation about India (we were on the same side). He was a quiet and meditative man but he certainly felt strongly that Winston Churchill had wrecked the chances of making a proper settlement in India.

I think it was the same combative element that recommended me to Nancy Astor. When she could not persuade her son David to come and have lunch in Claridges with one of her more exciting luminary friends she would fall back on me. Both there and at parties in her home in Hill Street and in Cliveden I always found myself sitting on her left, whatever the precedence should have been, because she wished to emphasize all points of her view by hitting me on my right shoulder with a clenched fist. As a result I was usually black and blue after any prolonged visit, but I did get to like David's brothers and I did meet a lot of rather exotic sheiks of Araby and distinguished though somewhat passé Americans (Bill Bullet for instance).

All this helped me considerably in running the Pendennis column, but my real interests were more in the field of international politics, and generally speaking by that time in the post-war world political decisions between nations were not made in Cliveden or Claridges. The basis for this form of information was the mandarinate of the Civil Service, particularly the Foreign Office and Treasury. Luckily I had fairly close connections there from my Washington days even though I was often critical of the policies that were being pursued. Sometimes I found that the mandarins were not wholly opposed to my views. But in what is now a fairly long experience in journalism I have always found when visiting a strange city that the best way to find out what is really going on there is to latch on to one or two of the best serious foreign correspondents (whether British or not) and get them to talk about their favourite topic which is the country that they are assigned to. Since I had not worked in pre-war or wartime Fleet Street this was very necessary to me and I was extremely lucky in being adopted by Donald Tyerman who had been virtually editor of the *Observer* during the war and had now moved to being deputy editor *en titre* at *The Times*. We had many affinities, including both being Geordies from the north-east of England, and I was a frequent guest at his house in Essex. When he left the *Observer* and felt rather isolated amongst the Blackfriars of *The Times* he set up a regular Tuesday lunch in one or other of the better and cheaper restaurants adjoining Fleet Street to which he invited a wide variety of friends. There were never more than a dozen of us but fair regulars whom I got to know well were David Low the cartoonist, John Beavan of the *Manchester Guardian*, Maurice Green of *The Times* (soon to become the editor of the *Daily Telegraph*), and George Stiedman of the BBC.

Because I was a newcomer to journalism proper I invited along quite regularly some of those who were seeking speedy ascent of the ladder or indeed putting their first foot on it. Amongst these was one notable crew to whom I had given a lot of introductions in America when they went on a debating tour of the United States representing Oxford University. They were a bright leftist Tony Wedgwood Benn who did not take up journalism in the long run though he worked at the BBC for several years before going into politics; Edward Boyle, an extremely intellectually powerful middle-of-the-road Butlerite Conservative who also went into politics but had grown rather tired of them in Harold Macmillan's day when he was a minister and sought an opportunity to go to the Lords and become Chancellor of the University of Leeds. He made a notable contribution within my sphere of interest as a member of the Pearson Commission. Kenneth Harris was at that time a young, bright, aspiring Welshman with no particular ideas about what his career would be though he suspected it would be politics. He wrote a book after the US debating tour called *Travelling Towns* which I put in front of David Astor, and Kenneth came onto the *Observer* staff. He has served there through thick and thin as foreign correspondent, interviewer-in-chief for the paper and, last, involved with the management after the takeover by Bob Anderson and the Atlantic Richfield Company (Arco). There was a good deal of journalistic horsepower trading at those Tuesday lunches and Donald Tyerman and myself became known as the Gabbitas and Thring of journalism, named after the famous marketplace of educational talent which has been the butt of so many parodies from Evelyn Waugh onwards.

The basis of my education in quality journalism and comment came, however, from the *Observer* though I had learned a lot for which I am very grateful from Kingsley Martin and Aylmer Vallance of the *New Statesman*. But the intellectual content of the *Observer* editorial meeting and its mixture of national origins made it one of the most fascinating places to listen and learn and perhaps not remain entirely silent that I ever knew until I went to the World Bank. It was at these conferences that we decided on the make-up of the leader pages in the paper. These included both the main editorial and the individual comments which were often quite crucial, as for instance when we wrote one in 1947 saying that King George VI should not go for his post-operation holiday to South Africa just after a government dedicated to what is now known as apartheid had been elected. For months afterwards and even at the time of the King's death in 1952 we were written to by angry readers who said they would never let the paper darken their doors again, and claiming that we were going to or had killed our beloved king. There were also two leader page articles to be disposed of, one of which was quite often written by a member of the staff under a regular pseudonym (such as Student of Europe for Sebastian

115

Hafner) and one of which was by some distinguished or learned outsider. Present for discussion were six to eight people who were likely to be given some assignment, and also an occasional 'irregular attender' who was present for his special knowledge of a topic that needed to be commented on. Never had I heard argument so free based on principle and the long-term results that we hoped to achieve in the world over the next twenty or thirty years, or so well informed about the difficulties for the country of procedures that we were trying to put forward. There was a lot of disagreement and quite a lot of hurt feelings, including my own, when we did not succeed.

The most striking feature of these conferences was the editor's chairmanship. David Astor as a presiding genius was so modest, so tentative, so little claiming to specialist knowledge of far parts of the world (he had travelled very little in those days) and yet so editorially decisive on the basis of principles he held firmly and thoughtfully that I came to admire him (though often disagreeing) more than any of my previous bosses. This has remained so till today.

But there is need for more than intake into a journalist's life. He must, after all, have an outlet. Here I was very lucky. First of all the *Observer* itself, in which I wrote comparatively little, was a highly respected newspaper, known to be free of party bias and capable of resisting it. The oddity of having the editor as proprietor (which was virtually the case) meant that as long as things went well they went very well and with a minimum of battling between the journalists and the proprietors (i.e. the Trustees who were virtually appointed by the editor). This meant that my comments and sometimes leaders were on the whole influential in the world of politics and foreign affairs and I did a number of articles from abroad, often on the basis of trips arranged through quite other organizations than the not very rich *Observer*. The *Observer* Foreign News Service, which sold articles appearing in the paper and special articles written mid-week by many members of the staff, was a most enthralling organization to work for. I have found in my yearly package of clippings regular coverage of the British scene and of foreign policy conferences and events in more than fifty good quality newspapers around the world. And not only around the world. The *Liverpool Post*, the *Yorkshire Post*, the *Scotsman* were all papers that bought the service; so were many of the Commonwealth papers – the *New Zealand Herald*, the *Hindustan Times*, Pakistan's

116

only national paper *Dawn* – as well as the *Straits Times* of Malaya, the *Jerusalem Post*, some English-language papers in Europe, a great number of Scandinavian papers which translated me into their own language, and before long *Ashahi Shinbum* of Tokyo. After the German press became a factor in European thinking, *Die Zeit* and I think one other were regular publishers of *Observer* material. I was able to express fairly personal views though I would never go against the *Observer*'s editorial line, partly because I did not wish to. The position into which I had so fortunately been slotted was far more advantageous in terms of prestige and influence in Britain and around the world than I could have ever expected. It suited my habits of mind in that I was not a scholar by inclination, trying always to check the very last fact against the very firmest standards; nor was I a lighthearted gossip, paying little attention to the long-term consequences of such efforts.

Above all I had both a worldwide and a large domestic outlet in the BBC on the Home Service and later the Third Programme, plus the overseas broadcasts which reached almost every part of the world in English or sometimes in translation. I had been 'discovered' by one of my great benefactors, George Stiedman, an awkward and sometimes cussed Yorkshireman but with an eye for what the BBC wanted; he was a magnificent trainer of people who knew very little about broadcasting. I owe him a great deal.

I remember Walter Lippmann, in London shortly after the war, asking me, in all seriousness, how the British public remained so comparatively well-informed, particularly about foreign affairs, when its popular press was so utterly frivolous, its middle-brow press pursued quirkish crusades, while the real quality press, which he admired, had so small a readership. I replied, without having given a great deal of thought to this matter, that Britain was saved from ignorance by the fact that it had the BBC which a great preponderance of the country regarded as their main authentic source of news.

The news in those days and throughout the past war had occupied more attention of the BBC than any other part of its programming. This certainly remained so for ten years after the war had ended. The news was sacred and suitably read by well known but of course unseen Delphic oracles. Then if comment was wanted on the sacred text it was done by outsiders – who were what the Department of News and Talks considered the most reliable. I fell rather neatly into this category of reliability myself because I had

117

not merely been a journalist for a comparatively short time but I had held a responsible official post as Press Attaché in the British Embassy in Washington. I was not a party man and I was 'reasonably talkative' while being able to moderate a debate between antipathetic ideologists.

The BBC served a very useful purpose in bringing out a consensus that carried Britain through the revolutionary changes of the post-war decade. It was in this time that Britain became a welfare state by the action of a Labour government, but with the backing of Iain Macleod's younger Conservatives in the One Nation group, and with several leading ex-Cabinet members of the Conservatives giving it full support, for example R.A. Butler and Anthony Eden. But how was this series of private agreements between the parties to be made apparent and binding on the general populace? It could not be done by the usual debates in the House of Commons because such debates are intended to seek out points of disagreement and concentrate on them; anyway, the populace did not then hear anything said in the House of Commons, and parliamentary reporting was either dull or rather facetious. Nor did the newspapers help with the working out of consensus. Newspapers which might indeed favour generally a moderate consensus sufficient to hold the country together in a time of considerable and revolutionary change sound their trumpet uncertainly by the frequent addition of 'but on the other hand'. In fact most newspapers are a little further towards the extremes than the individuals who write their policy statements.

The BBC was not in any way upset by these institutional crimps. Their duty, as they conceived it, was to try and get a balance of journalists (not newspapers) to discuss issues of the day and long-term trends of the period in a quiet non-sensational manner. This was often duller than the jousting which now is the essence of broadcast debate, but first of all there was no alternative to the BBC, and secondly there was a felt need for an independent debate between journalists of varying views. So the BBC's output in this period in current affairs talks was largely the discussions of four or five people, all concerned and with differing points of view about the question at issue, but not bound to the ideology of their newspaper or their party and able to hammer out as a rule a certain measure of agreement.

There was also at least one weekly fifteen-minute talk commenting on the news domestic or foreign, artistic or financial, by a well-informed and articulate commentator usually from the vales of Fleet Street rather than academe. I found that I did about one of these a month, which was fairly regularly reprinted in the *Listener* and thus reached a quite considerable audience. The commentary itself was occasionally repeated on the World Service from Bush House, but more often I would find myself being asked to participate in a discussion of the issue with which I had dealt, or alternatively to do a repeat performance more carefully addressed to a foreign as well as domestic audience. Eventually, at the suggestion of Ernest Simon who had become Chairman of the Board of Governors at the BBC in the early fifties, much abbreviated discussions and commentaries on individual topics were added every day to the sacred Nine O'Clock News (later to become the Ten O'Clock News). I was much involved with these short clarifiers and think they helped in the general task of disseminating information about the world to the sixty per cent of politically aware people in Britain who did not make the policies of the government but with whose support the government could only survive.

Just what contribution did I make to these discussions? I did not preach the detailed policy proposals of the *Observer*, though I hope that by being named as a member of the *Observer* staff I gave it a certain amount of a boost, and at least pointed the way in which the *Observer* was going. I remember, though, after one rather brutal debate, being asked by a far right journalist who had suffered under my moderation more than once before: 'William, just what role do you have to play in these discussions? Always a chairman, never a leader, holding us back from the radical changes that are needed, never suggesting how we could lead the world again as we did during the war.'

I replied: 'I try to make you all realize the necessity of co-operating with the inevitable; and to recognize what is very difficult for the British people to do – what the terms of inevitability are. I think we must recognize that we are going to lay down the burden of empire in the sense of being political and military masters in its areas, as we have already done in India, because we do not have the power to impose our will and would not find either the allies or the spirit of determination in the British people to restore that power to our arms. Those limitations of power are part of the inevitability. Secondly, one of the limitations on our future independent action is the fact that we need to give some additional power to our diplomatic dowry by a strong association with Europe – I believe the sooner we do so the stronger we shall show ourselves to be. This is necessary because we have not got the capacity to stand up to the United States, nor even to the Soviet Union, unless we do make some such arrangement with Western Europe, which will not destroy the Commonwealth and will in fact please the Americans as they showed in their original demands for action over the Marshall Plan.'

'And how, may I ask, is Britain going to demonstrate this new-found strength of hers after all the weaknesses in India, in Eastern Europe, etc. that this government has shown since the end of the war?'

'I would suggest that we begin by making use of this instrument,' I said, pointing at the microphone. 'It served us very well in the war and gave us a sort of leadership in Europe at that time which I too think we have rather thrown away. But if we can persuade the Commonwealth and Western Europe that we are a great power which has real intentions not of dominating but of leading Europe and keeping in touch and in good relations with the worldwide commonwealth I think we will be able to prove ourselves real leaders in the world at large.'

I do not think that I convinced him of what I was saying, but as it happened the producer had left the microphone and the recording live. Later I learned that this little exchange was circulated quite privately to a number of the higher officials in the BBC and in its Overseas Service. As a result I was asked to 'cook my cabbages twice' by repeating the gist of the argument in discussions on this topic with people mainly outside Britain. I had a number of excellent producers and I know that this item appeared quite widely, for example on *Talking Points in the News*, a regular and rather popular general discussion programme which I shared weekly with Harry Hodson the editor of the *Sunday Times*, Trilby Ewer who had been diplomatic correspondent of the *Daily Herald* since the end of the First World War (and is to be found in all the reference books as the author of what must be one of the shortest poems in the English language: 'How odd of God/To choose the Jews'), and John Beavan of the *Manchester Guardian*. The programme was produced by George Stiedman. There was another five-minute commentary which had been commissioned by one of the commercial networks in Australia and was produced by John Terraine who went on to do that marvellous film sequence on the First World War for television.

120

Another of my regulars was a three-minute summary of news and views in Britain for the Canadian Broadcasting Corporation – produced by someone then on his way out of the BBC, Tony Wedgwood Benn. He was a sympathetic, careful and helpful producer, though almost as exasperated as I by a ruling from higher up stopping a commentary on the course of the last three weeks of the 1950 election, which was due to be broadcast on polling day, at midnight, some four hours after the close of the polls. The broadcast was stopped in case it could be picked up between London and Canada and so influence any voter who might hear; say some telegraphic genius on a lightship in the middle of the Atlantic. The BBC at that time was strict about not saying a word about elections in any commentary spot during the period of the campaign.

The final accolade came from the Director-General himself. Sir William Haley asked me to write an article for the in-house BBC quarterly, on the topic of how broadcasting could properly be used in international relations. The only phrase that I remember from this quite long article was that 'political warfare through broadcasting has never killed anyone yet but it may have persuaded them to look at things from your point of view and thus changed, however infinitesimally, the balance of power in your favour'.

Hopeful Dialogue
1950–5

As diplomatic correspondent of the *Observer* I attended more or less all the international conferences in Europe, the Middle East and possibly further East if there was not a correspondent on the spot. The regular round of Council of Foreign Ministers who were allegedly making the post-war peace gave me an opportunity in January 1950 to visit one of the more interesting small countries of Europe. This was Finland, then under virtual Russian occupation, the windows on the trains all being boarded up while one went through Russian naval or air bases on the fifteen miles per hour expresses.

My main duty was to give the British Council's annual New Year lecture on the absorbing topic of 'The House of Lords as a part of British democracy', which was attended by quite a large audience of Finns, all members of English classes so that their questions were about my pronounciation rather than my political science. Having completed this task I was just enjoying a sauna followed by a dip in the snow when I received something rather unusual in Finland, which was a telegram from Great Britain. I opened it with some excitement and discovered that it was from the *Observer*, asking me to return at once and prepare to go to Colombo for the Commonwealth Finance Ministers Conference. By early next morning, after making my farewells to my hosts, including the Foreign Minister and the Prime Minister, I was duly booked through to London. I was sorry to have missed the sightseeing of Finland even in the almost total dark, but I promised to return again, which I did three or four times in the fifties.

I was thrilled at the prospect of going to Asia for the first time in my life and seeing the Commonwealth beginning to emerge under Ernest Bevin's tutelage as an instrument of economic development. There was little time to change from Arctic clothing into buying a new set of tropical clothing. However, that was fairly expeditiously taken care of and I eventually found myself with visas correctly stamped on one of the new British planes just going into commission, named the *Argonaut*.

It was a comfortable plane and very roomy, but it did have one sad defect which was that it preferred to travel by night and sleep away the daylight hours. Thus, instead of leaving London at about noon we left at about six o'clock and flew overnight to Cairo, watching the dawn rise over the desert. We were told to wait in the airport lounge but after about half an hour they had to tell us that we would not be taking off for another four hours at least. I asked if I could take leave of absence to go to the Embassy, and was given permission so I had the pleasure of having breakfast in the Embassy canteen with the then Head of Chancery (again), Donald Maclean. We eventually took off in the latish afternoon and got into Karachi in the early hours of the morning. We were provided with beds, which we needed, and I slept through until about ten o'clock in the morning.

Once again there was bad news. The *Argonaut* could not take us any further that day. Luckily I had the name and address of a friend who was working in the new Pakistan administration. Terence Creagh-Coen had worked in the Political Secretariat in the days of an undivided India and had been particularly friendly to many of the princes in the north-west. I spent more or less the whole day with him (since he did not seem very hard pressed) doing what was essentially my first survey of Pakistan's politics and economics.

Duly as dusk fell our plane took to the air again and arrived safely at Bombay early in the morning. On this occasion we were told that the delay would be only a few hours but in view of our hardships I managed to persuade BOAC to let us go around town in an airways limousine and see the sights. I also managed to see an Indian journalist who had once worked in London and whom I had known there. He gave me quite a lot of very useful information about the situation in the states surrounding Bombay.

We then had the unusual experience of taking off in daylight and arriving in Colombo in the middle of the night. So I got a good night's rest before turning up rather belatedly at the government headquarters where the conference was to be held. However, others including ministers were even later and the conference did not begin until the afternoon when we had had time to read all the guidebooks, economic survey books, etc. which were made available to us by what seemed a very efficient and rather Westernized administration.

At an impromptu lunch given by the government I found myself sitting next to the leader of the extreme left party, who spoke admirable English and told me he had been President of the Union at the London School of Economics. Over coffee I met the Prime Minister, Dudley Senanayake, who presented me with a very nice silk tie emblazoned with all sorts of Sinhalese symbols, along with some brass replicas of the same symbols which he handed to me smilingly saying, 'When I tried to put these on my outside door – your oak, I think you call it – at university in England in order to frighten away spirits I found it merely brought the proctors to my room to enquire whether they had any religious significance.' Then I was introduced to the leader of another party, I forget which, who explained that he had been Secretary of the Union at Oxford. Clearly the introduction by a governor in the thirties of universal primary and later secondary education had had its effects – not perhaps exactly as he had expected – on the Sinhalese people.

At about three o'clock the conference opened with a certain amount of panoply and I felt how lucky I was to be watching this meeting of the new Asian Commonwealth prime ministers or finance ministers, obviously dominated by Nehru, but with Jayawardene, the Finance Minister of Ceylon, taking the chair. The Asians were clearly, as they said in their opening speeches, glad to feel that they were now one of us and no longer subject races and wished to maintain that position, while also maintaining a genuinely friendly attitude towards the rest of the Commonwealth, in particular Britain. Ernest Bevin in his opening address played his role magnificently. He made it clear that speaking for the United Kingdom government he was really interested in the economic development (or reconstruction as he called it) of the less developed parts of the Commonwealth. 'Progress,' he said, 'depends mainly on the improvement of economic conditions, and progress we must have.'

The public plenary group then went into executive session, supposedly for ten days, but on Friday, four days early, it was announced that the conference would adjourn with a full and agreed communiqué by Saturday afternoon. The communiqué, which was handed out at a general press conference, was clear and explicit. The whole programming was modelled on the Marshall Plan and the Organization for European Economic Co-operation (OEEC) by which it had been framed. A copy of the full communiqué and some working papers were being telegraphed that night to Sir Oliver Franks, Chairman of the OEEC in Paris. There was to be a committee of Commonwealth countries like the OEEC but it was entitled and encouraged to co-opt others in the area whether they were full Commonwealth members or not. This made it perfectly clear that the real success of the programme depended on the accession of the United States, which in fact followed within a few weeks.

The machinery of the Colombo Plan was however not primarily a financial aid scheme. It was rather a technical assistance scheme with all participants giving technical assistance in training where they could, for instance for cattle rearing or for simple handing over of material from one country, rich or poor, to another. Under this national process there was meant to be a flow of technical and financial resources from the rich to the poor but Ernest Bevin was insistent that the idea of the exchange should not be held up by lack of finance. Above all, his words, repeated again and again, that 'Progress depends mainly on the improvement of economic conditions' was a very suitable lesson for almost all Asian peoples and was accepted by the Asian leaders as a sign that the old head of the Commonwealth was really concerned with their wellbeing and not just their military or economic support.

Pandit Nehru, who had an effective veto on any resolution in the congress, and whom I described as the 'gentle dictator' of the conference, used it against any form of arms pact which, he said, would not stop communism and would ruin most of the Asian powers. For the same reason he refused all attempts to get Asian leaders to recognize the Bao Dai regime in Indo-China. Bao Dai was regarded as a French puppet and Nehru was determined that no colonial puppets should be set up, or would last if they were set up, in the present revolutionary mood of Asia. But the gentle dictator was quite prepared to overlook some of the errors of the past, even at the meeting of Australia and New Zealand. They, Nehru declared, were not imperialists unless they changed for the worse. This was a very important reprieve, particularly for Australia.

Almost every leader was anxious to claim credit for the plan which had emerged from the Colombo conference. Both Percy

Spender, the Australian Finance Minister, and Jayawardene, the Sinhalese chairman of the meeting, spoke to me privately and gently, saying did I not think their name would be very appropriate. They were all bearing in mind that the first news of the conference in the broad world would be in the Sunday papers. I put them off equally gently by pointing out to the Australian that a plan which was called the *Spender* Plan had hardly a hope of getting any support in the American Congress. Similarly I pointed out to Jayawardene that he must recognize that his name would not compare in ease of pronunciation or even of memory with a short European name like Marshall. They both seemed to understand but went away sorrowful.

The real author of the Colombo concept and its implementation was Ernest Bevin. It is said that he has never received the credit due to him as the founder of the Commonwealth as an instrument of development. But perhaps on the next day, Sunday, he may have taken some comfort from the quite extraordinary tributes paid to him by the Sinhalese government and people.

The day was proclaimed a holy day: the sacred tooth of Buddha would be displayed to the multitudes at its resting place in the Temple of the Tooth at Kandy, a mountain resort which was also the site of Ceylon's major university. The route to the temple was up a well paved but very winding road which induced some nausea in most of us, including the Foreign Secretary. The scenery was marvellous and as we got ever higher the climate improved out of all recognition. I was very lucky in being assigned to the police car which immediately followed the Foreign Secretary's car, so when we finally arrived at the Temple of the Tooth, which was surrounded by tens of thousands of Buddhists, I was able to stay close to his party and get a good seat in the stalls.

Ernie, who was a very sick man, was also a very sporting fellow. He agreed to take off his shoes as he went into the temple, only exclaiming not wholly *sotto voce*, 'My God, 'oles in my socks! What would Flo have said.' He padded with Roger Makins and myself just behind him up the long winding staircase to the top of the tower which looked over the plains beneath and their countless thousands of yellow-robed priests and multi-coloured lay people.

The ceremony of unveiling the tooth was long and complicated but had a certain grandeur to it. The high priest (or whatever he was called) was dressed in pure cloth of gold with some gold brocade trimming, topped off with a gold dunce's cap. He con-

126

ducted the service in Sinhalese but whispered explanations behind to the English-speaking contingent. First he removed an encasement for the tooth covered with precious stones. Then followed a slightly smaller crystalline cover, followed by a brilliantly polished silver covering, and finally a box of gold. The priest paused for a moment before lifting off the lid and revealing the tooth. It was about four or five inches long and would have done credit to a shark. He solemnly lifted this up and turned to the four corners so that all the crowd could see it. The conches sounded everywhere and the people without exception fell to their knees. As the priest was facing us in his circumambulation with the now revealed tooth he said in a perfectly clear Oxford-accented voice, 'My, Foreign Secretary, but aren't we packing them in.'

The tooth was then re-covered by its jewelled boxes and replaced in its sacred and secure resting place. But all was not yet over. We descended the stairs, reassumed our shoes, and went along to the balcony of a nearby hotel where we could sit in the shade and watch a parade of elephants. This parade, it had been clearly stated, was an appeal to the gods for the good health of Ernest Bevin and his rapid recovery from his recent painful operations. As perhaps some 120 elephants processed by, all richly caparisoned with gold- and silver-lined cloths and with an infinity of bells dangling and jangling from every part of their being, someone tapped me on the shoulder from behind and said in what I had become accustomed to as good Oxford Sinhalese, 'I wonder when last there was such a parade of bejewelled pack animals as a magical cure for those haemorrhoids which have so far defied Western medicine.'

Next afternoon I saw the Foreign Secretary off on his train journey up the continent (he had been warned to fly as little as possible for health reasons). I flew straight to Delhi that evening to witness the proclamation of the Republic on Thursday. It was a wonderfully nostalgic occasion. I spent the day before the parade sitting on the balcony of Sir Sardar Sobha Singh's magnificent house at the end of Kingsway which by tomorrow would be named Jampath. We looked down into the peaceful depths of Burla's garden and estate – the scene of Gandhi's assassination only a few months before. The Sardar, however, was not reverentially eyeing that sacred but mournful place; he was looking through a telescope at the changes taking place at Lutyens' Viceroy's palace and secretariat on the hill half a mile away. The Sardar had been the contractor for the building of all of Delhi and this was in some ways his prize piece. He clearly resented very deeply the fact that they were taking down the three British lions which topped the towers of the secretariat, and hoped that his warnings against trying to carry the big stones over the arches had been heeded. They had not. Suddenly, with an awful crashing sound, two or three workmen carrying one of the single-stone British lion pieces disappeared through the fragile roofing of the dome and were lost to view. 'I warned them, I warned them. I told them they couldn't take away the British Raj without putting in some proper underpinning of our own.' The remark was symbolic of his and a lot of Indians' feelings.

Next day the city seemed to have been turned into a cantonment with soldiers encamped in every bit of shade. About midday we started moving towards the stadium where the parade was going to start at 3.45. It took about an hour for even such distinguished guests as the Sardar to be assigned to their seats. By a lucky chance the press seats were nearby and we were able to chat over the barrier between us. The Sardar said that the parade was an exact replica of a Curzon durbar in the early years of the century. Nothing had been changed in the order of march or in the ceremonies taking place in the great stadium parade ground, overlooked by the Red Fort which was once a symbol of Muslim rule. Experienced observers would notice one significant change: there were no units present from Muslim Pakistan.

As the President set off at 2.45 from the Viceregal Lodge (now to be the President's palace) in Curzon's old and ornate state coach, the front of the parade began to move into the parade ground. There were twenty-five separate units in the march past, ranging from the boys of the Punjab Regiment to the Sikhs and the Gurkhas. The bands all played full blast, varying from ancient Indian instruments to pipe bands. Every now and again something easily recognizable reached us – 'Hearts of Oak' from the Navy, and 'Colonel Bogey' from the Gurkhas – but a good deal of the music was played on traditional Indian instruments and was weird, wonderful and very stirring.

At 3.45 exactly the new President arrived on parade in his state coach. He was an aged Hindu dressed simply in his dhoti, a lifetime disciple of Gandhi, who had adopted and retained throughout his life a strict pacifism. Now surrounded by some thousands of soldiers he stepped for the first time in his life into a jeep and drove round the circle of troops which fired with perfect precision a *feu de*

128

joie which moved round the circle at exactly the point that the President had reached.

In the evening the celebrations continued, again according to Curzon's plan for the coronation of Edward VII and George V or both. There was a splendid display of fireworks and after they had finished the floodlights were turned up on all of Lutyens' magnificent buildings and statues. The lighting arrangements were equally unchanged, with the odd result that the centrepiece of the whole display was a brilliantly lit statue of King George V. Queen Victoria, Empress of India, Edward VII, and even a rather modest statue of George VI stood out like the gods in some Wagnerian opera. The next night when the fireworks and the display were repeated I noticed that someone had inserted a fairly dark piece of red cellophane in all the floodlights covering the British monarchs, so as to give a modest display to some Indian statues. The trouble was that it was a Hindu custom to represent Indians in life size which made them look tiny and insignificant beside the monumental statues of past viceroys and sovereigns.

It had all been something of a muddle (but then muddle is the essence of India as Aziz remarks in Forster's *Passage to India*), combined with the strict military discipline which the British had imposed on the Indian Army. It was in fact the last great ceremonial display of the British Raj, handing over through its military operations to a Hindu pacifist.

Back home in Britain the election had taken over public attention completely. The *Observer*, facing its first election under the current editor, had decided to remain non-party and our first editorial said a newspaper does not have a vote. But we tried to make our coverage as extensive and interesting and fresh as possible for those readers who did have a vote.

From my broadcasting background I introduced two exceptionally bright electoral scientists, later to have nationwide fame on television: Bob Mackenzie from the London School of Economics and David Butler from Nuffield College, Oxford. They suggested an interesting forecasting gimmick which was known as the cube rule. In a rather complicated way it explained that the difference between polling prospects and actual election prospects could be calculated by some mathematical magic. The 'cube' did not disgrace us on our results. We also featured, with their help, some of the more interesting statistical and political workings of the electoral process. With all of this in our minds we actually dared to take a full-page advertisement in two issues of the *Economist* (because of paper shortages advertising display space was extremely difficult to get). I remember that I wrote the first line of the copy (but no more), which was what I think is called a tickler. It read, 'We are all psephologists now.' Further down the page this novel word was explained as deriving from the Greek word for a small round stone which the Greeks used as their ballot in voting.

This did not seem the time to carry on a crusade in Britain about the Colombo Plan and the economic future of Asia. I was allowed to do a couple of wrap-ups of the whole set of events in the *Economist*, and used the overseas broadcasting services of the BBC extensively, since they were very glad to have some copy dealing with the outside world and not with Britain examining its own electoral entrails. But I did prepare for some sort of a crusade to establish that the old Empire had now become the New Commonwealth which was to concentrate on helping defeat the poverty of the less developed countries with at least as much priority as restoring the prosperity of the old dominions and the European countries of the Marshall Plan. In several lectures at Chatham House, the Royal Empire Society, etc. I stressed to the best of my ability that we would lose south-east Asia if we could not find food, preferably grown indigenously, for the eight million extra mouths that were to be found in the Indian subcontinent alone. I began at this time to make a great deal of noise about the population problem (which was extremely little understood in Britain or Europe). I also stressed that this should not and could not be a matter of expanding exports from Canada or America or, even less so, from Europe itself; it must be done by making some use of the population explosion and getting peasants to produce food for themselves and their neighbours, not in collectives or vast prairie farming but on their own land surrounding their own homes. It was a great pleasure and support to find that the United States fully agreed with this point of view. At the time, and indeed ever since Truman's Point Four speech in his 1949 inaugural, American aid authorities had stressed the importance of self-help and had urged on the rest of the Western world that more money should be diverted towards development and it should be used for agriculture and food production rather than industry and the production of goods and for export.

Equally, Britain needed to realize that such relatively small-scale development and not extensive military pacts would alone hold back communism in Asia. The UK in particular should continue to repay the 'sterling balances' which were debts run up by the UK government in India during the war, and try to use the leverage which these very large sums of money amounted to to ensure that they were not diverted by either country into military efforts and general rearmament against each other. But I always expressed the fear that the Kashmir dispute might finally break the peace in the subcontinent and we should do everything we could to prevent that happening.

Thirdly, I made the point very strongly, and fairly unpopularly, that there was no way of trying to maintain good relations with 'liberal Asia' by giving any support to colonial efforts in the Asian sphere. In particular we should not associate ourselves with the French attempt to maintain their colonial empire in Indo-China. This was not out of any jealousy of France's empire but simply because we had learned from Nehru that such efforts would alienate his country and many around it from the more liberal protestations and actions of Britain and many of its allies.

But Britain was still having some problems. Australia was not fully behind us in our attempts to move out of a military posture in the area, because they feared they might be abandoned in the process. America to some extent leapt into the breach on Australia's behalf but unluckily the United States, which five years ago had been the leading Western anti-imperialist, had now been branded as the chief imperialist-militarist power because of its expansion of colonial outposts in the Pacific and its insistence that its quarrel with Russia was the most dangerous and important aspect of world attentions, which must be given priority over anything else. Britain spoke against this but there were some doubts whether she was acting in accordance with her principles when she devoted so much effort to the suppression of communist guerrillas in Malaya fighting the established Malayan constitution. This was in large part forgiven, however, on the grounds that the guerrillas were non-Malays and that Britain was only standing behind the nationalist government of Malaya.

In general I maintained that the Colombo Plan had made the Commonwealth an engine for development. It helped to save the errant relationship between the whole vast mass of India and the British Raj – in a sense by abolishing the British Raj and in another sense by establishing a far better relationship, not of military power but of economic collaboration. By making the Commonwealth a partnership in development the Colombo Plan helped to save southern Asia and bring the Australians and New Zealanders firmly into an economic collaboration of equals, with their leadership being exerted in their own region and not in the Middle East and Europe which was essentially Britain's region.

As soon as the election was over, with the Labour majority reduced to single figures, the problem became how to deal with some of the urgent actions which were being presented to us from Europe. Clearly the Marshall Plan was working and Europe was beginning to come into profit again, but was it turning into some form of common market which would ensure that it was a strong economic force in world trade?

Britain was not thinking much about this but was thinking, to her credit, about Commonwealth trade and was in fact beginning to see that her run of supremacy in world trade, which had begun in about 1588 with the victory of the Armada, was starting to come to an end with honour in the Second World War but almost total exhaustion in the peace that followed it. The *Observer* was not by any means popular in suggesting this rather sad line and was bitterly attacked by the right wing of the Conservatives when we suggested that we could not hold our worldwide empire together, nor defend it, but must get defence from NATO and the US, and economic help from the Marshall Plan and the US. The American Administration was clearly beginning to regard us as a country which had lost an empire and not found a role (a phrase used much later by Dean Acheson and bitterly attacked by Harold Macmillan when he was Prime Minister).

The Labour government now faltering in its last months was determined not to stir up trouble within the party by making any efforts to join a community which would include Germany, and a rearmed Germany at that. Hence the policy was to pay no attention to the requests from Europe, including surprisingly strong requests from Monnet's economic group in France, to consider future association.

I went across to Paris on other matters in the first week of May 1950 and just had time to slip out to the elegant house and offices occupied by Jean Monnet, whom I had known quite well in the

Embassy in Washington where he worked during both wars. He began to harangue me while making fierce little charts on a sheet of paper as he went along. He had decided that Britain was never going to come into any sort of community status with Europe, and making concessions to Britain was a dead loss because the government simply did not listen or reply. Therefore he had decided on a different tactic. While Ernest Bevin was in hospital and the more moderate Kenneth Younger was acting Foreign Secretary he would try and explain the quite difficult hurdles that Britain had to face if it wanted to keep a long-term economic association with Europe. He wondered if we could persuade Kenneth Younger to attend a lunch meeting with as small an entourage of Foreign Office battleaxes as possible and talk this over because on 10 May he intended to make a formal proposal to most of the European powers that a steel and coal community should be formed which would in essence so interrelate the French and German industries that they could never go to war against each other again. The nations that joined this coal and steel community would have to join without reservations because there simply could not be a separate set of rules for different members of the community.

I had to make a hurried getaway but promised that I would do my best to set up the lunch that he requested, and it was duly arranged in London for 8 May. Monnet was effectively in the chair, Kenneth Younger and his private secretary represented the Foreign Office, the *Observer* was represented by David Astor and myself, and there was also present an old friend of Monnet's from Washington days, Lord Brand, who had been head of the Food Mission in Washington, and was now head of Lazard Frères in London. Monnet repeated the arguments that he had made to me a few days ago and then got a prepared response from Kenneth Younger asking for much more time to make such a serious decision. Monnet responded by saying that there was no time for a later reply, we were already behind time in these matters in our relations with Marshall Plan operatives who were pressing all of Europe very hard to start forming a community. He then went on to argue with great power that Europe was at last ready to move, and if Britain was not, Britain would simply be left out and this could not be in its interests as a powerful and expensive heavy industry country. But he had become absolutely used to Britain regarding itself as the natural leader of Europe and then doing no leading. This was a last chance and after this Britain would have missed the bus.

133

There continued to be a lot of opposition from the Foreign Office, but Kenneth Younger did say that he had some sympathy with the Monnet plan and he would try and propose it. He said modestly that he was only acting Foreign Secretary, and therefore there was bound to be some veto power from other senior members of the Cabinet, but he himself would try to present Monnet's proposals as thoroughly as he could.

I do not of course know exactly what went on in the Foreign Office but I did learn subsequently that a large part of the old and powerful Foreign Office thinkers in the Economic Department and the European Department, and indeed in the American Department, were strongly opposed. Eventually Roger Makins said that he thought in all the circumstances it would be best if the proposals were allowed to mature until they were properly prepared for consideration by Britain. A telegram to that effect was sent off through the British Embassy in Paris to Monnet that evening. A day later, on 10 May, all the proposals were formally put forward to the European governments by Monnet and were accepted by most of the community.

About two months later the Coal and Steel Community was fully established and when Monnet moved into his new office in Luxembourg there was only one telegram on his desk. It read as follows: 'Congratulations on your success in establishing the Coal and Steel Community. May I come and discuss it with you thoroughly in the next few days?' Signed Roger Makins.

Another more or less effective lunch party that I gave in those days was at the request of a very old friend working in the French Embassy in London. He asked me if I could arrange a very private meeting with Ambassador Alphand who had recently returned from the French Embassy in Washington to undertake the delicate task of preparing for the rearmament of Germany. The others present were to be Toby Low, who as a brigadier had received the first surrender of a German general who was commanding the key position of Aachen, and the general himself. I was asked if I could give my word not to publicize this in any way; the need for secrecy was absolute and one reason for choosing my house for the meeting was that it was out in the Notting Hill area on the edge of Ladbroke Square where there was unlikely to be anyone looking for three moderately well-known faces. I made no protest at this explanation for choosing me.

We met and had a cheerful, rather gossipy lunch, recalling old and hardly happy days. I then said that I would take my coffee to my study and leave the three gentlemen to talk by themselves. They talked for about an hour and a half, and I am proud to say that no word of this leaked, partly of course because I heard none of the conversation myself. But I did gather from Toby Low that he had warned that for Britain to join a European army, which was the objective of this meeting, was likely to be very, very unpopular with both the political parties in Britain. I later learned, however, that a lot of discussion had taken place which was useful in avoiding a strong opposition to a European army by Britain itself. When Anthony Eden had to pick up the pieces after the collapse of the European army, he found the notes that Toby Low had given him were very useful in preparing his position which was still that Britain would give all support to a European army, but would not promise either to join or to keep troops on the Continent. It was clear that if there was going to be a European community, whether of a military or commercial kind, it was going to meet with a great deal of opposition from Britain. This struck us at the *Observer* as a very dangerous situation because America was determined to bring all Germany's potential power into co-operation with the OEEC and the Marshall Plan, NATO and heavy industries. What David Astor particularly feared was that if America found Britain standing out it would, before very long (in his phrase), transfer the contract for running Europe from Britain to Germany.

It seemed very necessary to me therefore that we should concentrate our attention on educating the British about the merits of the Germans and the Germans about Britain's real willingness to accept them as part of the European community. But the Germans must be persuaded that they were to be genuine partners and not leaders of a revanchist war against Russia. For particular British political reasons they needed to accept some limitations on their political, military and economic progress.

The first Königswinter meeting in full array with German politicians, journalists and businessmen could not have been held at a more fortunate moment in the spring of 1950. All the German complaints about how Britain was holding them back so as to seize their industry and transfer their advanced machinery to Britain (as, to some extent, France had done too) came into the open and were responded to, partly by the British complaints about German attempts at domination in Europe by both military and commercial means.

135

Of course nothing was settled, no blinding agreement burst on any of these minds, but there was the beginning of a discussion between individuals of like sorts, including on the British side some quite strong anti-German thinkers. The process of re-understanding rather than reconciliation had begun, most slowly in Britain which was the one country in Europe that had not been defeated and overrun by Germany.

Within three months, when Europe's attention was firmly fixed on its indigenous defence within NATO, there was suddenly a threat from an almost unknown source in Asia. On 25 June 1950 the North Koreans invaded across the 38th Parallel, striking quite deeply into their Western-oriented half of the country now known as South Korea. Who was to blame for this? America, the Old Commonwealth and, as a statement by Pandit Nehru made clear, the new Asian Commonwealth regarded this as an assault by Russia and its ally China. Owing to a miscalculation by Russia, which was boycotting the Security Council because of the failure of that council to admit Red China to its proper seat in the Assembly and the Security Council, the vote was overwhelming for the United Nations' military response against the army of North Korea.

Few of us in the *Observer* knew much about the Korean political or historical situation. Our main expert on the area was an old man, O.M. Green, who had edited the *South China News* for many years before coming to us on retirement. But luckily for us, 25 June was a Sunday, and after a brief call to David Astor we agreed that I should try and put together from the resources in the office and from Dennis Bloodworth our correspondent in Singapore a sort of mini Marshall Plan article filling the editorial page.

By nine o'clock in the morning I was in Chatham House with its wonderful library service, getting some of the basic facts into my very ignorant mind. In the afternoon (since Mondays are an *Observer* holiday the office was not open or full) I went on my trail of those embassies which were anxious to persuade one of the rightness of their government's cause. By Tuesday material had come in from our correspondents abroad, and a faint outline of the issues which faced us in Asia was emerging. In the next few days we worked on this material, which covered not only Korea but China, Malaysia, Indo-China, etc.

While I was still polishing up this large piece based on book-learning we met in the editor's room to decide on the leader article which was to be our approach to the whole divided Asian scene. I had emphasized strongly some lessons I had learned at the Colombo conference that we must not try and make military alliances within the Asian groupings because they would fail to bring any unity to the various powers in that region, and O.M. Green had equally emphasized the necessity of keeping some links with the new People's Republic of China. But there was general agreement that we must keep faith with the New Commonwealth to ensure that it had an improved life at the end of colonialism, which the editor emphasized was in fact a school for democracy.

David Astor often reiterated his belief that we needed to be as anti-communist as we had been anti-fascist, an idea that had been imposed on him by Arthur Koestler and George Orwell. But he also made it clear that we were not at war with communism and what we wanted to do was to ensure in particular that China was enabled to become (what he later called) a Tito to the Kremlin. He also emphasized that we must avoid above all allowing passionate patriotism to become linked with a strong communist ideology so that independence of the colonial masters meant enslavement by the communist ideologists.

In the next few weeks we began to see the difficulties of pursuing the policies that we were proposing. General MacArthur, now commanding the United Nations forces in Korea, had long been the real leader of the new isolationist and anti-eastern Asian forces at the end of the world war. He had kept those forces under his command and had done nothing to let them be interfered with by the White House, or the Russian allies. On this occasion it was much the same. He had rushed forward across the Yellow River because he wanted a victory. He had therefore brought the Chinese into battle against us and had had to retreat very rapidly. Now he was actually proposing that atomic weapons should be used against the Chinese.

It was at this point that Attlee, realizing that the whole future of world peace might lie in the balance, and urged on by a remarkably united parliament, flew to Washington after requesting an interview with Truman. There was the usual battle between the White House and Congress, but Attlee was a very good negotiator and managed to persuade Truman to make a statement that action with nuclear weapons would not take place until Britain had been consulted. The Secretary of State Dean Acheson took the President

137

aside and pointed out that the one condition Congress had insisted on was that there should not be any promise to put the power of decision over nuclear weapons in the hands of any other country, however close an ally. Truman had to back down and Attlee had to be content with an understanding that the United States would not act unilaterally unless it was absolutely essential. What was unfortunately true was that this left MacArthur with a great power to force the President to act. In Britain and Europe and many parts of Asia it appeared that the command of the United Nations forces was not in the hands of the American President, let alone in any way under the control of the United Nations, but in the hands of a violent and imperious American general.

The Attlee government continued to try and fight as a loyal ally by the side of the United States, but there was a great deal of British resentment at the feeling that we were being led by the nose. The Keep Left section of the Labour Party continued to battle against British involvement with a belligerent American Administration, and it was perfectly clear that Aneurin Bevan himself was working towards a breach with his Cabinet colleagues.

The removal of MacArthur in 1951 did not basically change the policies of the United States. Congress had become convinced that China was the equivalent of Russia as an enemy in the East. Britain's view was rather that China could be a false ally to Russia and become an independent communist state, forming close connections with the Asian dominions. That was the main policy of the Asian Commonwealth at this time. It seemed, though it was kept very secret, to be the only way in which to prevent a vast coalition of communist powers against the Commonwealth, and perhaps overwhelmingly powerful opponents to the whole Western world. It was still possible that America's nuclear lead (no longer a monopoly since Russia had exploded her bomb in 1949) could achieve victory, but what was victory in a nuclear war?

In Britain there was considerable anxiety on both sides of the House. In a foreign affairs debate a leader of the moderate wing of the Labour Party, Sir Hartley Shawcross, who had been Attorney General, suggested that what was really needed was some means of discussing the issues in a federal council of sorts which would make it possible to review issues with the US before they were explosively revealed on the battlefield. There was no NATO for the Pacific, and therefore no NATO Council in which to discuss such issues.

In the *Observer* we had always supported some sort of confederation of the Western nations and we gave our full support to this, saying that it should be helpful to the Americans as well as supportful for us in Europe. There was alas little chance that America would co-operate in an election year with Senator McCarthy at his height in demanding to know who had lost China and who were the spies in the State Department and the Defense Department. I visited America for the *Observer* during the spring of 1952 and was appalled by the power of McCarthy's blackmail and his use of television to corrupt and accuse. I thought at the time that it was one of the most dangerous periods in American history and one in which Europe was completely at the mercy of America. I could only hope that a few brave men would stand up against this imposter, but I must say it took a long time for that to happen. Once it began, McCarthy's decline and fall in the face of the democratic habits of the United States was very encouraging.

In early March 1953 I was invited to be part of the British delegation, headed by Hugh Gaitskell the former Chancellor and Patrick Gordon Walker the former Commonwealth Secretary, to the fifth unofficial Commonwealth conference. This was a series of conferences which had been arranged by Chatham House and the Institute of International Affairs over the past twenty years. At this conference a group of about sixty people, ex-Cabinet ministers, professors, businessmen and clergy, sat round a table in Lahore in Pakistan discussing 'Why does the Commonwealth exist? What can be done to preserve it?'

There were equally important delegations from the other dominions, including four white South Africans representing in varying degrees of fervour the apartheid doctrines, and some white representatives from Southern Rhodesia. But there were of course no black Africans present since none of them or their countries had yet received full independence. That was not to say that there were no blacks present. Trinidad was represented by a very distinguished black Trinidadian, Sir Hugh Wooding, then a KC and soon to become Chief Justice of Trinidad. Wooding had been invited to the conference by Chatham House and not by any independent government. It seemed to me at the time to be a pity that Chatham House could not have invited one or two more independent non-white future leaders.

But nothing struck me more forcibly than a universal distrust of

America among Asians. On world strategic problems the Commonwealth divided dangerously neatly into the Old Commonwealth and the new Asian members. For instance, in discussions on NATO, Australia and New Zealand, though distant from Europe, looked at the problems of association with America and defence against Russia in a way that coincided almost exactly with the British view. India and Pakistan were reluctant to express any view at all on NATO. So far as either country had a view, it was that NATO was to be distrusted because it was an alliance with imperialist America.

The conference's two-day debate on race relations was a remarkable occasion. Afrikaners, West Indians, Africans, Indians and Canadians all took part in frank discussion that never became heated. Asian members were prepared to accept a great deal: they agreed that some separation of races was tolerable; they accepted the fact that Muslims and Hindus had split into separate states in India and Pakistan; and they admitted that backward people could not be given immediate equality. But they resolutely refused to accept the idea that there could be permanent or prolonged subjection of any people by European leaders.

The main thrust of the conference as I remember it was the future of black Africa. It was recounted in an essay by Philip Mason in his book *A Thread of Silk*, certainly the most illuminating and novel report that I had seen. Since I do not have any notes I will very immodestly quote what Philip Mason wrote: 'There were businessmen, journalists, an economist, and three members of Chatham House on the British delegation as well as William Clark, then of the *Observer* . . . a brilliant talker [who] played a big part in the discussion and here developed what he called the Clark Doctrine. This was the prophetic theme that Britain, if forced to choose, would prefer the friendship of black Africa to that of a South Africa that stayed obstinately white. Black Africa was then still almost entirely colonial and Nigerian oil was in its infancy so that the doctrine was truly prophetic. And it was a valuable point to make because many South Africans harbour – or then did – a feeling once expressed to me by a Rhodesian.

' "Don't you think," he said to me, "that before long the white Western powers will wake up to the facts, see where their true interest lies and come to the help of the whites of South Africa?" He wanted to make being "white" the only value that counted in friendship.'

The Indians and the Pakistanis spoke little about this subject on which they were somewhat sensitively poised, but in the closing of the conference, the chairman, Sir Firoz Khan Noon, who during the war had been a member of the Viceroy's Defence Council, said with delicacy that almost none of us round the table were wholly innocent of some measure of racialism but that we must proceed towards a greater measure of equality, pursuing the political paths first.

At the end of the conference I felt it had been extremely useful to me and probably very useful in bringing together people of wholly different views within the Old and New Commonwealths. I had learned much more about Pakistan and its society. The city of Lahore was a rich cultural area with one of the most magnificent museums of Muslim art that I know. There was the university where I lectured and was lectured at, and I realized what an old but fiercely competitive civilization the Muslim religion supported. I also went up to Muzzaffarabad where I found the basic tribal antagonism towards Hindu India and realized what was the real base of the country's battle with India. Finally, I foresaw for the first time the deep racial antagonism that was growing up in Africa and to a somewhat lesser extent in the Caribbean. The road to a free and equal Commonwealth was going to be more bumpy than I had supposed.

The autumn of 1953 and winter of 1954 took me through the Indian subcontinent, the Middle East, Turkey and much of Europe, into the complexities of Muslim politics and Middle East confusion. One particular journey left an odd memory. Crossing the Arctic circle is like crossing the Equator or the 38th Parallel. It is a slight disappointment because things look so very much the same on the other side. Still, it was not without a tremor of excitement that I walked into a hotel in Finnish Lapland to spend my first night in the Arctic. At the desk the clerk's face lit up when he saw my passport, and in faultless English he asked: 'Can you say what the prospects of Arsenal are this season?' In his hand was a football-pool form (in Finnish) which he, like everyone else in the hotel, was assiduously filling in. This was my first experience of something that was to be borne in on me wherever I went in Scandinavia: almost everyone spoke English, but the England that they knew was not Westminster and Stratford but Tottenham Hotspur and Sheffield Wednesday.

It is dangerous to generalize about Scandinavia, but I felt that the great days of supremacy would never return; four countries with a total population of fewer than 20,000,000 could not, even united, make a Great Power. And they were far from united. Norway and Denmark were part of NATO; Sweden was neutral; and Finland, passionately attached to the West, was imprisoned in the strategic grasp of Russia. Finland was never happier than when she welcomed all the nations of the world – East and West – to the Olympic Games in 1952; Sweden still dreamed of leading a Scandinavian bloc or even larger neutral third force; Norway (and to a lesser extent Denmark) worked and prayed for a real Atlantic community. Each nation dreaded isolation, but there was no basis for union in an area divided by the Cold War.

If 1953 seemed like a year of hopeful international conversation, the winter of 1954 presaged a very different kind of diplomacy. It became clear that the policy proclamations were going to be made by John Foster Dulles and that they were going to be very tough. Two or three days before Eisenhower's State of the Nation address in January 1954, Foster Dulles gave one of those disastrous speeches, off the record, but as far as Americans and particularly Congress went, they were to be the main source of information. The gist of JFD's programme was to declare that there was going to be no appeasement of those who threatened the United States. On the contrary, there would be massive retaliation – which meant that there would be nuclear retaliation; and Dulles went on to hint that he had intentions of using it in Vietnam which he saw as part of the communist conspiracy to conquer southern Asia. Eden sent puffs of protest, but Dulles was laying out his policies to protect himself against any charges of softness from Congress. Mendès-France made a series of private bids for atomic threats from Dulles, which were strongly opposed by Britain and equally strongly resisted by Chou En-lai for China. As a result a conference was organized in 1954 in Geneva of the major powers concerned and accepted reluctantly even by the US.

Geneva was a new conference venue and I wondered at the time whether Geneva would become a political term like Versailles or Munich. It appears to have been prophetic dreaming. But at least the Geneva conferences would never share the reputation of the Congress of Vienna which ended the Napoleonic wars in an atmosphere of waltzes and intrigue. There may be intrigue at Geneva, there are certainly no Congress dances. I have never attended so glum a conference, at which there was so little entertainment, so little official good will to oil the wheels of diplomacy.

In some ways the conference was like a zoo, with the crowds clustering around the rarest specimens. At that Geneva conference, the most followed and least communicative man was Pham Van Dong, the Foreign Minister of the Vietminh would-be government that was waging its all-too-successful war in Indo-China. There were well over one thousand press representatives at Geneva – easily outnumbering the delegates – and the communist powers seized this opportunity. At the Maison de la Presse there was a small, well-organized group of communist pressmen who carefully buttonholed those of their colleagues whom they considered waverers.

Upstairs, in the press conference halls, a more open wrangle took place for the minds of newspapermen. Next door in a room filled with the waverers from India, Egypt, Burma and Thailand, Huang Hua, the Chinese spokesman, 'commented' on the Western speeches. In the corridors even the cold weather, with snow in May, was confidently attributed to the American H-bomb explosions.

The United States delegation seemed to be isolated and prisoners of a small group of violent Senators led by McCarthy and Knowland. The private views of the Americans were so sane and balanced, and contrasted sadly with what they had to say in public if they wished to avoid Congressional investigation. It was very noticeable that on his last days in Geneva Dulles loked even grimmer than before, while General Bedell Smith, who had been sent out to replace him, seemed quite jaunty and cheerful. A fellow delegate, I seem to remember, warned me not to draw any conclusions about changes in American policy: 'The fact is,' he said, 'that Dulles is going back into the Washington prison while Bedell Smith has just escaped from it.'

I have since tried to recall why visiting this conference was so worthwhile an experience. Partly, of course, it was the chance of meeting many of the people who make Western policy, though on this occasion they had little new to say. But I must confess to a sheer tourist's delight in actually watching Molotov, or seeing Chou En-lai in his five-ton Russian armoured car (a version of the 1939 American Packard, I noticed), and in observing their entourages: the Russians still in blue serge lounge suits, the Chinese in smart grey serge with button-up collars; the North Koreans, for some unknown reason, in purple Homburgs, grey coats and enormously wide 'Oxford bags' that seemed a relic of the 1920s. But above all these interesting irrelevancies there was a sense of being present at a great historic event. It was not just a pageant of the nations, with each participant speaking his appointed lines; it was the first real meeting of world powers since the Second World War.

While I was travelling the world and observing the increasing pace of international conferences attempting to grapple with the future of the world as we knew it, at home the debate on a comparatively minor and local revolution was beginning to occupy the minds of politicians of both main British political parties. This was the question on breaking the broadcasting monopoly of the BBC by the introduction of commercial television. The subject had been rumbling along for many years. To begin with, discussion had been curiously blinkered, as if the only alternatives were monopoly or commercial competition. At this time the only effective attack had been on centralization, with the result that a great deal of power had been devolved on the regional offices of the BBC, in particular the Scottish and Welsh regions, and neither listener nor performer had gained much benefit from this limited competition. Many years previously a plan for a thoroughgoing competition had been outlined to the Beveridge Committee by Geoffrey Crowther and Sir Robert Watson Watt but failed to proceed any further due partly to the cost and partly to the then lacking technological development.

I have always regarded the broadcast medium, be it radio or television, as a most important political and cultural power and, at the time, felt extremely strongly that the influence of pure commercial broadcasting was not beneficial. A number of committees, notably in Australia, had investigated the problem and had found against it. In 1932, the Australian Broadcasting Commission was founded to take over certain commercial stations where considerable abuses of their licence had taken place. At about the same time that the Beveridge Committee was sitting in Great Britain, Vincent Massey was chairing a Royal Commission to examine Canadian broadcasting and they also found that the BBC system held up extremely well against either a pure commercial system, as had existed for a while in Australia, or the mixed system then broadcasting in Canada. I wrote at the time: 'Commercial broadcasting can drive out public service broadcasting. Since no one really wishes to destroy serious broadcasting of the BBC type it is preserved by government subsidies, but it loses its mass audience, which is delivered over to the commercial interest.'

In October of 1954 I found myself very much closer to this whole subject. I was editor of the Conservative Party Conference Record and it had been decided to make a film for television purposes of the Blackpool conference. Up till now neither party conference had been seen in action by the British public. The 1954 conference was televised on closed circuit in its entirety, but this version was seen by only about half a dozen people concerned with editing the film. Having myself watched the politicians for six hours a day for three days, I felt that if the whole conference had been put on the air for the general public to watch at will, it would have done the party no harm and I hoped at the time that the next year would see both parties permitting at least part of their conferences to be shown live.

The editing proved to be a mammoth task and, at times, something of a nightmare. One of the worst must have been compressing fifty minutes of Winston Churchill's oratory into a quarter of that length. Some parts of his speech were gay, some grave, some eloquent and some quite dull, but the whole had been worked over with his infinite capacity for taking pains. In compressing it we felt as if we had been suddenly asked to throw away three-quarters of the pictures in the National Gallery and had been given just one hour to do the job.

After this experiment – and it is odd to think that once again by pure chance I had been part of one of those first-ever occasions – I believed that it was a success, but that such success depends on the honesty of the camera and of the conference organizers. It undoubtedly affects the mood of a conference; it makes it more staid, just as the introduction of a tape recorder in the home dries up the conversation. Watching the cameras travel over the conference hall, one felt like the driver of a police car on a crowded road – a sudden attention to duty and unusual politeness afflicted those who saw that they were observed. 'We are all television stars now,' said the chairman hopefully in his opening speech.

For years I had been seeing all these politicians from the front of the press box. I was now to see them backstage and, no longer the receiver of calculated leaks, to change sides; the poacher turned gamekeeper.

145

6

Downing Street
1955–6

The part of my life that I spent at Downing Street is a story of disillusion. I was disillusioned by – and even felt let down by – a prime minister I had previously admired, though no doubt there were mitigating circumstances arising from his health, his colleagues, his party, his wife, and his political experiences before he arrived at No.10. I was disillusioned also by something much deeper than the personal failings of Sir Anthony Eden: the realization that Britain, whose main task, as I saw it, should have been to push two parts of the world together, to be a bridge-builder between the rich white Commonwealth and the poor black Commonwealth and the rest of the still poorer Third World, in practice was still caught up in an old imperial dream, its leaders – or at least those of its leaders who held political office – largely unaware, though the facts stared them in the face, of the fundamental shifts of power and influence produced by the Second World War and the end of empire.

Eden's was the last British Cabinet dominated by men who had come to maturity before the First World War. They were its survivors. They all, not excluding Butler, with his family background of India, possessed an exaggerated view of what Britain in the mid-1950s could do on its own; and they lived in blinkers, with a very outdated vision of where their country's true interests lay. In this, a large part of the electorate followed them; and – astonishingly to me – still does.

I entered Downing Street with excitement, and if not with high at least with modest hopes. In June 1955 a fly was cast in my direction by an old acquaintance from the Commonwealth Relations Office, Sir Anthony Rumbold, at – characteristically – a party for a visiting Siamese dignitary. Two months later, the Prime Minister's private secretary rang me from Chequers at my country cottage ten miles away and asked me over for the night. I guessed at once what was up, and found myself delighted at the prospect. I drove over to Chequers to arrive at 7.30. One solitary policeman in a sentry box almost at the house asked my name and seemed to expect me. Philip de Zulueta and a WAAF sergeant were at the door to greet me and I was shown up to my room, which had a key in the door labelled 'Prime Minister's No.2 closet'. Inside was a fourposter of stifling comfort and a pleasant view over a tiled garden.

When I went down for drinks I found the main sitting room – a vaulted hall once open to the sky – gloomy and covered in rather second-rate 'family portraits', presumably of the Lee family. Eden came down very brown, very healthy, wearing a dark blue shirt and green silk scarf, followed later by Lady Eden looking pretty and relaxed.

The three of us (plus de Zulueta) dined together, a good meal, with the cutlet bones collected for the dogs, a golden retriever and a black poodle. We talked about wines, on which Eden was quite an expert, and I was reminded of the saying that he was the best hostess in London; he was certainly adept at small talk. He spoke of Baldwin's advice to him when he first entered Parliament: 'Don't ever make fun of the party opposite; you may have a better education, but they know more about unemployment insurance.' He said of Neville Chamberlain: 'History will write him down a good deal, he was a very mean man.' Sam Hoare he despised more than I expected as fussy with no grasp of bigger things.

After dinner, in a smaller room decorated in white, we got down to business. The PM explained rather lengthily why the present man could not go on; also that he lived rather far away – in Brighton. So he wondered if I'd come: 'The one thing that I have in common with Winston is that I like people I know' – which was his excuse for taking a diplomatic correspondent as his press adviser.

I simply said, 'Yes, I will take it, whatever the conditions,' and went on to explain how much I felt in agreement with him about an informed democracy and relations between the classes in Britain. We had a brief word on pay and allowances, about both of which he was apologetic.

I had, I suppose, an over-enthusiastic view of the Prime Minister when I accepted his offer. He had been a boyhood hero. In the sixth form at Oundle in the 1930s, I thought him the bright and shining light of hope: interested in the League of Nations, which I was keen on; anti appeasement and in favour of what he called 'a better ordering of humanity's way' (a phrase that I think Attlee later appropriated and used in a letter to Truman in 1945); and the one person who recognized that if war was to be avoided – as I, being a potential victim, certainly hoped it would be – then old ideas of total national sovereignty would have to change. None of these great themes, however, featured in my first business encounter.

A week after the announcement of my appointment – with the press oddly interested in knowing my exact salary (£2,500 p.a.), possibly because that is the modern way of denoting rank – I was summoned to Chequers to lunch with the two Edens and the principal private secretary. What the Prime Minister wanted to talk about and ask advice on was a Cabinet reshuffle. He wanted to move Butler from the Treasury and make him Lord Privy Seal and Leader of the House (to which Butler had already agreed), to put Selwyn Lloyd at the Foreign Office instead of Macmillan, and to make Macmillan Chancellor. But when was he going to do it? An important international conference at Geneva was coming up; so was an autumn budget. Therefore Butler and Macmillan could not be moved until these events were over. But could such important moves be kept secret for so long, especially given Butler's notorious loquacity? Then the Prime Minister said: 'Will they think I can't make up my mind?' Here, before I had even done something about the carpets and chairs in my office, I was made aware of what was to be a continuing, even dominant, theme of my Downing Street days: Eden's indecisiveness and, equally important, his anxiety about being thought indecisive – a psychological trait that played its part in the Suez crisis a year later.

That I must have been worried by this trait from the beginning is shown by a diary entry for 3 October 1955, my first real day on duty at the office: 'Before lunch I went up to talk to the PM who was spending the day in bed, wearing his green sweater and chatting away about this and that. It's a lovely bedroom on the fourth floor looking over Horse Guards Parade. On the wall is a small glass plate showing a bomb hole. I asked the PM if it was what I thought and he replied a bit huffily, "Oh, I suppose so. I didn't do it, the Old Man did it." No love lost there.

'We talked desultorily about the press, then were interrupted

The *Observer*: the author interviewing Bertrand Russell, and (*bottom*) David Astor, proprietor and editor of the paper, at the same meeting

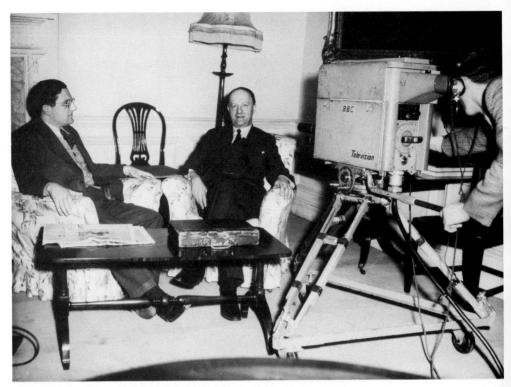

An early 1950s budget broadcast by R. A. Butler. William Clark was the first TV interviewer to put a Cabinet minister on television

At work in the *Observer*'s Tudor Street offices in the 1950s

World Bank triumvirate: Robert McNamara (centre) with his vice president for development policy Hollis Chenerey and William Clark on Martha's Vineyard

William Clark's real service to Robert McNamara at the World Bank was to introduce him to leaders and politicians of the Third World. This meeting between McNamara and Julius Nyerere, the first President of Tanzania whom the author knew from his first visit to Africa twenty-five years before, was a typical example of his role at the World Bank

A formal photograph of the executive directors of the World Bank in full session. William Clark kept several of these photographs and they charted his progress from managerial to executive rank within the Bank. Robert McNamara is at the extreme right; William Clark is sixth clockwise round the table. The photograph was taken on 7 January 1975 when the author had been appointed vice president in charge of external relations

The stages of William Clark's career always induced caricature on the part of his associates, invariably focusing on one of his inimitable clichés. This farewell memento, from the staff of the World Bank, also managed to crystallize his studied eccentricity of dress and alarming casualness

An early group shot of the ODI team, taken at The Mill, Cuxham. The author has his hands on the shoulders of Teresa Hayter and Andrzey Krassowski. Tom Soper is at the back between the heads of Adrian Moyes (left) and John White

'A weekend in the country ...' William Clark used to cajole his guests into having a drink at the Cuxham village local, The Half Moon. Second from the right is the architect of colonial independence, Sir Andrew Cohen, first Civil Service head of the Overseas Development Ministry in the 1964 Wilson government

The author greets British Prime Minister James Callaghan at Rich Neck on the Chesapeake Bay during the PM's visit to President Carter in the 1970s

The Queen at a Commonwealth Secretariat reception in 1982/3 chats to the author

The author's Christmas cards, usually a collage of the more compelling events or locations of the previous year, became a great tradition. This example provides the title of his memoirs but, curiously, is undated

with a message that Eden wants to send to Bulganin about arms for Egypt. I was pleased to notice that though, understandably, the Americans were worried about discussing the Middle East with Russia, Eden was determined to go ahead. "If we'd waited on the Americans," he said, "I'd never have gone round Europe after EDC (European Defence Committee) smashed; we'd never have had a Geneva conference. They're always unprepared to act." I was pleased not at the action itself, but at the sign of decisiveness. After all, so far we'd not had much luck. He originally decided on a special session of Parliament for an autumn budget. That died, and was replaced by the idea of Parliament meeting a week early. That died, and has been replaced by a change in the order of business in the first week. The same erosion seems to be affecting the call-up changes. I do hope the PM is in control, but I'm not yet sure.'

Next day, my doubts deepened: the 'urgent' message to Bulganin was delayed for thirty-six hours, and was 'a bit watered down at that'. Six weeks later I wrote in my diary: 'Macmillan has been away at Geneva and tonight has gone off again to Baghdad. The PM has had me announce that *he* is in charge of the Foreign Office. He is; but is he in charge of the country? I am a bit uneasy at the way we seem to be drifting – economic affairs don't seem good to me.'

Downing Street possessed an air of exceptional informality. In Washington I had been required to send typed minutes to the Ambassador, and to call him Your Excellency. In Downing Street I sent notes to the Prime Minister written in my execrable handwriting, and received them back with his scrawls added in red ink and initialled 'A.E.' No. 10 is in fact the downstairs rooms of a country house, so that there is a curious ambiguity about it. All the private business was conducted in the far north end of the house, where the sun never penetrates; and the Prime Minister, at least in my time, did not have a desk, only the Cabinet table. One result was – and I think this is true of all recent Prime Ministers – that Eden used to retreat two floors up, above the state dining rooms, to the little flat at the top, which was more or less created for Winston's war. But that part of the house was not the Prime Minister's but Clarissa's. Not unlike Winston, and not primarily because of ill health, Eden used to conduct a lot of business from his bed. We used to have little troubles like finding that the most secret telegrams had been made into his bed. One inconvenience of this room, which was like a large bed-sitter, was that it had no filing cabinets – and nor had the Cabinet Room – so that if you wanted to get a file you had to phone down for it. Fortunately the Registry, housed in long tunnels under No. 10 and No. 11, was superbly efficient, able to retrieve a file in minutes. A good deal of business was done in the mornings while the Prime Minister was having his bath. The typists would have to come up with their shorthand pads from the subterranean basement where they lived, which was known euphemistically as the Garden Room.

The garden also belonged very much to Clarissa, who spent a lot of time sitting in it. I think it all belongs to No. 10, but also serves No. 11, which leads to boundary disputes. It was while in her deck chair there listening to the radio that Clarissa found the Third Programme blocked by what was fairly clearly a transmission from a Commonwealth Prime Ministers meeting inside the house. She raised this bad-temperedly with me, saying she wished we would not stop her listening to concerts. I made enquiries and discovered that we had put in boosting equipment so that the Prime Minister of Rhodesia, Sir Godfrey Huggins, could communicate with Salisbury. His private messages to Rhodesia were heard not only by Clarissa but also by a taxi driver on his radio, who reported it to the police.

We were a small team, seven professionals in my day. The private secretaries knew their jobs and strictly observed their proper hierarchy, in spite of the informality, without trying to invade one another's territory. And the switchboard was of unmatched ingenuity in raising anyone almost anywhere. I remember Mountbatten being discovered on a Swedish ski slope, and myself being discovered at square leg during a village cricket match in Oxfordshire. The machinery of government itself ran less like clockwork. Eden always insisted that matters should be brought to Cabinet only if they could not be dealt with down the line; but the first Cabinet paper I saw concerned the raising of the status of sanitary inspectors, and the first Cabinet report 1 saw – a simple little Mimeographed paper, baldly summarising the discussions and conclusions and, no doubt by design, all sounding very unanimous and dull – was mainly about whether they dared to pull down Decimus Burton's gate façade at Hyde Park Corner. Around this time much press speculation was caused by a Cabinet meeting that dragged on to the unprecedented time of ten minutes to two in the afternoon. The Middle East? The economy? It was, in fact, the proposal to build a road across Christ Church Meadow in Oxford, a problem that could have been resolved in time for lunch, one might have thought, since the Prime Minister came from Christ Church and the Minister of Works from a lesser college.

I was soon made aware by Sir Edward Bridges of an underlying weakness of the administration, which was the tension between Eden and Butler: another circumstance that played its part in the Suez disaster. Bridges, the head of the Civil Service, looked like an eccentric don, with a boyish haircut, brushed forward, and spectacles pushed on, over, and above a determined nose. He came to my office shortly after my arrival, and the talk turned first to the ramshackle machinery of government and its undue dependence on Bridges himself, on Norman Brook, the Secretary of the Cabinet, and on David Pitblado, the canny, unruffled Scotsman who was the Prime Minister's principal private secretary. Bridges then raised the matter of Butler. Like other outsiders, I had of course assumed that difficulties and rivalries existed among those at the top of this administration as of others; even so, I was surprised to hear the head of the Civil Service stressing to me, a newcomer, the necessity of avoiding quarrels between the Chancellor of the Exchequer and the Prime Minister.

A few days later I found myself having a long conversation with Butler, the first of many. 'It was most odd,' I noted in my diary, 'because he talks all the time in a curious rather high-pitched monotone as if he were hypnotized.' It was a devastatingly frank talk. I told him I knew about his new position after the reshuffle and he asked did I think it was a mistake to give up so much – the Treasury and all its experts, the special position of Chancellor, etc., even perhaps No. 11 – to deal with a lot of dunderheads in Parliament instead of the fierce intellect of the Civil Service. I said I was sure it was right. I reminded him that Bonar Law had kept the right to No. 11 when he became Lord Privy Seal. The need, I said, was for someone in the government to look out and direct policy, keeping ahead of the crises, finding out what the UK needed of the future. But I added that it would throw a strain on his relations with Eden because they would be closer together and more disputing the same territory. RAB said he always got on well with Eden; he was not a genius, but he was very shrewd and perhaps a great PM – absolutely straight, and never did anything except for the national interest. 'I've always thought he was a winner since the thirties.' RAB was more worried about the relations of Eden and Macmillan, where there was friction.

RAB said he felt his April budget was too easy, but he had been over-persuaded both by his unanimous expert opinion and by Churchill, who thought it could be easier still. He was worried as to whether he would be made much more unpopular by his autumn budget. I said yes, but only temporarily. He had been hurt by the attacks on him at the party conference at Bournemouth and said, rather pathetically, that those days in a hotel had left him feeling his wife's death. I thought that in spite of his smug assumption that we were all much better than the rest of mankind he would be easy to work with.

Not long afterwards he telephoned me to complain that he was being publicly criticized for delaying his budget. That was not his fault, he said, it was the fault of Eden and his colleagues, who had insisted on delay. Other people would have resigned. (Butler, Monckton, Salisbury – they all seemed to think about resigning once a week.) Then came his budget, which was savaged in the Commons by Gaitskell and much criticized in the press. RAB did well in a censure debate, and instantly recovered his sparkle; but three weeks later he was again down in the dumps. On a single day, a Sunday, he telephoned me three times worrying about his future; he told me in the morning that he could not possibly stop being Chancellor at the moment because he must see through the consequences of his budget: 'There is the matter of honour as well as convenience' – he meant the Prime Minister's convenience. By the evening his mind had moved on and he was worrying if he would have enough to do in his new post as Lord Privy Seal and Leader of the House after he left the Treasury. But, said I, Sir John Anderson and Herbert Morrison had both played important roles as Lord Privy Seal, surely? No, said Butler, that analogy did not apply because they had both had considerable economic responsibilities which was not going to happen to him because 'they're afraid now of taking anything away from Harold (Macmillan)'. RAB was also worried about his future staff and his future office. I later explained to the PM that what Butler needed was love and a feeling of being wanted. Eden looked at me in amazement and said, 'By God, maybe you're right.'

Eventually, three months after – to my certain knowledge – a Cabinet reshuffle had been decided on by the Prime Minister, it happened. It could pehaps have been more smoothly conducted. Just before Christmas I came back from Hemingford, where I had been recuperating from flu, to be in at the last stage, arriving at the office at 11.15 a.m. to find total chaos. The Cabinet was supposed to meet at 11.30 but the PM was still in bed with the same virus I had had. Lord Salisbury had resigned as Lord President of the Council because there were too few peers in the Cabinet, and had started a regular 'down Coronets' movement. Alec Home, Secretary for Commonwealth Relations, was on the point of joining it and was asking for a secretary to dictate his resignation. None was supplied, to stall that. But De L'Isle (Secretary of State for Air) was firmer and anyway expected to resign, so he got a secretary and wrote a letter of resignation which he carefully sealed, marked 'Personal for the Prime Minister', and handed to David Pitblado. David waited a moment till De L'Isle left, then opened it, and we started to compose a suitably sugary reply for the PM to sign. A good deal of the rest of the day was spent in trying to find synonyms for 'devotion to duty' and 'splendid job', while the resignations drooled on about 'chance for younger men'. There was a torrent of honours to placate everyone – baronetcies for sacked under secretaries, viscountcies for ministers, e.g. Harry Crookshank. He had no idea this was going to happen to him (did he never read the papers?) and was deeply hurt at the offer of the mere Chancellorship of the Duchy of Lancaster. He told the PM in Cabinet that he did not want any job. Eden was now able to increase the number of peers by giving the Duchy to Selkirk, leaving the Paymaster Generalship for another peer. Salisbury's suggestion for Paymaster was Quintin Hogg who was approached at 3.30 and eventually given till 6.30 to think it over.

The afternoon was taken up with the PM seeing (in bed) the under secretaries, while the Chief Whip, Patrick Buchan Hepburn (who was to go to the Department of Works and be replaced by Ted Heath) saw others, especially the expellees. Each had ten minutes (I had set 7.30 as the deadline for first editions) so it was rather like a National Health Service dentist doing 'fillings and extractions'. Meanwhile, David Pitblado and I worked on the guidance which I would give the press. It was delicate because it had to satisfy RAB that he was being promoted to virtual Deputy Prime Minister while reassuring Macmillan that nothing of the sort was happening and that as Chancellor he would be fully in charge of *all* economic affairs. RAB, with whom I had a short talk at No. 11, was terribly anxious to ensure that he got credit for not running away from that autumn budget. He was quite cheerful and already talking about how busy he would be in the new post. 'I've been very calm,' he kept on repeating.

During the evening the draft of what I would say to the press (which the PM went over with me in detail) was circulated to ministers concerned, and from then on I got bleak little bleats from one side or the other asking me to emphasize their side of things. The Treasury was really afraid that RAB's departure would bring sterling toppling down, and so had arranged to telegraph the press statement to all posts. At about 5 p.m. it was suddenly discovered that the Chief Whip had lost three of his flock and could not contact them. Eden exploded and all was very glum; there was talk of putting off the under secretaries till the next day, but I begged to have the whole thing in one and to begin by 7.30. Heroic efforts got the Cabinet list, honours, and letters of resignation Mimeographed by 7.35, and I got over to the House of Commons and Lobby Room by 7.45. To catch the first editions meant finishing by eight o'clock and we succeeded – my deputy Alfred Richardson bringing in the big batch of copies at about 8.01. I think all editions were caught. The under secretaries remained, but we put them out as a separate list. One of them, R. Wood, was still lost at 10.00 p.m., but at 10.15 he drifted back and we put his name in at last. Quintin finally felt that he could not afford £2,000 a year so the Paymaster Generalship was still vacant.

It was striking how haphazard the whole procedure was. People got jobs quite chancily. The office was littered with lists of posts and two or three names opposite them; it was not till later that I could be sure who finally had which job.

Just after I noted in my diary that Butler was 'as edgy as ever' and that the Prime Minister was 'capriciously interested in detail and so neither relaxes nor gets rest', I went one evening early in January to Carlton Gardens to see Macmillan at my own request. The press, especially the conservative press, was increasingly hostile, with Lady Pamela Berry stirring up hostility to Eden at her husband's *Daily Telegraph*, and Randolph Churchill in the *Evening Standard* doing his utmost to cause trouble for the man he privately called 'jerk'. The Conservative Party too was restless, though less violent than the press. I found Macmillan calmly reading a novel in a rather bare study. I asked him what we could do to help the Prime Minister and government; for instance, could he make a statement somehow recalling how much we all owed to Eden? He agreed, but then he happened to mention that he was dining with Winston Churchill the next day, so I suggested that perhaps Churchill could make such a statement. Macmillan said he would try.

'I see why his civil servants are so devoted to him,' I noted in my diary. 'He is a kind, wise, unruffled avuncular old man.' Macmillan was worried by Eden's inability to relax and his looking over the shoulder of ministers, especially the Foreign Secretary. He said he had been rung up several times by mistake in the last few days because the PM wanted the Foreign Secretary. Macmillan was afraid that Eden tended to over-react to press attack and, rightly or wrongly, that Clarissa fed his sensitivity. As Chancellor he was appalled by the problems before us; he thought he might have to introduce physical controls such as import licensing all over again. He wondered if he could get the Prime Minister properly interested in that side of things. He must also have been wondering, as he calmly read his novel, about his chances of succeeding a Prime Minister who was getting no support in the conservative press, and not much support from his two principal colleagues. I did not put it in my diary, but I think it must have been on this occasion that Macmillan made the (in retrospect) chilling remark that it would be 'interesting to see whether Anthony can stay in the saddle'.

Macmillan's remark about Clarissa reinforced a hint I had just had that she might be going to cause me trouble. On the very first day of 1956 I went over to Saturday lunch at Chequers and found Eden in a vile temper because a public row had blown up about the sale of tanks and arms to the Middle East. The government had discovered in the early summer that tanks sold as scrap were ending up in Middle East countries, and at once stopped licences. But because these deals, in a way that I never learned, involved some dirty business by our security forces, the government had not been able to make a clear and convincing statement about what had been going on. Now Eden felt he had to say something publicly, but had not been able to find anyone on the telephone – it being Saturday morning – to help him. We rang up various people throughout lunch, chiefly Selwyn Lloyd, with the Prime Minister driving us all on. Then during a walk after lunch he raised some of his other worries: the forthcoming visit by Khrushchev and Bulganin, how he was proposing to make it more businesslike by concentrating on talks, with just a courtesy call on the Queen, but how he feared that even though he hoped the visit would be a 'contribution to peace', Lord Salisbury would again resign. (The trouble with Salisbury was that he, and Lady Salisbury still more so, felt that he ought to be Prime Minister or at least Foreign Secretary instead of being merely Lord President of the Council.) Then as we sat in the gloom of the

Central Hall Eden said, 'Clarissa has been saying to me that my reputation has suffered over the budget far more than RAB's and that really you oughtn't to favour RAB at my expense. It's no good you saying that everyone is all right except the Prime Minister, who just dithers.'

To divert him I showed him a brief I had prepared for RAB when he was due to see the Lobby as the government's spokesman. Eden read it through. 'That's nothing to do with RAB . . . That's my idea . . . All this is what I was going to say in my Bradford speech . . .' I tried to explain my difficulty; how could I produce to the Lobby the spokesman for the government if I had to confine him to his own field in order to stop him seeming too like a prime minister? Eden then got very low, and revealed his distress at the lack of support he felt he was getting from the Conservative Party. 'Of course I don't care about this at all,' he said, demonstrating how much he did care. 'If they want, they can get rid of me and go back to Winston.'

Plainly, the source of the Prime Ministerial gloom was Clarissa. Over drinks I tackled her about her upside down view of the comparative popularity of RAB and her husband, telling her that in fact Butler was much more criticized than the Prime Minister. Her reply was: 'Of course RAB is criticized more, but that criticism is justified and the criticism of Anthony isn't.'

This episode neatly illustrated, I realized later, the nature of Clarissa's role as the Prime Minister's wife. She never interfered 'downstairs' at No. 10, but she resented criticism of Eden as being absolutely intolerable. She kept the door like a tiger, rarely allowing any but true and staunch friends to see him. It might have been better if she had. If, for instance, she had allowed him to see and hear the criticism of people like Sir Walter Monckton, who was loyal, her husband might have written more plausible memoirs. On one occasion Clarissa said in my presence, 'I see Hugh Massingham in the *Observer* yesterday was taking the RAB line; I think he gets all his information from RAB.' Eden's response, when she had gone out of the room, was to say to me, 'I think you should probably stop seeing Massingham,' which was the exact opposite of what he should have been telling me to do; if Massingham was getting all his information from RAB, then there was every reason why he should start getting some from us. Eden had a very low boiling point and he found it a considerable strain to run one of the roughest offices in the world; the main duty of the private secretaries was to soothe him. Clarissa, on the contrary, tried to stir him up by drawing his attention to press attacks on him.

Although Clarissa was a Churchill I do not think her marriage was dynastic; and she was not specially political. Her friends were from quite another world – Auden, for instance, and Stephen Spender, who was often in and out. But she was, partly because she was non-political, an extremist: she really thought that someone like Ian Jacob, the intellectual soldier in charge of the BBC, must be a red. She did not understand the *modus operandi* of politics. But she was forced into a horrid position by that wholly horrid man, her cousin Randolph Churchill. He used to ring up, always got through, and left her invariably on the verge of hysteria, tears, and fury. My sympathies over Randolph's harassments were entirely with Clarissa.

Randolph was not a rational man; he hated there being a successor to his father. When the Prime Minister was going across the Atlantic to the White House in January 1956, Randolph was in Southampton for the *Evening Standard*. I said, essentially to the hoi polloi of journalism, that if they wanted to see the Prime Minister's suite I would be happy to show them round; to which Randolph, who was drunk and in the audience, said, 'I don't want to see it: I saw it in the days when there was a *real* prime minister.' He was a detestable character. It was around this time that I knocked him over at a dinner party given by a Dutch correspondent. Randolph arrived late, drunk, and started laying into David Astor, who actually at that time was giving him occasional work on the *Observer*, a last resort for Randolph. He said that David Astor was a traitor since before the war, referring to David's friendships with members of the German opposition. I said to Randolph that he really must stop talking like that about one of my best friends who in any case was helping him. Randolph took a lurching swing at me, I hit him in the chest and he, being drunk, collapsed, spending the whole of dinner asleep on a couch in the sitting room. After dinner he woke up, saw me, could not remember what had happened before dinner and asked me to give him a lift home, to which I replied, 'I think you can afford your own tumbril.' I did not have a car anyway. He was pure malice. Primarily he was a bully; and he enjoyed teasing his female cousin.

Another worry of the early days was Princess Margaret, and whether she was or was not going to marry Group Captain Peter Townsend. Looking back, the excessive national anxiety about her matrimonial plans seems not only a sign of how far Downing Street, and the country at large, was still living in a vanished world, but also how Downing Street can become obsessed with a matter of almost no importance at all. Townsend was divorced, and in some court circles regarded as a social climber. If Margaret married him, she would have to give up her position in the line of succession to the throne. All this naturally aroused great popular excitement, and also great perturbation at No. 10. Almost the first day I arrived, an anxious Ian Jacob from the BBC sought my guidance about how the Corporation should handle this 'crisis'. I had no idea what he was talking about. Next thing, the Prime Minister wanted to talk to the Archbishop of Canterbury. But how could the Archbishop be got into Downing Street, since it was not thought to be wise for it to be publicly known that the PM and Cantuar had seen one another? This conundrum brought into play Sir Anthony Bevir, who had a little room in No. 10 opposite the lavatory, where he made bishops, regius professors, etc. Bevir was a quaint, don-like figure, much addicted to snuff, to waving his hand as if playing an arpeggio on the piano, and to asking repeatedly, 'Is that fair? Does that make sense?' to passers-by. He was about sixty, and due to retire, but considered irreplaceable because after fifteen years (having started in the Colonial Office in charge of the Gold Coast) he had built up a vast knowledge of the inner recesses of the Church and the establishment. Faced with the problem of getting Canterbury from Lambeth into Downing Street, as it were invisibly, we all instinctively turned to Bevir. His inspired suggestion was that Canterbury should enter through the front door but bring two bishops with him in order to demonstrate that episcopal, not royal, matters were afoot. The Prime Minister turned down this ingenious idea.

Eden's overriding concern was that the affair might damage the Crown. Much more likely, in my view, was that if Margaret decided against Townsend the populace would assume that true love had been thwarted by the Church – with Downing Street in support. Eden behaved very honourably in all this, stressing that Margaret must be allowed to do as she chose and must not be punished if she did decide for Townsend: she must be allowed to keep her royal wages, for instance. He first said he was going to talk to her himself and tell her she must hurry and make up her mind one way or the other, though he never did. I urged that the princess, obviously lonely and distracted, with disagreements between herself, the Queen Mother, and the Queen burgeoning, should talk to the Archbishop. Eden opposed this idea, for reasons that are still obscure to me.

Constitutional problems loomed. David Pitblado was set to work and produced the formula: if Margaret decided that she wished to marry Townsend she would have to write to the Queen, lay down her succession rights, and ask permission to marry. The Queen would then ask all dominion governments to agree, including the British government. What would have happened if some dominions had agreed and some not, Pitblado, I think, had not worked out; but the question did not arise. Religion, the princess told the people, had caused her to reject the group captain, and the only thing thereafter for Downing Street to decide was whether Townsend, who had gone to Brussels while the announcement was made, should or should not be put up at the Embassy for a few days by Christopher Soames to protect him from the press.

Thirty years on, this drama stands out as the event that for the last time simultaneously and automatically brought into play all the pieces on the traditional English chessboard – Crown, Prime Minister, Archbishop, *The Times*, Lord Salisbury. It was as poignant a colophon to a dead era as Suez itself.

In his memoirs, *Full Circle*, published in 1960, Eden says that the policies he upheld and pursued as Prime Minister were based on his earlier experiences. 'I held responsibility for the conduct of my country's foreign policy . . . from 1935 to 1945, with a break of eighteen months from February 1938 until the early autumn of the following year, due to my resignation from Mr Chamberlain's government. I returned to Cabinet office, in company with Mr Churchill, on the outbreak of war on September 3rd and became Foreign Secretary again towards the end of 1940.' He was again Foreign Secretary from the autumn of 1951 until he became Prime Minister in April 1955. He was in office for twenty years, and Foreign Secretary for nearly ten. Why then, with this long experience behind him, did he disintegrate?

First, his health. In 1953 Eden's gall bladder had been removed and the bile duct damaged. It was repaired at the Lahey Clinic, but although for some time things went well, two or three years later – it is not clear to me exactly when – the condition treated by the American operation (which was the third in one year) began to return. The condition is known as cholangitis, which means

159

inflammation of the bile duct. Sufferers from 'biliary structure', according to one expert whose opinion I have read, are liable to become 'introspective, querulous and suspicious'. What happened – though we were only partly aware of it at the time – was that these attacks of cholangitis, unexpected and brief, produced a sudden high fever and left Eden for a day or two tired and flat. His doctors on these occasions checked his blood pressure and prescribed amphetamines which, though widely used and recommended at the time, were later virtually abandoned because they were held to cause over-activity, sleeplessness, aggressive outbursts, and an illness resembling schizophrenia. However, Eden was never what one would call 'ill' – as a doctor who treated him later put it. After his resignation he was accepted for life insurance on favourable terms, and lived until he was nearly eighty.

It would be charitable to blame the condition of his bile duct for the vileness and unpleasantness of his temper. This defect was one of the best-kept secrets about Eden. I heard not a whisper of its existence until I went to Downing Street; he enjoyed a public reputation, of course, as the most considerate, charming, and calm of men. But in private, under pressure and hostility, he used to become perfectly terrible. The aftermath was worse. As the head of the Foreign Office News Department, Sir Gerry Young, told me when I took up my post, 'It isn't so much the swearing at you that you'll get tired of, but the awful oleaginous apology later.' I came off comparatively lightly, perhaps because I was not part of the familiar Civil Service. In any case, since he was getting a bad press it was understandable that he should whip the messenger who brought him the bad news or the person who failed to prevent it from appearing, which was me. Much more serious was the way he treated even the most distinguished and senior civil servants – inlcuding the head of the Civil Service, Sir Edward Bridges. I remember Eden telephoning Bridges and saying, 'Well, Edward, I suppose I've got to try to save this country while you traitors try to break it down in every way you can. Poor old England. Poor old England.' Bridges told me later, 'That was the point at which I said, "Prime Minister, I think it would be better if you thought this over and called me back." ' Eden's terrible fits of temper were part of the family history. I owned almost the only copy of *Memoirs of a Bad Baronet*, which circulated round the upper echelons of Whitehall. Eden's father was mad. Even so, Eden's bursts of temper deeply shocked me.

Past experience, as well as health, contributed to Eden's inadequacies. It was often said that he had been too long a bridesmaid and never the bride. The saying contains some of, but not all, the truth. The trouble was not that he had had so long an apprenticeship but that he had been trained throughout his ministerial life to be a number two. He was not a number one under Baldwin or Chamberlain. He was peculiarly unable to run the Foreign Office under Churchill, and by the time he became number one his health had gone; and it was his health, I think, that stopped him making a new life for himself as number one. He had lived in office for a great number of years, but never in anything like the supreme office, and had never been allowed to deal with the major problems. Churchill, on reaching the top, discovered a new lease of life, and he was much older than Eden, who was not yet sixty and had a long life ahead of him. But Eden's health had given way. It was no secret inside No. 10, which is why we tried to keep him calm and why it was particularly dismaying when Clarissa's constant refrain of 'George, be a king' spoiled all our efforts. Had his health been better, had he not succeeded to the top job when he was feeling quite ill – though subsequently conducting a good election campaign in May 1955 – he would have reshuffled his government earlier. His failure to do so gave him a reputation for dither, which was justified. The press does latch on to people's failings, and they soon latched on to Eden's.

By the time I had been in Downing Street for six months, disenchantment had begun to set in. I was disappointed by Eden's lack of grip on home affairs; he seemed to know even less about economics than I did, and it was my impression that he did not have much good advice on economic affairs from either of his Chancellors, Butler and Macmillan. Eden had never had a home ministry. He was a 'one nation' man – though never a member of the political group that called itself by that name – which is why he fought against the abolition of milk and bread subsidies that Macmillan advocated as soon as he became Chancellor. Macmillan of course had the whip hand, because you cannot sack your Chancellor in his first two months (nor, incidentally, would a decent Chancellor do something against his Prime Minister's wishes). Except for his notable defeat by Macmillan on bread and milk, Eden managed his Cabinet pretty well – helped by the fact that he could play off Butler and Macmillan against each other.

Yet it was clear by early 1956 that Eden was losing his sense of

161

purpose, and that the government was in serious trouble. By the end of February the Cyprus crisis was full upon us. In early March General Glubb, commander of the British-trained Arab Legion in Jordon, was sacked by King Hussein, which was a shocking blow to our prestige throughout the Middle East. The Baghdad Pact was breaking up and so was our whole Middle East position (Selwyn Lloyd was fooled in Cairo and stoned in Bahrein). The Opposition demanded a debate, which took place on 6 March. We had staked our policy on getting the US to retrieve the situation by throwing in its lot with the Baghdad Pact. As might have been expected in an election year, it refused, so we knew the debate was bound to be difficult. In the event, it was far worse than I had feared. Eden said nothing worthwhile. He became angry and then began petulantly to answer back to jibes from the Labour back benches. It got worse and worse, and in the Gallery where I was sitting next to Sir William Haley, editor of *The Times*, we both froze in horror. It was unreal, a nightmare. The Bevanites began a calculated laugh, which was rude and offensive beyond belief. The Prime Minister crumbled under it all. ('Noisy, noisy' was his only rather ludicrous comment to me afterwards.) There was a tremendous revival of press attacks on him, including a vitriolic piece by Randolph Churchill in the *Standard* saying that the time had come for RAB and Macmillan to replace Eden. Rumours to this effect reached me from all sides, so I went to see Macmillan in No. 11. He said he would speak to Eden about his great disapproval of Randolph's attacks, but I felt in fact that Macmillan was a bit shifty, and wondered to what extent he was intriguing.

A horrible air of dissolution hung over all. The Prime Minister was short-tempered (though not to me), withdrawn, and anxious. The collapse of Middle East policy proved very trying for him, both because it was his policy and because there was no Foreign Secretary (Selwyn being away on his travels) to look after the details. As always, Eden worried about every aspect of affairs. Britain's base on Cyprus was unsettled by a guerrilla war, and on 9 March Archbishop Makarios was abruptly deported, after evidence reached Eden that he had close links with the EOKA guerrillas. 'Everywhere this fantastic attention to detail,' I recorded in my diary. 'Preparing his speech on Cyprus he wants detailed proof of Makarios's guilt – no lifting up of his eyes to the long term. Now he is rattled and sleeping badly and convinced of failure, I, too, wonder (with the press) how long Eden can last.' Two weeks later I wrote: 'The PM is pretty tired and fretful. Not surprising in view of all he has been through. It affects me in that I see less and less of him, and feel more and more cut off from his views. Luckily I can still get government views, but that particular extra which is his view I cannot get. Does he really have views or is he a hollow man? Is he really opposed to Macmillan's rather strict economic policies? Does he really put "one nation" above all else? I don't know, and I realize how vague his impact is on me. Is that my fault? Does he not trust me? Or is there really no one behind the door, where "the Consul is busy"?'

The first anniversary of Eden's taking over the premiership in April 1955 was also the end of my first six months in Downing Street. It was time for stocktaking. We were about to enter the quadrennial winter of the Western world, when the American sun is obscured by election clouds. It was a constant source of surprise to me how bad our whole planning with the US was at this time. There was no regular machinery for consultation – NATO had ceased to be very important and anyway did not deal with the Middle East. Officials at the US Embassy in London were merely used as messengers, and so were useless as a means of consultation. We had decided, after the events in the Middle East, that Nasser was no longer to be trusted and so the whole basis of our past policy in the region was changing. But clearly nothing good would come of this unless we could carry America with us. This meant that our decisions to ditch Nasser and build on the Baghdad Pact were telegraphed to Roger Makins in Washington. After a week he managed to see Dulles, whose reply was that in election year he could hardly afford an open agreement with us so it must be *sub rosa* – and anyway he could not join the Baghdad Pact without giving a cast-iron guarantee to Israel of her frontiers.

How did we get that far apart? Why did we ever go so hard on the Pact? Because we hoped the Americans would do better, and we did not know their views before we acted. What was horrifying was our impotence in Britain, which had nothing to do with whether Eden was a strong prime minister. The fact was that Britain was weak, especially in the new cold war of economic aid. We could not make it worthwhile for Baghdad to stay with the West, nor Persia where there was bound to be trouble soon. Nor India nor Ceylon. America could do this; but in election year would not.

Facing us were the Russians, in some ways at the peak of their powers. Clearly they were technologically and in other ways doing splendidly; they could make glittering offers to small states such as Egypt which needed technical aid. The European alliance was cracking, with France involved in a war she could not win in Algeria, and Germany becoming tougher and less amenable. A weak and divided West was facing a clever and united East. As a result the weak spots were going – the Middle East in particular. What could *we* do? Unless we changed our whole way of life so as to adapt our economies to helping the world – very little.

When I reviewed the political set-up in Britain the main criticism I had was that it never seemed to be ahead of events. I could detect no grand design. The fact that the Prime Minister was no orator and hated making speeches all added to the difficulty because he never stood back and looked at the picture. Winston did. Attlee probably did not, with similar results. We had no clear economic policy for the country. We had not made up our minds whether to let prices rise so that inflation would be mopped up, or to try and hold prices so that wage claims would not be pressed. Perhaps oddly enough this failure to have an economic plan was rather successful; it resulted in the 'one nation' theory of the Prime Minister's surviving in spite of everything.

As so often, Eden succeeded in getting his way not because he dominated the Cabinet, but because he tipped the balance this way or that. By accident rather than design, he was in the classical position of having two rival claims to the succession who could be relied on to keep each other down. In the first few months it was RAB who was trying for the succession. He lost it because the autumn budget was a failure and he did not understand how to deal with failure, though it was not his fault that it did not succeed since he wanted a far more drastic budget and earlier. Eden refused him this. Macmillan had the same ideas as RAB and managed to force the end of bread and milk subsidies through the Cabinet. If his budget succeeded in stopping inflation he would be the obvious successor to Eden, but he would find an implacable enemy in RAB. All these three, Eden, Macmillan and Butler, watched each other like hostile lynxes.

Eden lacked the certainty of leadership, and so the loyalty of his colleagues. And he lacked the priceless gift of any trace of a sense of humour. The private secretaries sometimes refused to take things up with him because they knew it would worry him and cause an explosion. Always at the back of everything was the fear that he would lose his temper and we should be sworn at. Other ministers were not above behaving in a similar manner. As I noted in my diary: 'I do find the habit of ministers of being bloody when things go wrong (because they cannot lose their tempers publicly they do it in private) a trying feature of this job. Success is theirs, failure is ours. I see now why civil servants get so desiccated. Perhaps the secret of all these people at the top is that they have vertigo, but out of a feeling of "the show must go on" they smile in public and are sick off stage – on us.'

Despite my growing misgivings about Eden, I still felt that if he went there would be extinguished a light which might lead his party to sane policies in relation to the modern world. I wrote in my diary on 19 June: 'The strain of being polite on paper to someone whose sole manifestations to me are snappy notes via private secretaries, or saccharine remarks to my face, is getting rather hard to bear. Yet for all my personal dislike of the PM (with which is associated some feelings of guilt at this disloyalty) I do realize that in politics he stands for what is best and most liberal and central. It is he who has seen the possibility of reducing our vast burden of conventional arms in the light of the hydrogen bomb and the change in Russia; he has seen the change from Cold War to the trade struggle and told the nation about it; he has prevented the Treasury and the party from starting a cold war with Labour by freezing wages without corresponding restraint on employers. What I don't know for sure is whether he is appeasing Russia too much (e.g. his refusal to allow any comment on Khrushchev's speech for fear it might harm Anglo-Russian relations); and whether the more "liberal" economic policies he pursues are strong enough for the situation we face.'

The fact – if it was a fact – that I had lost the Prime Minister's confidence I attributed to remarks made jestingly about the government and himself getting back to him; or perhaps, I thought, to Clarissa. All such anxieties were soon forgotten, however, when the Suez crisis got under way a month later.

On 13 June 1956 the last British troops left the Suez Canal which they had guarded for so long. The administration of the Canal remained in the hands of the Anglo-French Suez Canal Company. On 23 June, Colonel Nasser was elected President of Egypt. On 26 July, Nasser nationalized the Suez Canal Company.

I shall let my diary tell the story of what followed. Re-reading it after thirty years it strikes me as more Mr Pooter than Mr Pepys; but despite the gaps and inadequacies, it does bring back, at least to me, a quite vivid and rather authentic feel of those very odd, frustrating, and in many ways agonizing and appalling three months in Downing Street that were also – as one knew even at the time – a turning-point in British history.

Thursday/Friday, 26/27 July
After dinner I was rung up to be asked if I had heard that Nasser was going to nationalize the Canal. I hadn't, but spotted a first-class crisis. I went down to No. 10 at about 10.30 and met the King of Iraq just leaving ('Ah, Disraeli,' he said, looking at me stuck in the corner of the passage where the bust is). From then till 4 a.m. it was frantic. PM, Home, Selwyn, Kilmuir the Lord Chancellor, and Salisbury, plus Caecia from the Foreign Office all in tails, Mountbatten and Templer (Chief of the Imperial General Staff) called in (in black tie), Chauvel and Picquot of France in lounge suits.

(This was the meeting at which Eden made it absolutely clear that military action would have to be taken, and that Nasser would have to go. Nasser could not be allowed, in Eden's phrase, 'to have his hand on our windpipe'. It was also the meeting at which the Chiefs of Staff told Eden that although Britain could deal with Cyprus or Mau Mau or with atomic war, it could not deal militarily with a little local episode in the eastern Mediterranean. I felt ashamed that our nakedness should be thus revealed to the French and American representatives present – although one of the private secretaries kept writing notes to Eden pointing out that not all those present were Privy Councillors.)

Sunday, 29 July
The last few days have been very hectic and today is the first rest I've had. Even more to be pitied is the PM though he has clearly risen to the occasion with exhilaration. He is the only member of the Cabinet who has held a position of comparable responsibility at a comparable period of crisis, and it makes him feel his superiority. (*Per contra* I think the Chancellor feels his years a bit. Certainly he bit off my head yesterday for asking the Treasury Press Office to hold their notice about freezing Egyptian sterling, even though I was acting on instructions.)

I spent my fortieth birthday lunch yesterday drinking sherry with PM and Clarissa and eating sandwiches. By that time, after constant ministerial meetings, the broad decisions and alertings had been taken. The Navy is being alerted and I had the task (in conjunction with the Vice Chief of Naval Staff, Admiral Davis, since Dickie M. was away entertaining the Queen) of seeing that it did not leak out. The only leaking spot (the Chief of Naval Intelligence!) was duly stopped and it hasn't leaked. I gather from PM that other military dispositions are being taken – Clarissa said to him rather ominously at lunch, 'You will do a TV before sending the troops in, won't you?'

The PM has sent a long message to Ike saying, in effect, we must act this time and stop Nasser or else the whole thing collapses in the Middle East. The answer (which I have not yet seen) seems to have disappointed the PM. But Bob Murphy (of the State Department) has been sent across and so we'll see.

What will we see? Certainly this is the most critical moment in my tour of duty. It is certainly the gravest for Eden, for if he does not act strongly and effectively he will be out. But how can we really act strongly? The US has a veto there. What strong action short of getting rid of Nasser is any good? If we get rid of him, how do we replace him?

Tuesday, 31 July

A day filled with Cabinet meetings and Chiefs of Staff attending. Walter Monckton (Minister of Defence) is ill so Antony Head is taking his place, but none of the other service ministers are called in and presumably are ignorant of what is going on. Certainly those Cabinet members outside the 'Egypt Committee' are not kept in the least informed, so that Alan Lennox-Boyd (Colonial Secretary) has revolted and asked if he could please have some information because it affects his colonies.

I find it difficult to be up to date because the papers fly so thick and fast. I see the Egypt Committee papers though not the Chiefs of Staff's papers. Clearly we are preparing a very big military operation, but under what circumstances it will be brought to bear is not clear to me.

Bobby Allan (Eden's Parliamentary Private Secretary) was much disturbed this evening by the fact that Selwyn Lloyd had been far too bellicose to the 1922 Committee on foreign affairs. Apparently he really almost declared war, and got a great hand for doing so.

Suddenly in mid-afternoon a message was received that Dulles was coming over – whether to restrain or encourage us was far from clear.

Wednesday, 1 August

A rather ominous committee, the 'Defence (Transition) Committee', consisting of all permanent under secretaries under Brook's chairmanship, has been set up (or, to be more exact, has emerged automatically from its cocoon). Again many Cabinets and Egypt Committee meetings. Then Selwyn reported that Dulles would give full support to our tough attitude if only we agreed that Russia should be invited to an international conference of Canal users. The PM on the whole agreed with this (at least, he gave powerful arguments for it, though he had previously been set against). So he summoned a Cabinet very hurriedly at 7.30. Owing to a muddle, just as he was setting off by car to the House, Brook plus four ministers drove up to Downing Street. So PM and all decarred again and held the meeting at No. 10. Cabinet of course agreed. Duncan Sandys (Minister of Housing) arrived at the PM's room at the House at 7.35 and said, 'If I can be on time I don't see why the others shouldn't be', only to be told he was late and at the wrong place.

Thursday, 2 August

Last day of Parliament and a day of chaotic preparation. PM was working away on his speech upstairs in the morning, while the Cabinet met briefly under RAB ('just say I assumed the chair'). At twelve noon PM went in for his speech and there was a boring interval while MPs used the 'captive audience' to air grievances on the Seychelles, etc. At about 12.15 the PM got up to speak. I had had to tell him at about midnight that Dulles could not agree an early communiqué about the proposed Canal users conference in time for the speech ('trouble about Foster is, he is not straight'). So it was really rather a thin affair, but he brought it off pretty well.

On the way down the passage this morning Antony Head – looking very glum – told the PM that he had regretfully to ask for a Royal Proclamation calling up some Class B reservists. He only needed a few hundred (for specialist work in ports), but he had not discovered this until ten o'clock. The PM protested, but by noon it was duly in his speech. Then the problem of getting it to the Queen arose. She was at the races at Goodwood. Adeane (her private secretary) had to take a car down, get her approval (she had no private secretary with her) and telephone us. It came through about 4.10 p.m. and Head went into the House and read it out, then he and RAB dashed up to the Lobby and told them what it meant.

I went down to PM's room again to attend a meeting of the Egypt Committee. I had got the agreement of Mountbatten and Head to release some of the more obvious information which the public could see with their own eyes. But the PM opened the meeting very irritably by saying, 'I think we should say as little as possible.' Mountbatten tried to urge that something should be said, and then Field Marshal Templer disagreed with Boyle (Chief of Air Staff), who was solidly against any news at all. Head looked glum and apologized afterwards, but the damage was done and we agreed to say nothing. Of course it all appeared in the nine o'clock news (landing strip being prepared, etc.).

Friday, 3 August

Cabinet at eleven, and at twelve I was told to stand by to come in with Chiefs of Staff. In fact I met them in the waiting room and explained that if we wished for voluntary censorship we must as a *quid pro quo* offer some news service. Mountbatten agreed more or less enthusiastically, the other two looked puzzled. I then went with them into the Cabinet Room. Macmillan was briefly urging that we should aim at a total economic blockade of Egypt. No one seemed to understand what he was after so the Foreign Secretary and President of the Board of Trade nodded and that was agreed. Then we got down to publicity. It was discussed with no sense of reality and *no* understanding of the working of agencies – everyone agreed the press ought not to say too much for patriotic reasons, and that was that. Both Mountbatten and I tried to intervene, without effect. I was instructed, however, to call together the editors to see the PM. This was done between 12.30 and 1.00, and I wrote a note for the PM urging him to offer some *quid pro quo* to the press if he asked for restraint.

The PM began with a little survey of the situation, then went on to offer every sort of help with military information! I was a bit horrified at his own extension of my suggestion, but undoubtedly it all went quite well because as a result the press began to backpedal and say – not too much information, for gawd's sake. Finally we all agreed that Admiral Thompson should send out a D-notice limiting mention of numbers of troops and their destinations. I took this back to the Defence meeting and Admiral Thompson (a quaint figure with white hair and a smooth fat face) was duly instructed to send out a D-notice. At the same time the Service ministers agreed on a form of daily press conference.

Bank holiday weekend, 4-6 August
Very busy on the telephone. The Foreign Secretary suggested that
he should make a TV appearance. This at once fired the PM to
demand that *he* should. Very foolishly I suggested that the PM
should wait till events were more developed and let the Foreign
Secretary do a sound broadcast first. For this I got a royal rocket on
the telephone, including being told that I always worked for other
ministers, etc., etc. Eventually it was agreed by all that the PM
should do it.

Tuesday, 7 August
It is appalling to realize what effort is taken up by preparing such a
speech. The person who writes the first draft (in this case Guy
Millard, one of the PM's private secretaries) makes all the policy,
then a tedious process of fiddling starts, in which words are altered
by departments, by George Christ (Conservative Party), by Norman Brook, etc., etc. All act as if it were a legal document, while I
inform the press that he will speak merely from notes.

Gerry Young confirms my own feeling that the first fine careless
rapture in the press has almost entirely died away, and the weasels
are at work asking whether we should be so bold. *The Times* letter
column shows this very clearly; the Labour Party in particular
cannot face the idea of the use of force. All my instincts are against
force and for United Nations action, though I fully realize that this
may prove fatal to us. The sad fact is that, in the present state of
international law and order, nationalism, which may destroy the
world community's interest, is sacrosanct and Nasser could get
away with theft before the UN. Equally, if Nasser does get away
with it – in fact if Nasser is still dictator of Egypt next year – the
Eden government is doomed and British (and probably Western)
influence in the Middle East is destroyed.

Gerry Young was instructed today to say that acceptance of the
invitations to the Suez Conference did not mean acceptance of the
principle of nationalization. Nor does it, but the PM is trying to
keep that quiet so far as possible and when he saw the result in the
evening papers there was a violent explosion. As a result the FO
reversed itself and issued a denial – which I saw on the tapes at the
Athenaeum at about nine o'clock. At ten I listened to the news, and
the BBC failed to get it right. At 10.07 the PM rang up in a great
state: 'Are they enemies or just socialists?' I got after them and it all
turned out to be pure muddle.

Wednesday, 8 August

PM worked at his broadcast virtually the whole day. I sent up a few suggestions which were mostly taken, but at least I didn't have to sit for hours in the bedroom producing a speech by committee. I only had to go up once. There was a circle – Guy, George Christ, Norman Brook, Bobby Allan – sitting round the bed like a TV panel team.

Macmillan has put in a paper about using Israel as a threat to Egypt, which is causing great controversy in Cabinet. The idea that we must not drive the Arabs into Egypt's arms persists, though I think it is now a little hopeless. Still, the Iraqi and Iranian support for Egypt is explained away by the FO and they *may* be right.

Sudden explosion at six o'clock when PM saw the evening papers containing Gerry Young's statement on the record that 'we believe in peace'. I knew that he had been instructed to say that by the FO, on Michael Wright's request, to help Nuri es-Said, Prime Minister of Iraq. But listening to the PM screaming at the FS over the phone I noticed that Selwyn gave no support to Gerry (who commented later that he did not expect any support from that sort of a politician).

The broadcast itself went quite well. There was a great deal of complaint by PM that the lights were too hot, too bright, etc. So he had to wear his spectacles! After it was all over we went back to No. 10 and all had a drink and pulled everyone's character to pieces. I remember it was generally agreed that Grace Wyndham Goldie (of the BBC) was a well-known socialist.

Thursday, 9 August

A rather ominously quiet day. At about 5 p.m. the PM blew up over the evening papers which had headlined 'hitch in air lift to Med'. This is in fact true and due to the Libyans having kicked up rough over our plans for using them as a base (in other words, all the bases we pay so much for are worth nothing to us on the only occasion we might wish to use them). But the PM had been assured by the Minister of Defence that nothing would leak out. Hence the explosion. Then at eight o'clock when I'd gone out to dinner he rang up again, said why hadn't anyone told him, etc. etc. It was a peculiar example of hysteria.

I went back to No. 10 after dinner in time to have a brief chat before a 'secret' ten o'clock meeting began. Brook was nobbling

Monckton to tell him that the Chancellor planned to try and get building controls back, under cover of this emergency (he has been trying this for some time, just as he plans to get a division or two out of Germany by the same means).

When the meeting broke up at midnight the PM was all sweetness and said rather naïvely that he was only anxious to avoid giving the impression that there was order, counter-order, disorder.

Then Brook drove me home and came in for a drink and we had one of the frankest and most interesting conversations of my life. He began by saying that he had felt he must warn the PM that the idea of using force was growingly unpopular. 'How do you do it in this age? Call together Parliament, send in the troops and get a positive vote of perhaps forty-eight in Parliament, and a vote against you in the UN? It just isn't on.' We agreed that Britain now found herself almost isolated, the Arab world against us, Asia against us, America wobbly, the Old Commonwealth wobbly, only France as an ally and she is a definite liability with world opinion. Clearly Brook is advising against aggressive action, but I don't know if he'll win. As he said, the bluff etc. is all very well until this Armada sails, then we are committed because it can neither turn back nor sit offshore. (So the thing to watch for will be the sailing of commandeered passenger ships – that will be the balloon going up.) As he left, Brook sighed, 'Our Prime Minister is very difficult. He wants to be Foreign Secretary, Minister of Defence and Chancellor. Of course if there is war,' he added, 'he will have to be Minister of Defence.'

I feel now that there will not after all be war because the country couldn't be held together on it. But whether the present government can hold together on a policy of peace I am very doubtful. Guy Millard thinks we can get away with bluff – I am not sure but think not. I fear that nerves will crack – the Labour Party, the centre press, the Conservative Party, and finally the right-wing press and only last the Cabinet. Personally I think an attack on Egypt by us would ruin our standing in the world, but if Egypt gets away with this 'act of plunder' we shall be economically ruined by Middle Eastern blackmail. One can only hope that we can do what was done in Persia, i.e. yield but overthrow the government eventually and put in its place one a bit more willing to play.

The forgotten fact is that the nuclear deterrent has really made even small wars too horrible to contemplate. Therefore we must rely on some form of international police to stop the Nassers, even if that only means ourselves with a special constable badge, which is what America/UN was in Korea.

Monday, 13 August
Went up a bit late and almost immediately was called over to a meeting at Ministry of Defence where we dithered on about press control. Certain facts are now becoming clear: ministers want the press to be quiet about our military preparation because they are politically embarrassing; but fool themselves into thinking they are only asking for military censorship in the national interest.

I had a talk to Richard Powell (Permanent Secretary, Ministry of Defence) who is very depressed by the whole outlook. He sees our present plans as ending up in a massive invasion, which will turn world opinion against us, and be violently unpopular in this country. So unpopular in fact that it may not take place and by the same token AE may be thrown out.

PM rang up in the afternoon to say that he noted a growing softness in the provincial press; could I do something about it? I agreed as to diagnosis and later in the afternoon spoke to the London editors of *Birmingham Post, Westminster Press*, etc. I found, as I expected, that their doubts went far deeper than appeared on the surface.

Dined with the unworryable Chief Whip. Ted (Heath) is sure no one will revolt and it won't cause much bother in Parliament because there are no leaders on the Conservative side to cause trouble. But the Opposition are now demanding the recall of Parliament and it looks as though we shall have to grant it.

Freddy Bishop (principal private secretary to Eden) back from Chequers tells of terrible tantrums over the weekend with him slamming the door and PM bouncing out of bed to shout at him.

Tuesday, 14 August
Just before Cabinet I saw Walter Monckton who is also depressed by the prospect of military op. and feels that the senior civil servants are against it. But he realizes that to row back now would be fatal for the government. My own feeling is that we must avoid seeming to change our tough attitude but try to make it clear that our toughness was never meant to be aggressive. This will not be easy.

The softening up process goes on pretty fast. The *Daily Mirror* has shifted its front and come out for no force at any price.

From Three Worlds

In early August, Britain, France, and the United States invited the nations principally concerned with the Suez Canal to attend a conference in London, with a view to setting up an international body to run the Canal. Twenty-two nations accepted, though not Greece, or Egypt; Nasser denounced the scheme as 'a conspiracy'. The conference was arranged for 16 August.

Wednesday, 15 August

There was a constant ebb and flow of Foreign Ministers throughout the day, including Dulles looking as wizardlike as ever. The best news of the day was a secret report that Nasser was really on his uppers and would find it hard to resist us. 'If that's true, we're home,' commented Guy.

One problem was whether or not the PM's opening of the Suez Conference should be televised or not. I was against it because I feared it might be rather neutral and a flop. He said it would not be neutral and indeed wrote a 150-word speech which underlined the seriousness of the situation very well. So we decided on TV.

I spent a good deal of the day trying to convince the press that there really was a serious emergency for us, that the issue was literally one of 'life and death'. I don't feel this has been got across yet – as the PM said at one point this morning, people still talk about the danger of our alienating India, or worrying Africa, but the fact is that if we lose out in the Middle East we shall be immediately destroyed.

Lunched with Bill Buchan to meet a Miss Begby who is something to do with the 350th anniversary of the founding of Jamestown. Harold Caecia and Lady C. were there – he is trying to appoint James Morris as his PA. We walked back to the office together and were joined by Alec Home. We were speculating on where the real crunch of the conference would come and Alec thinks it will be over payment of Canal dues. If payment is made to an international body *outside* the control of Egypt then we shall have permanent and clear control by cutting off the money.

Went to the theatre (Arts) to see a bad play, which was anyway interrupted by PM ringing up to complain bitterly about an anti-government programme that the BBC planned to broadcast on the Light Programme tomorrow. Could he stop it? I said no – at any rate he should not.

Thursday, 16 August

Having decided that PM was to do the opening of the conference on TV I went off with him to Lancaster House at about 10.50. This got us there much too early and we had to wait in a queue of cars for a time. Then we were shown by Samuels (the FO secretary of the conference) into a waiting room, where Guy, PM and I waited. PM was remarkably cool. There's no doubt that AE is at his best when a crisis looms blackest. His 150-word speech on this occasion was excellent, designed to provide the headlines needed for the formal opening ceremony – 'a very grave situation'.

Dashed back to a Home Office meeting on censorship of the press. It was a curious exercise held under the chairmanship of Frank Newsam (who afterwards told me frankly that his object was to find ways of telling the ministers that they couldn't do anything, but without seeming to be purely *non possimus*). It was clear that – as Monckton said the other day – the civil servants were pretty well against the whole line of policy. I was struck with the extent to which the BBC was regarded as completely under government control. This is showing up over the Salem programme. PM has written to Cadogan (Sir Alexander Cadogen, Chairman of the BBC governors) fiercely over last night's lamentable programme. Other ministers – including the Chancellor and the Colonial Secretary – are even fiercer and are looking up the rules to see how they could control broadcasting. I produced a note for them ending, 'These powers have existed for thirty years but have never been used.'

Friday, 17 August

Sent for first thing to hear more anger against BBC. Someone has foolishly told Lennox-Boyd that the programme with Salem etc. was designed to balance the ministerials. The result at PM's level is passion and determination to teach them a lesson. I was therefore ordered to summon Cadogan and whoever else was in charge, but I protested that it was only worth talking to Ian Jacob. So eventually I was told to get him back from his holiday in Suffolk. I did so and got a rocket from him, but eventually he came. I guessed from the atmosphere it might be a pretty rough meeting and so I got hold of Jacob first and cooled him off, then I had a few minutes cooling the PM off (he was being heated up by Chancellor and Col. Sec.). The result was that both PM and Jacob told me afterwards that the other had been very calm and polite. Indeed, I am wondering if his journey had been really necessary.

Just as I was leaving last night I saw on the tape that EOKA had agreed to call off the terror campaign. I at once asked the PM to try and get out a comment. But it wasn't till eight o'clock that it came in from the CO and then it was a stupid statement, so nothing was done today.

Saturday and Sunday, 18 and 19 August
Spent a lot of Saturday being rocketed by PM because of a story in the *Evening Standard* (p.7!) that PM was thinking over Menon's suggestions. (Krishna Menon, India's representative at the conference, was in fact busy undermining the proceedings by backing Nasser and proposing a purely advisory international body with no powers at all.) 'Why aren't you watching the evening papers?' etc. PM is very easily rattled at present. On this occasion he spoke to me, Bobby Allan and Foreign Secretary, all of whom in various ways got after the Beaverbook papers with the result that by the weekend they were convinced that PM wanted to force India out of the Commonwealth!

Sunday I had a good try at getting across successful British operations in Cyprus against the guerrillas and after a very active afternoon felt that I had got the press to believe that we were being active. On the other hand there will be some trouble at our suggestion that EOKA has been 'defeated'.

Monday, 20 August
A good press on Cyprus. Busy ministerial day, but somehow the conference has now taken over and No. 10 is not the centre of affairs. At least not till the evening when a reception for the conference was held (PM told me rather sadly that of course it would happen that he found he had got the Dutch and Indonesia ministers stuck in a corner together). I had a few words with Shepilov (Russian Foreign Minister) who is charming but as hard as nails; also with Haley who is going off soon to America. Chip Bohlen (US Ambassador to Moscow) also there, very dubious about any attempt to pressure Nasser, on the grounds it would unite Arab-Asia against us.

Previously I had gone to ITV and looked at their lighting to see if it wouldn't improve on BBC's. It is far less glaring. I gather they have newer cameras.

Tuesday, 21 August
Read with some cold shivers the Foreign Secretary's note on the problems that will face us after we have won the military operations in Egypt. If we intend to establish a friendly government, how much can we leave to it without destroying it? I still find it quite impossible to believe that we really shall do all this – *macht-politik* seems so distant from the quiet tantrums of No. 10.

Again the evening papers were full of stories of our retreat from a forceful position, which is a beastly nuisance.

Lunch at Albany with Douglas Clark, who is editing the *Sunday Express*. He is very confident that the country would respond to a demand for forceful action.

Kenneth Clark and Dilys Powell have resigned from ITA because of HMG's refusal to grant £750,000 for cultural programme. RAB has been rung up and told to try and prevent trouble.

I also had words with Jack Rennie who is now in charge of PWE for Middle East. Apparently he is putting more emphasis on black radio.

A message from PM to Nehru trying to get him back on the lines.

Wednesday, 22 August
Question of recalling Parliament is now acute because if it is to take place next week a decision must be taken in the next forty-eight hours. The general ministerial view is that once Parliament is summoned it's going to ask a lot of very awkward questions about our possible military movements. At present these could not take place before 15 September which is a long way ahead of Parliament which is planned for 28 August. I think it is bound to be put off.

Mountbatten tackled me this morning about the recall of Naval personnel. Admiralty feel they cannot do this under 1950 (Korean) proclamation even though it is legally valid. M. wants to know if we can avoid a fuss if there's a new proclamation. I think not and that a quiet re-affirmation of the old one is best for all.

Just before lunch (yet again a group of Foreign Ministers at the conference) Dulles came steaming in at PM's request for a brief talk. The object is to get him to agree to serve on the group which goes to Nasser to tell him about the conference proposal to set up a board, which would include Egypt, to run the Canal. He is unwilling, but the Scandinavians will not easily be persuaded unless he does go.

For this afternoon's Cabinet (or rather Egypt Committee) Harold

Macmillan solemnly walked out of No. 11 and acknowledged cheers, walked briefly to FO and then back to No. 10 to acknowledge cheers. He is clearly cutting himself a big swathe at the moment, in the expectation that he might – just might – succeed Eden. In fact AE's health is holding up quite well, though he has had Dr King in to give him various placebos for some time now. Dr K. told one of us that it was really all a matter of nerves!

Certainly he remains pretty easily triggered and Clarissa seems to upset him at every turn. She came in at 6 p.m. to tell him that Menon and Casey (the Australian Foreign Minister) were on the BBC that night. He at once rung up poor Alec Home and brought him back to brief Casey (a very weak brother). No one consulted me, though I knew about it *and* knew the whole thing had been pre-recorded!

Dined with Beadle the new head of BBC Television. He is quite prepared to put a coaxial cable into No. 10 for television, but thinks it would prove rather an unnecessary expense. I raised with him the question of ministers appearing on TV, and I think as a result he will approach RAB.

I was able to warn Lobby at 4.00 of the statement on an amnesty in Cyprus, and so got them interested. Results were excellent as conference end was held up twelve hours and so Cyprus got all the leads.

On 23 August the Declaration of the London Conference was published. R.G. Menzies, the Prime Minister of Australia, was appointed by eighteen powers – India, Russia, and Ceylon abstaining – to convey their proposals to the Egyptian government, accompanied by the representatives of Ethiopia, Iran, Sweden, and the United States.

Thursday, 23 August
A very interesting lunch at Albany with Home. He is firm about the need for force. But he regrets (and thinks Brook does too) the hurry with which the PM pushed that vital decision through Cabinet without time for a proper discussion. In fact I gathered the whole Cabinet is a bit weak and searching almost desperately for a moral basis for action. In particular RAB is discouraged by the whole outlook, and has come back from holiday a very damping influence. The worst part is the thought of bombing which may really revolt the conscience of the nation, but which is, he says, necessary to control the air. He asked me what my estimate of public reaction

would be. I said that I thought the country would divide pretty closely, about 60:40 for action (after it had been taken), but that nonetheless it would split the party, not in the House but in the country, where many Tory supporters were very 'liberal' in foreign affairs, and would be shocked by this. Alec agreed glumly. I asked him why everyone was so gloomy about Casey and he said that Casey was determined not be taken for British with the result that he was always leaning over backwards to avoid pulling our chest-nuts out of the fire. He had said to Home, 'I'd gladly eat a lot more dust to save the peace.' What worries me is that we are putting all our trust in Menzies and I really wonder if he is either (a) firm or (b) representative of his country. Home also said that Canada was terribly wobbly and India, including Nehru, as bad as could be. Nehru always spoke of 'my friend Nasser'.

A good deal of effort now is going into trying to find a proper pretext for taking military action. This is because we need to justify our action, though its real basis is the *suprema lex est salus populi*. I gather Harold Mac. is very fertile about this. One idea is to bring an Israeli ship through; yet another is to remove our military stores from the base and bring them through the Canal. Also Bob Dixon (Sir Pierson Dixon, Britain's representative at the United Nations) is being asked to study the problems of 'informing' the UN Security Council before we actually invade, the theory I believe being that we would say that we are being strangled, that the possible closing of the Canal was a threat to the stability of many nations and therefore we would act.

One very awkward fact is that the US has supplied us with a lot of military material for use only in NATO areas. This is now part of our armed forces and will be used in the Mediterranean *outside* NATO. The PM is enquiring what this means for all our imperial responsibilities.

Duncan Sandys bellyaching because he does not know military plans, nor the justification.

Friday, 24 August
Caught PM in bedroom at 9.45 and got him to urge on Foreign Secretary the value of doing a brief broadcast interview for TV. This was agreed, was done, and was, I think, a useful contribution.

Then to Defence (Transition) Committee which consists of heads of all departments. A formidable group of grey heads, the effective Civil Service cabinet of this country. We agreed to recommend that no attempt should be made to impose a censorship of opinion, and that even military censorship would be very difficult to impose and ineffective in operation.

After lunch Alastair Buchan (of the *Observer*) came in and told me his latest dope which was that the object of the Menzies mission was to climb down from our high horse and save Britain's face. I was horrified and asked him where he got this from: it was Lange, the Norwegian Foreign Minister. I hope I got him put right.

Then I was suddenly sent for by Freddy Bishop. When I got to the private secretaries' room there was the PM looking ghastly worried. It was the Egyptian destroyers. A piece of paper was shoved into my hands by the PM which was a note from the First Lord (Lord Cilcennin) saying that the destroyer at Portsmouth was asking to leave at 4.30 (it was 4.28) and that Cilcennin wished to say that 'it had been referred to a higher authority'. Foreign Secretary was said to believe that we could requisition them (shades of Winston in 1914). I said that above all we must not 'refer it to a higher authority', i.e. the government itself, unless the government could act. To act, said the PM, was an act of war. By this time RAB had come in; he agreed. Cilcennin was sent for. Kirkpatrick (Permanent Under Secretary at the Foreign Office) said requisitioning was impossible after all. The PM went back into the Staff meeting with Keightley (C-in-C, Middle East) etc. We stood around until First Lord arrived and then all told him he must just let them go. He agreed. I was told off to check it all up with the Chief of Naval Intelligence. I did so and the flap was off.

Monday, 27 August
In conversation with Walter Monckton it became clear that PM is pressing Cabinet to decide for the immediate use of force. WM said that at last Friday's Cabinet he had had to speak up when PM and Chancellor were trying to rush things through because he could not agree to press the button *now*, which made war inevitable. He told me that he had spent the day with Macmillan on Sunday being toughened up. What PM and HM seem to want is agreement to go in if Nasser refuses to accept internationalization. WM refused. This has all made him feel very low, no longer essential and he will have to go when the crisis is over.

Tuesday, 28 August
Haley to lunch. A most cordial meal. On Suez his main anxiety was

that PM should not rush things too fast, i.e. should go through all the hoops including the Security Council. Only if force were *seen* to be a last resort could he carry the country with him. On journalism generally he was interesting in his belief that only the elite did matter in politics, the half million who read the *Sunday Times* and *Observer*. The popular press didn't matter much, and couldn't be expected to influence real politics directly. Their worst influence was indirect, e.g. by their sports pages where they gave the impression that everything was the result of quarrels and deals, not of good or bad game-playing.

After lunch I formally advised PM against seeing editors until there was a new situation to report on. I also said that I thought Parliament might be the best place for him to speak first. He took it very well.

Dined at the Savoy with Charles Curran who is now writing the *Spectator* political column. He is giving our line very faithfully but somewhat unconvincingly.

Wednesday, 29 August
Norman Brook is trying to persuade PM to go on five days' holiday between now and the end of the Menzies mission. By evening the PM agreed and I hope to go too on Thursday night. But PM is obviously afraid of adverse publicity and insisted that I should say he would be back early in the week, though I hope it may be Thursday before he is back.

Bob Dixon to lunch (we had to meet outside to avoid his being seen coming into No. 10). We talked over the question of going to UN. In fact since the early part of the week I have seen papers suggesting that we should go to Security Council. Foreign Sec. is strongly for this; PM is very reluctant, sees all sorts of trouble ahead if we do and would prefer to go to NATO or WEU (Western European Union) – which I regard as quite absurd because it would satisfy no one. Bob D. feels that government underestimates dangers of Security Council. He said the Iranian delegate will certainly feel that he is more a representative of the Arab states than of Iran alone, and so may well vote badly. Yugoslavia will certainly vote badly. Also he fears that the procedure will be tangled and it may be hard for us to avoid compromise resolutions, restrictive resolutions, etc. In fact the danger is that UN will only confirm Nasser for some time in his possession. Bob saw PM later in the afternoon.

Chancellor held his press conference today, doing the exact opposite of what I advised, i.e. on the record with a speech directed plumb against the TUC. I feel sure that the result will be to heat up the feeling between TUC and government. Yet he sent across an urgent note to PM begging me to avoid giving too much vigour to an article Curran is planning for the *Daily Telegraph* on 'what would happen if Nasser won'. I was told to beware of frightening confidence in the pound by stressing the problems arising from loss of oil.

Gerry Young came in about 7.00 very worried by a statement to be made that French troops were going into Cyprus. I agreed it was very difficult to justify, but I thought if it was put out about 8 p.m. and embargoed for midnight it would not get too much editorial comment. The official excuse 'that the French had asked for a site on the base to protect their nationals' is a bit thin.

Thursday, 30 August
PM got off about 10.15 a.m. to Broadchalke. He thought the Cyrpus affair had done no harm, and wondered whether or not the Ministry of Defence mightn't do more to play this all up as a serious affair. (I trust they won't.)

Saw Ian Jacob just before going off to my cottage at Sheepbrook. He is very anxious to get the opening of Parliament televised.

Friday, 31 August–Monday, 3 September
This was my alleged holiday. It began at about 8 a.m. on Friday with Haley ringing up to express deep concern about a despatch from Washington in the *News Chronicle* saying that the US was thinking of hauling us before the UN. He knew that we planned to go of our own volition and feared that this might misfire. I got telegrams sent off by No. 10.

Then Hugh Gaitskell pressed for the recall of Parliament and after a frantic lot of telephoning RAB drafted an announcement saying we couldn't do so till after Menzies had reported. I put this out 'from No. 10' from Sheepbrook.

The PM in a passion about a leader in *Birmginham Post* attacking the Cyprus move – which is generally attacked today. He supposed no one was doing anything in the office about it – I had in fact done something and said so – but realized I must go back in the morning.

So on Saturday back all morning at No. 10 where a weary group of us dealt by telephone with a raging PM. Harding (Field Marshal

Sir John, Governor and C-in-C Cyprus) wanted to return from Cyprus on Sunday and had to be told not to!

Weekend at Hemingford; very enjoyable but constant phoning. The PM has got so irritated with the press that he wants to give a press conference (like Macmillan!), a 'speak to the people some-how'. I had a long talk with the Chief Whip as to means of stopping this and eventually agreed to plump for the Lobby.

Monday a.m. I went up to Wyton Aerodrome and spoke to the PM at length on the scrambler there. I hope I have persuaded him against a public speech and perhaps for a Lobby. Spent the rest of the day touring Northamptonshire with my nephew Nico (Nicholas Herbert, now Lord Hemingford) and Bob Higgins.

Tuesday, 4 September

Back to work; very tired. Iverach MacDonald asked me to lunch at the Garrick. He seems very well informed and 'sound' on the whole Suez issue, which is a mercy as he will be writing *The Times* foreign leaders. When the PM got back about 6 p.m. I saw him at once re editors and again advised against and said the Lobby would be best. I do not really believe that the Lobby is all that good, but at least it keeps the PM's name out of sight.

Wednesday, 5 September

Further pressure by PM and Cabinet for him to see editors to 'explain frankly' to them. The difficulty is this: ministers believe the press would alter its line if they only knew as much as they do; fact is that they would not and if told more of government's plans would only be more virulent. Therefore I feel that I must stop PM using up his cards on tricks he cannot win. If there is a war or a retreat, then will be the moment. It is not easy to urge this, but I must say PM has been very good in accepting it.

We also experimented today with the TV cameras in the upstairs study. PM and Clarissa were delighted at the lighting which was much, much better. But PM is too short-sighted to read the teleprompter. A pity.

The most devastating thing I saw today was a copy of last night's telegram from Ike. It seems at first sight to be an absolute ban on our use of force, arguing very strongly along *Observer* lines. It is this which has brought the PM racing back, almost in despair. I have now seen a draft reply (by Kirkpatrick) which is really a very noble bit of prose saying we would rather die fighting than live with a thumb on our jugular vein. This is also supported by long analogies with the Rhineland 1936 episode, which is clearly in the forefront of the PM's mind.

Thursday, 6 September
Great rush at Cabinet to get out the recall of Parliament before Gaitskell's shadow cabinet could do it. The decision (for Wednesday) was taken at noon and I had it back on the No. 10 tape by 12.18.

It is now clear that the Menzies mission has failed, and that the original demand that we should go in if Nasser refused internationalization (the demand Monckton resisted) has been dropped. Instead we will go to the UN though the French dislike the idea of this very much indeed.

The background to the next diary entries is as follows. After the failure of the Menzies mission, Britain told the French and the Americans that it was on the verge of taking its case to the Security Council, to seek endorsement of the Anglo-French view that Nasser's nationalization of the Suez Canal was illegal. Dulles demurred. Instead, he proposed a Canal users' club, with a headquarters in Rome, to which all Canal dues should be paid; but he was reluctant to give the club any teeth. The French regarded both the appeal to the UN and the idea of a users' club as procrastination – devices to avoid bringing matters to a head with Nasser.

Friday–Sunday, 7–9 September
Need for a meeting with French owing to real disagreement with them over UN. So Mollet and Pineau are invited for Monday.

The message to Ike has now gone off, as well as long message to Dulles about UN.

PM off to Balmoral so I got a little rest at Sheepbrook though PM rang up on Sunday evening to worry about the documents which are being put out by Australia House at 9 p.m.

Fairly busy telephone weekend. Editor of *Birmingham Post* rang up in a worry and wanted to see the PM before the debate.

Monday, 10 September
PM rang me up late last night about the documents issued from Australia House. Did they contain the Nasser answer, etc.? I was

able to reassure him that they did. Indeed the collapse of the Menzies mission has been the main news today and well played in the papers. Now that it is clear that Parliament is to meet on Wednesday the fear of a sudden war is disappearing.

Lunched with Max Ways at *Time*. He feels that the whole British case on Suez is simply not understood in the US. He suggested therefore that we should try and get an article out of the PM for *Life* written by Ways but clearly attributable to the PM. He was most complimentary about my briefings to US correspondents, which is encouraging.

Day was filled with diplomatic activity trying to clear up the policy which was eventually to be explained in PM's speech. Astonishingly it is still very far from clear what our policy is to be. Late this afternoon a strong telegram went off to Washington saying that by 2.30 on Wednesday the PM had to announce a policy. Very well, what was it to be? We had gone along with Dulles over an appeal to the Security Council, then at the last moment Dulles had said he could not support us. Then he had hinted at a users' association. We were prepared to support this if Dulles really favoured it, but only if he made it clear that he was prepared to go along with us in it. Otherwise we would certainly go to UN. (The idea that we would use force seemed to be dropped from this telegram.)

The American news seems a little more hopeful. Ike's latest message speaks of the necessity of cutting Nasser down to size, but protests at the idea of doing it by force on the grounds this would in fact fail and only make him an Arab hero.

The French PM and FS turned up in the late afternoon so that we could tell them that there was little chance of our setting out on Operation Musketeer at present. They had been unwilling to come and to some extent were fooled into it by our promising them Menzies. In fact M. didn't arrive till after dinner (he has Gyppy tum) and then mostly saw the PM alone. M. having refused my request to do a set piece at the airport for BBC/ITV suddenly thought better of it and did so. I had forgotten to cancel the TV arrangement which worked excellently!

Tuesday, 11 September
The French have been proposing Anglo-French union again. We feel it is impossible at present because of the Commonwealth (I must say it might be the *coup de grâce* since the Commonwealth

opposes our forcible Suez policy almost without exception – NZ is pro and Australia split). Gladwyn Jebb (UK Ambassador to Paris) talked to me about the French – couldn't we get the press, or BBC or ministers to say something to indicate that they (the French) were not old-fashioned imperialists. I said I had urged that Mollet should see Gaitskell, and I gather that has been done, but I'm dubious about the results.

French meeting went on all morning and about 1.15 I was told the communiqué was ready – Mollet had agreed to see the press at 12.30. In fact it was 1.55 before I finally got it out of the Cabinet Room, having spent the time going round Selwyn, Bobbity (Marquis of Salisbury), etc. trying to get them *not* to alter words, and, when I failed, going round Mollet (a quiet Attlee-like figure), Pineau (less pleasant) to get them to agree the change. It was a dull communiqué and no one has the least idea of what big doings were abroad.

In the afternoon I had a long talk with Vaughan Reynolds of the *Birmingham Post*. He was plainly worried by the PM's belligerency, but anxious to support him. I hope I gave him some help.

At Lobby at 4 p.m. I gave details of Parliament's procedure tomorrow. Then at 5.00 saw the American correspondents. At 5.30 Charles Curran and at 6.00 Iverach MacDonald. I was in an awkward situation because, fantastically, we *still* do not know what the Americans will reply about the users' club, nor therefore what tomorrow's speech will say! At 11.30 p.m. the office was still vague.

The Suez pilots are being called out now, with the full agreement of both governments, but not – I think – at our instigation. The FO had no clue what to say on this crucial matter.

Wednesday, 12 September
Quiet morning awaiting the debate. I got in a bit early and found the telegrams which had been coming in to No. 10 from Washington throughout the night. Dulles has taken our threat of war seriously and has therefore agreed to come in and back the users' club pretty fully. Forms of words between him and us are agreed.

Egypt Committee at eleven agreed on this line. What I do not fully see is what our relationship to UN will be. We are to send a latter to President of Security Council but not yet let the UN be seized of the case. This seems an error in tactics, and I begged Bobby Allan to try and get more about UN put in. PM spoke to me at lunch about his speech and I said as much again, but I don't think he took it seriously, even though the speech was being written over lunch.

The speech to a crowded House, all of it full before Prayers, went very well. Gaitskell was less good than on 2 August, and did appear to have been pushed rather far by his own left. After the two speeches I felt that the split in the country had been irretrievably widened, the PM's introduction to the users' club could not have been more belligerent, which will make it a difficult article to sell; Gaitskell's advocacy of the UN could not have been more pacifist, which also adds to the trouble.

When I got back to the House about 9 p.m. I found the FS in the PM's room. He greeted me by saying that Dick Crossman had just denounced me as 'a sort of Egyptian Burgess and Maclean . . . Nasser's secret agent' because of my alleged habit of giving out military information to the press! Gaitskell earlier in the day had also spoken very roughly about the press leakages from Foreign Office and Downing Street. The Lobby were amused by this.

Bob Boothby wound up very amusingly and did a good deal to heal the breach. He said that he really did not see how the government could have acted better. On coming out, PM was in very good shape and said that he agreed and did not see how anyone could have done better; he was sure every action had been quite right.

Went back to Fleur Cowles' flat in Albany and heard Victor Borge give a most amusing turn with the piano. Sat next to Peter Ustinov (VB asked, 'Could I borrow your beard?').

Thursday, 13 September
The belated Cabinet minutes from Tuesday reveal that there really is a severe split in the Cabinet. Chancellor said plainly that he thought the users' plan should be a prelude to the use of force, that any delay would be economically catastrophic. Min. of Defence equally clearly said that he thought it should be the prelude to negotiation or UN appeal. I can't say that I know which way the Cabinet made up its mind. I doubt if it did.

Earlier I had asked PM again if he would help out *Time & Life* on their article. He rang up Clarissa who is becoming his unofficial and wholly bad press adviser and asked her advice, and then more or less refused. But he did find time to see Iverach MacDonald to explain that his leader (saying that the country wants to go to the UN) was wrong.

RAB later in the afternoon said to me, 'Really, the trouble is that the House and the country cannot understand why the man who created UN and the man whom UN created (Selwyn) will not say a word warmly for it.' I agreed, and clearly that was the spirit of the Lobby so I put in a note to the PM urging him to be warm and clear about UN. When I returned from Lobby I found a group of ministers all very gloomy because Heald (Sir Lionel Heald, a former Conservative Attorney General) had spoken forcibly for UN and so PM felt he must go further than he wished (in view of French and American views) in promising to go to UN.

Afternoon and evening of chaos as the speech for winding up was prepared. Eventually a careful offer of appeal to UN was worded, but at the last moment the PM was badgered by Gaitskell into stating this before the proper point in the speech. Indeed he seemed to say that if the Egyptians frustrated the users' plan he would go to UN *immediately*. But the last word was lost in shouts and when *Hansard* asked what he had said de Zulueta said he did not know so 'Interruption' is what appeared.

Friday, 14 September

The press was not too bad on PM's speech, though the phrase 'climb-down' did occur rather frequently, in spite of my efforts. It is not quite true since we had intended to go to UN though not perhaps in quite the way its advocates suppose. Just before Cabinet (at the H. of C.) Walter Monckton said he was still worried that PM would use loophole to start trouble. It seems that, after all, the popular view of PM being restrained from being a wild man is not so far out.

The Cabinet was about Plan G – the current plan for UK going in with European federation. I gathered later from RAB that he had made a great speech against it on the grounds that it would be ruinous to the party. Home had also stated the Commonwealth problems – and spoke for the Colonial Secretary, who was in the House dealing with Cyprus, in favour of delay.

In the evening down at Sheepbrook *The Times* rang up to say that they had a letter from Hugh Gaitskell asking PM to 'preciser' his remarks on when he would go to UN. I rang Chequers and Chief Whip and told them all about it but did not rouse the PM.

Monday, 17 September

A slack day for us while the FS prepared for the meeting of Foreign

Ministers. PM got back latish and held a brief Egypt Committee meeting, but the Chiefs of Staff who were supposed to be preparing Musketeer II were not ready and so there was no after-dinner meeting. Instead the PM and FS got together to discuss the problems of publicity. As a result they rang me up and we had a talk on the phone.

I do feel that the government case is in some danger of not getting put fully and I have urged on RAB the necessity of getting more government speakers. The fact of the matter is that government foreign policy has now become a straight party issue and we must deal with it accordingly. This has thrown the BBC into trouble because it doesn't know what to do about 'ministerial talks'. Gaitskell has asked for time more or less equivalent to that given the PM and FS and has been refused on the grounds that he had the right to demand a reply and did not exercise it. Now the BBC has agreed to put Gaitskell on *Press Conference* this Friday and give Selwyn a whack the following week. I suggested on the phone that Selwyn should do an end of conference 'news' broadcast on Friday as some counter to Gaitskell, and that instead of a *Press Conference* he should do something less open to questions. This was, I think, agreed, though clearly PM doesn't care a damn what Selwyn does.

Tuesday, 18 September
Lunched with Leonard Miall and persuaded him to use Selwyn on *Panorama* on Monday. It is a programme with a far larger audience than *Press Conference* and should do him proud.

The Cabinet held its second meeting on Plan G for British association with the Messina Powers in Europe. Clearly the general view is that it will be very dangerous for us to stay out because we risk a German-dominated Europe, but it is very dangerous for us to go in for fear of a run on our reserves (again because the D. Mark is a harder currency) and for fear that it will hurt the Commonwealth connection. Also of course the party is a problem since it is bound to be worried by any deviation from the true milk of Empire trade. Peter Thorneycroft (President of the Board of Trade) is the strongest advocate of the plan (devised by Otto Clarke I believe), and Butler regards it as too extreme and too fast. PM sees the dilemma and has allowed the Chancellor to take the whole thing up with the Commonwealth ministers at the IMF/IBRD meeting in Washington this month.

In the afternoon Curran came in to talk over his *Spectator* article.

189

He was very bitter about the defeat which he felt was being imposed on Britain by Dulles – i.e. the retreat from our tough position. Though he said little that was not wholly obvious he opened my eyes to the facts of the situation of public opinion. I wrote it all down on a piece of paper to try and clear my own mind, which showed that the public felt that the government which had intended to be warlike was slowly but surely being pacified by Dulles and would finally have to go reluctantly to the UN. Then I followed this up with some suggestions on how to mitigate it. In the afternoon I asked Norman Brook to come in and see my notes and have a word, as I really feared – and wanted to tell him – that we were building up to a disastrous let-down. He was glum but emphasized that all was not yet lost, and that force had not yet been abandoned.

Dined with Leola Epstein, the Barffs and Wrights and Gordon Hutton. At home later David Campbell and friends dropped in but somehow I was continuously telephoned so got little talk.

Wednesday, 19 September
Again a relatively slack day for us, while the Conference of Canal Users went on at Lancaster House, just audible like a distant battle. The news at lunch was very bad indeed, everyone seemed to feel that somehow the Americans were letting us down by giving way on the pilots, etc. Then about 6.30 Selwyn came in saying that Dulles had made a very firm speech in which he had spoken of the need to maintain law and justice even if force or the threat of force were needed. This seemed to restore morale a bit though the odour of defeat is still pretty pervasive.

During dinner I was rung up by the Admiralty and asked to go down there to talk over *Empire Chubb*. Earlier in the day this had looked like a *casus belli*, and it was worrying to see how pleased everyone was at the possibility. Mountbatten came popping out of the Chiefs of Staff meeting to order a search of the whole Med. for this ship which seemed to have been hijacked by the Egyptians in Benghazi. By evening it had become clear that the ship had put in at Malta after having lost most of its crew who were suborned by the Egyptian Consul. One difficulty about our putting out the story, which was the problem that faced me, was that the Libyans – our allies – had acted as enemies. I read all the stuff in the First Lord's room before Quintin (Lord Hailsham, the new First Lord of the Admiralty) came in, and then I advised that we should get Reuters to put it out. I then got hold of Tony Cole of the Foreign Office

News Department; he came round about midnight and I told him enough to get his correspondent cracking.

In conversation with Quintin he spoke of the horror with which he had first viewed the plans for Musketeer I, in particular for bombarding. He feared that had it been carried through the wrath against us would never have been assuaged.

Thursday, 20 September
A day of deepening depression. At lunch I showed my estimate of the situation and lines of attack to the PM who agreed heartily with it though denouncing the analysis of what people thought as 'unfair'. He seems to feel that accepting the Users' Association has been a bit of a mistake though if we can make the clause on payment of dues effective, he said, it will be just worthwhile.

Lunched with Iverach MacDonald who is also a bit depressed by the news. But *The Times* still stands by us. He shocked me by telling me that Norman Robertson, the Canadian High Commissioner, had confided in him that Dulles had only produced the users' plan because we had said that unless Egypt accepted the Menzies plan we would invade.

Saw the dominions correspondents at five o'clock and found them *very* critical and downcast, and particularly anti-Dulles. I see great dangers in the strong anti-Dulles movement which is building up.

Went to ITV cocktail party and talked to Tom Driberg who is just back from Moscow and Burgess.

Friday, 21 September
Had the usual rush of weekend correspondents and also saw the Americans. It was a ghastly day with all the worst expectations turning up. Dulles pulled rug after rug from under us, and watered down the Canal Users' Association (renamed SCUA because CASU means arse in French) till it was meaningless. Tony Moore (of the Foreign Office) came in halfway through the afternoon almost in tears about the whole thing – how could we prevent it all seeming a total disaster? Then Pineau came in and seemed almost on the edge of dissolving the alliance. To keep him sweeter there was announced agreement that PM and Foreign Secretary would go to Paris next week, and (unannounced) that Queen would go next year. By sheer luck at this black moment the Russians have come to our rescue by announcing that they have cancelled the visit of the

Bolshoi Theatre ballet unless we are prepared to release Nina (a defecting ballet dancer). This is stealing the headlines.

Drove down to Sheepbrook in the Chequers car and was met by Margaret Tyerman and Ron Harris.

Saturday and Sunday, 22 and 23 September
Rather continuous PM calls from Chequers. He is getting very tetchy indeed. The theory of the weekend is that PM is not doing all the work and Salisbury is sitting in to help. There is little or no truth in this. PM rings up on Saturday in a great state about something in the press (I forget what) . . . can't get hold of RAB – whose phone is out of order – then RAB rings up plaintively. He and I talked over the future prospects of speakers, since I have been urging for some time past that more ministers should speak more often. The first great success of this policy was the Lord Chancellor David Kilmuir's speech on Saturday which I had mentioned to Harry Hodson and which the *Sunday Times* published in full.

PM also very worried by some criticism of our policy I passed on from Iverach MacDonald, and poor IM was forced to ring him up on a scrambler from No.10.

Week 24–30 September
Got a good deal of holiday, i.e. all Monday and Thursday and half Wednesday. The pressure has gone off Suez and interest is swinging to Nina and more seriously the party conferences. Strangely enough, though intelligent people know that we have suffered quite a defeat, the PM's retreat seems to be well covered and it does not look too bad.

But inside the government there is some despair. As far as I can judge, the PM and others still would like to use force to destroy Nasser, but dare not against American wishes and without a pretext. Nasser is too clever by half to give a pretext. So we are left without an outlet for our fury.

On Wednesday PM and FS went to Paris. I saw them off at the airport where the PM said a rather good piece into the cameras. I gather since that at the meeting in Paris the French were very anxious to use force at once and the PM had a difficult task in persuading them to hold their hand. As a makeweight the Queen was persuaded to make a Royal visit, which nearly got ballsed up because no one remembered to consult President Coty. On Friday the PM (on the phone from Broadchalke) was very enthusiastic about the youth and vigour of the French.

Lunched with Julius Holmes to talk over Cyprus which he is attempting to mediate as US representative at NATO. He is strongly against the NATO solution, and really fears that if the Karamanlis government falls it will be succeeded by a communist government.

Monday, 1 October
A day of October misery. Left Sheepbrook in pouring rain with the beginnings of a bad cold. Greeted on arrival at No.10 by news that the PM was wanting me. He had rung me just after midnight to complain about lack of speakers ('of course there's no sign of a speech by RAB'), and wanted to go on with the grumble. Once again he wanted to appear on TV and rather weakly I did not oppose him in view of the general complaint about lack of government publicity. Yet I feel sure that this is not the way to go about it; it is too direct, too propagandistic. The ministerial speech which may – or may not – be reported is the thing that is needed and neglected. Luckily it seems to be the present view at the top that the failures of publicity are party and not mine. RAB, whom I saw later in the morning, is rather distressed, and O. Poole (Oliver Poole, Chairman of the Conservative Party), whom I also saw, is obviously under pressure. I gave the PM a note urging that a 'line' on the long haul of Suez should be worked out and given to ministers outside the Suez group and to others at the party conference to avoid confusion. He approved this and approved vehemently the draft outline I put before him, and passed it to RAB for urgent action.

PM is also worried by stories from Washington that seem to indicate that the Chancellor has been pushing Plan G very hard on the Commonwealth. If he has, he has certainly exceeded instructions. I suggested that it would be necessary to give a press conference to get things straight as the press was confused and yet very interested. PM seemed a bit reluctant because in fact Cabinet has not agreed on the time yet; all put off till Chancellor returns. Anyway his plane has been delayed till tomorrow.

Lunched with Bill Ormerod and went to Romanoff & Juliet.

Tuesday, 2 October
Chancellor got back early this morning and I spoke to him about

the need to clarify. He said rather wryly that everyone seemed already to have said rather too much about it. After his meeting with PM and Thorneycroft I was called in to discuss this point. I said that there were three main reasons for a conference: 1) the press and public were confused and might start barking up the wrong tree; 2) a conference the next day would rather dim the end of the Labour Party's conference on foreign affairs; 3) the subject of a customs union with Europe would provide a counter-topic to Suez, especially if we are to make it appear as an initiative. The PM was reluctant because he thought it might cause trouble with the colleagues, but agreed eventually.

Later in the day I went with Chancellor and P. Thorneycroft to Chancellor's room in No.11 and we chatted about this 'initiative'. HM obviously regards it as the climax of his 'European' days, and spoke longingly of a European–Commonwealth meeting with Winston in the chair. Thorneycroft was more worried about the party attitude, though he can really claim to be the main sponsor of this plan. He feels that it is necessary to get on the record the safeguards, e.g. on agriculture.

While talking to HM the PM rang through and asked me to go and see him – upstairs in bed. He was bitter about Dulles *Press Conference* in which JFD seemed to have accused us of 'colonialism' over Suez. However, we agreed to say nothing publicly, though I spoke to *The Times* which wrote a sharp leader, and the PM wrote a piece into his speech which I know will come out before he gives it. He also asked me most privately about a rumour he had heard that I had told Bob Boothby that only the PM could brief him on Suez, and that he would not do so because he was not prepared to give the time. Luckily it is quite untrue.

Earlier I had talked with Harman Grisewood about the BBC. The Cabinet has now set up a committee chaired by RAB to discuss how to take more control of BBC Overseas Service; clearly with intent to take it away from the BBC. At the same time the FO (which has some real experience of the matter) merely asks that a senior FO official should be associated with the process.

Wednesday, 3 October
The Times leader on Dulles is very strong, and Ted Leather (Conservative MP) came in in the course of the day to say that he was anxious to have a real bang at Dulles too. I said that we were officially taking a very hands-off attitude but that we had been hurt

by his statement. I did not mention that in the early distribution of telegrams was a very contrite apology from Dulles via Makins. JFD claimed he had been pressed unexpectedly on a question but admitted 'it was a very bad blunder'.

The most exciting moves at the moment are over Iraq–Jordan where an old plan for Iraq troops moving into Jordan to stiffen it against Israel, and at the same time to save it from Egypt, is about to go into effect. Miraculously the Israelis, when consulted, have agreed it is okay. So with luck it should take place soon. The deeper concern is that we seem hardly able to fulfil our own obligations under the Tripartite; as long as the Egypt threat remains we have to keep Musketeer mobilized.

Cabinet met for nearly three hours, but spent exactly five minutes deciding *not* to televise the Royal Opening of Parliament. The formal reason is that it would seem to bring the Queen into politics through her reading of the Speech. The real reason was conservatism. Yet in 1953 Winston had been for it. I had urged that this should be a bargaining point for getting BBC interested in Parliament, but I got nowhere.

Late in the evening just after I had been talking to Min. of Defence about getting publicity about the value of reservists, I heard from War Office that there had been a 'mutiny' in Cyprus. They wanted to put out a brief note exactly to that effect, but I dissuaded them and it was watered down a bit.

Thursday, 4 October
Cyprus is big news. PM working now on speech and seems very tired.

Friday, 5 October
A busy day in which I kept on hearing of the extent to which the Labour conference had gone left; it was a triumph for Bevan, a defeat for Gaitskell (though some query that last). Got away early to catch the 4.34, though the PM was leaving only a few minutes later. But when I got down to the cottage and rang back I was put through to Freddy Bishop – unscrambled – and he told me that the PM had collapsed at University College Hospital where he had gone to see Clarissa. He was there with a severe chill. We decided to say nothing that night and surprisingly got away with it, though I was rung by the Press Association to ask if he had *left* for Chequers (he had) and by the *Express* to ask if Lady Eden was in UCH (she was).

Saturday and Sunday, 6 and 7 October
Busy, boring days dealing with a flood of queries about the PM
after I had put out a notice at ten o'clock. In fact the PM seemed as
active as ever, sending messages via Guy and Freddy at regular
intervals.

I am wholly exhausted myself and have determined to go on
holiday soon.

(This account of my last week in office is written up shortly after
the event. I kept notes daily but was working too hard and too late
to write them up at night. There is therefore some hindsight, in that
I know as I write what the climax will be.)

Monday, 29 October
There was of course a mass of mail, and telegrams, but no sign that
any crisis was in the wind. But when I went down to the Private
Office things were rather different. Freddy Bishop looked completely worn out and very jumpy. At about 11 a.m. the PM
returned, I went down to the Private Office and when he opened
the double doors between that and the Cabinet Room I slipped in to
greet him. He seemed very surprised and not too pleased to see me,
but he looked less worried and calmer than usual.

Ten minutes later Freddy came into the second room of the PO
where I was reading the Dead Dip (papers that had been dealt with
by the Prime Minister) and asked me if I would walk down to my
own office with him. He was even more obviously upset and had
difficulty in delivering his message from the PM. 'I know,' he said,
'this goes against all your traditions and the agreement under which
you came here, but the PM has told me that I must keep you out of
the Private Office; you must stay down at your end of the building.
I know that's very difficult but there is so much going on about the
Middle East now that is peculiarly secret; in fact I don't know it all
myself.' I protested that I simply could not do my job that way. I
absolutely relied on reading the PM's input and output which
simply could not be sent down to my office, and I relied on asking
private secretaries questions. Freddy was sympathetic but firm and
begged me not to make a fuss, but wait a few days and then we'd
both talk to Brook. I agreed angrily and with a feeling of
apprehension. I felt that in my fortnight's absence I was being eased
out.

Gloomily I read the Cabinet papers for the past fortnight. It was

196

mostly about the legislative programme, and particularly the great squabble over whether to include reform of the House of Lords. Salisbury, who is allegedly ill, was smuggled in for the meeting on this and won the day by his advocacy of House of Lords reform against a lot of opposition. Annoyingly there was nothing recorded on the Middle East (except the F. Secretary's dull account of his visit to UN) as all of that was recorded separately in confidential annexes. On enquiry I learned that these were not even the usual kind (which I see) but were confined to copies for the PM and the Queen.

I lunched by myself and came back through the garden gate where I ran into a biggish meeting waiting to go into the Cabinet Room. It included Keightley (whom I was surprised to see back in England), and the Service Chiefs. Mountbatten came up to me very conspiratorially and said, 'Well, I don't envy you your job in the next few days; this will be the hardest war to justify ever.' Several other ministers welcomed me back saying I was back just in time.

I remained a bit puzzled by all this; later I got instructions that I was not to mention the Service Chiefs' presence at the meeting and particularly not Keightley. I had little to tell the Lobby at 4 p.m. but it was pleasant to see them all again. The meeting at No.10 went on till late afternoon.

I left Downing Street quite early and went to Lancaster House for a reception for the Norwegian PM. I had a word or two with Denis Healey and Chris Mayhew (Labour MP for Woolwich East) and a longer talk with Quintin Hailsham. I said to Q. that I seemed just to have got back in time. 'I know much less than you suppose,' he said, and added, 'and what I do know makes me profoundly unhappy.' Then I walked back home with Jim Griffiths (deputy leader of the Labour Party), talking about colonial students.

Soon after I got home, while I was reading a mountain of correspondence, the Admiralty rang me to say that their Press Office was getting a mass of enquiries about a British invasion of Egypt. As soon as I hung up the *News Chronicle* rang me to ask if I knew anything about this and I said no. With foreboding I rang Freddy Bishop to tell him of the report and ask if there were anything in it. He laughed and said no. Then about eight o'clock Ian Trethowan rang me with the correct news that Israel had invaded Egypt. I again rang Freddy who ran upstairs to tell the PM just before the dinner for the Norwegian PM (just like the last sad dinner for Feisal when I sent the news of Nasser's seizure of the

Canal). Later Freddy told me to say that the PM was very surprised and had summoned ministers for 10.30. I told the press this by telephone throughout the evening – they all suspected we knew about the attack at the time of the afternoon meeting – but I vigorously denied this though of course the suspicion was strong in my mind.

Tuesday, 30 October

Got into the office early. It was completely changed. There was in the Private Office an air of exhaustion and relief, and incidentally the idea of my keeping out of the PO seemed to have been dropped entirely.

I saw at once the long cables which had been drafted overnight to the Commonwealth and America. The one to Ike was vague, but made it clear that we couldn't regard Israel as simply the aggressor in view of Egypt's past record. The one to Menzies was extremely specific. It said that at last the pot had boiled over, as it was bound to in view of Nasser's ambitions and his association with Russia. The time had therefore clearly come for action. We had warned Israel not to attack Jordan, but made it clear that we could not offer the same guarantee to Egypt; as a result Israel had attacked Egypt. We intended to intervene to take over the Canal and a strip ten miles on either side, and would issue an ultimatum to both sides that day saying we intended thus to separate the combatants.

I was completely flabbergasted by this idea which was wholly new to me, and seemed at once to prove that all this was a deep-laid plot of some age. At least I see what Mountbatten meant yesterday.

About 10 a.m. a long message from Ike came in (crossing with the one from Eden) showing what a strain this was putting on the American link. The President had sent for Coulson (the British Chargé d'Affaires in Washington) last night, he said, to concert tripartite action against Israel; he was amazed to find that Coulson excused Israel and was clearly instructed to lay the blame on Egypt. Ike was determined to go ahead with action against the aggressor through UN and still hoped we would join him. Later in the day another telegram from Ike acknowledged Eden's earlier message in a fairly friendly tone.

About this time Brook looked in and read the latest bunch of telegrams of all sorts. He said, 'What strikes me as wrong is that Israel is too early and has no real pretext.'

There was an early Cabinet meeting at which the colleagues were told what was in store for them. I gathered later from Monckton that Duncan Sandys and Lennox-Boyd were enthusiastic for it. He and Heathcoat Amory (Minister of Agriculture) were very dubious.

When Cabinet had gone in I had a word with Ian Bancroft (RAB's private secretary) who told me that he was wholly in the dark about things. RAB had said 'all this is not for innocent eyes' and kept papers back from him. Ian said he thought initially the whole thing had been carried on solely in the PM's office.

Pineau and Mollet arrived in the morning and there was a lot of discussion in the Cabinet Room and upstairs. The statement was worked out bit by bit and I saw it in its virtually final form with the two ultimata to Egypt and Israel at about one o'clock when David Butler (of Nuffield College, Oxford) joined me for lunch. I said to him I was profoundly depressed by what I knew, and it would all be made more awkward by the fact that I could not talk about it.

After lunch I went straight back to No.10 and found that the statement was unlikely to be ready at 3.30, so I went to the House and passed this on to evening papers, warning them that it would be a very important statement. At 4.00 the PM came over to the House and talked in his room with some ministers for several minutes. Gaitskell and Griffiths were asked in just after 4.15 and given Mimeoed copies of the text which I had prepared for the press. At 4.30 the PM rose and the copies were handed out, but there was an agonizing pause while Shinwell raised a point of order about debate. The statement was then read very quietly and the House discussed it very quietly for ten minutes, then the temperature began to rise, as they realized that they were faced with ultimata that expired in twelve hours. (I remember passing a note to Bob Carvel, political correspondent of the *Evening Standard*, in the Gallery saying that I presumed it ran out at 4.30 a.m.) Eventually it was agreed that the PM should make a further statement at 8.00 and there should be a debate.

As I went out of the Gallery Iverach MacDonald said to me, 'I don't like it; I don't like it at all . . . this is what the PM talked to me about ten days ago and I like it less and less.' So apparently the PM has not kept his counsel all that well.

Went up to the bedroom where the PM was working on his speech. He was very worried about the American reaction and I read him some stuff off the tape about the beginning of the UN debate, which worried him further.

However the actual statement at 8.00 went not too badly. I

slipped upstairs and got a bit and then came down to the office at the House. One of the messengers was there alone, answering the phone. He said it was the American Ambassador so I took the phone and asked if I could help. 'Yes,' said Aldrich, 'it's a note from the President and I have been asked to deliver it by telephone since we are about to publish it.' He then read me the note which I took down in longhand on bits of paper in pencil. When it was complete I begged Aldrich *not* to publish it verbatim, and in any case not before the debate in the Commons ended (it was 9.15). The note was very bitter and cold indeed, and I feared it might create trouble in the House. Aldrich said he had the White House on the other phone where Dulles and Ike were talking. A few minutes later he rang back to say they had agreed to postpone the announcement till 10 p.m. and it would not be verbatim.

I sent a copy into the Chamber and gave a copy to Head who was mooching around awaiting a call from Nicosia. Head and I had a brief talk about the future problems of defence and publicity. It is his belief that security is a greatly over-estimated virtue in the modern services – what is wanted is that the enemy should know just what weapons we have and how powerful they are. That is the meaning of deterrent (I remember Ivelaw Chapman, the air vice-marshal, saying that some years ago).

At ten o'clock after the debate ended we almost all trooped over to No.10 to await the result of the ultimata. A pleasant, cheerful FO character (whom I don't know) said: 'It's rather fun to be at No.10 the night we smashed the Anglo-American alliance.'

The PM was anxious to publish the gist of the earlier communication with Ike, and I prepared to do so, but we never got further than that. As the night wore on the news on the ticker from New York grew worse and worse. Bob Dixon telephoned in despair to say that Lodge (US Ambassador at the UN) was gunning for us hard and we were certain to be condemned by the Security Council; it would mean that he had to use the veto. Selwyn Lloyd (who was with Pineau) instructed him so to do quite cheerfully. Indeed both Selwyn and the PM seem curiously euphoric today. The big decisions are over and they seem calm and detached. Selwyn about one o'clock asked me and Tony Moore what the press reaction would be. I said: puzzled, with *The Times* moving against us.

It had become clear by this time that Israel had accepted our ultimatum ('Very good reply from Israel,' said the PM to me, 'see it's played up'), and that Nasser would not accept it – he said as much on the radio. So I went to Brook and said that I thought we could now take it that the ultimatum had been rejected and so expired, i.e. we were now free to use the necessary force we had threatened. He agreed, we caught the PM and put it to him about 1.30 a.m. and the PM agreed to my guiding the press in that direction unofficially. I duly did so to the agencies.

I got to bed about 2 a.m. but the phone rang absolutely continuously till 5 a.m. so I did not get much rest.

As I had left No.10 I whispered to Brook, 'A long and bad day's work.' He looked at me with his sympathetic, meaningful stare.

Wednesday, 31 October
I have few notes and only a very confused recollection of this immensely busy day.

I had a meeting of the group of PROs (Service and Treasury, Col. Office, etc.) which had been meeting fairly regularly with me during the crisis. The Air Ministry man made it clear that the whole operation would be a softening up exercise by bombing for a day or two. I gather the bombing will be of airfields to keep down their planes, but it is bound to hurt cities a bit too (later in the day I learned that the bombing of Cairo airfield was only just averted today at the last moment because it was discovered that American evacuees were crossing it). Clearly something needs to be done to explain *why* we are beginning this operation 'to separate the combatants' by bombing the cities of one of them. Later I got messages to Head urging him to intervene in the debate and explain, but he refused.

Gaitskell made a quite brilliant speech in the House denouncing the government's policy, which several of the older Gallery hands thought the ablest attack on government policy they'd heard in twenty years.

Later I saw the American correspondents and did what I believe to be my best effort to date in explaining policy – even though it was one I am increasingly alarmed about. I took the line that the strain of Anglo-American relations was fully understood and was a calculated risk which we took because of the general failure of earlier co-operation with America. It seems to have been assumed by all who listened that this was the official line, though as usual I had no briefing at all.

Stories about collusion with Israel are beginning to appear in the American press. I have drawn PM's attention to the great danger of these, but of course he is not in a position to do much about it. Tony Moore is sure that the Americans have cracked the Paris-Tel Aviv correspondence.

There are two bits of evidence that support Tony's thesis: 1) in his first note Ike said ominously that American intelligence had noted an enormous increase in cipher traffic between Paris and Tel Aviv, as well as undisclosed arms shipments from France to Israel; 2) Coulson reports that Dulles spoke to him on Tuesday in a cold fury and said he had positive proof of British and French complicity.

In the House later, Walter Monckton asked me if I would come to a ministerial meeting in the FS room at 10 a.m. to discuss publicity. He (WM) would take charge of this for the Joint Services.

At lunch this day RAB substituted for PM at the British Newspaper Editors Society (or something). He made an off-the-record speech on Suez bitterly attacking the Americans for their refusal to co-operate with us, over the Canal, and over long-term economic affairs ever since 1951. In the car going back he again reverted to his old theme that the PM was mistaken to ignore the UN. I took the opportunity to say it was rather dangerous to be so anti-American.

Thursday, 1 November
There is a curious peace now at No.10. The PM looks tired out, but there are no rows, no drubbings, and apart from constantly writing speeches to reply to the Opposition in the House, not really much work. The war machine has taken over.

At 10 a.m. I went over to the FS room and joined a group of ministers: FS, Colonial Sec., Commonwealth Relations, Monckton, Head and three Service ministers, plus Kirkpatrick and Burke Trend (deputy secretary of the Cabinet). We discussed methods of getting Service information co-ordinated, especially with the French. I urged Head to get a really senior officer in charge of information by Keightley's side.

Then in a pause the conversation was turned by FS to our policy towards the UN, which was likely to condemn us as aggressors before long. Kirkpatrick seemed under the impression that we would be bound to leave the UN or be expelled unless some other way could be found quickly. In the conversation I suggested that we might say – on the Korean analogy – that we had acted for the UN and would be glad to accept a UN commander eventually.

Selwyn added to this the idea of asking UN troops to join ours. It was generally agreed that UN couldn't do this and so it's impotence would be shown up. But the chance remained that it would do it and Head kept on reminding us that the first objective of this whole operation was to get rid of Nasser, and that would never be done by the UN. Kirkpatrick reiterated that leaving the UN would be a bitter pill for public opinion too. Eventually I thought the idea was rejected, and so I was amazed when I heard it appear in the PM's speech in the censure debate. I at once tried all I could to get the press to notice this as a very significant passage.

After the ministerial meeting I had a brief word with the PROs in my room and then went to Walter Monckton's new office as Paymaster General, which overlooks the Horse Guards Parade in the old Treasury. We had a brief personal talk first, in which I was surprised to hear myself say that I felt I might well have to resign as I thought the policy bad and disastrous. WM, as I rather expected, agreed, said he had only stayed with the ship at the strong request of the PM and because he felt that much was necessary. He said he would go as soon as he decently could after this was over – if the government did not fall first. (This was really the first time I had realized that I couldn't stomach the hypocrisy of the whole policy.)

We were then joined by the PROs and had a general discussion of how to handle publicity, in which we agreed to leave as much as possible to Nicosia. The FO News Dept. head (a new man called Peter Hope) raised the question of how we could hold Iraq as an ally as long as we were so obviously aiding Israel (Michael Wright from Baghdad is screaming in the same direction). It was agreed that anything we could do to play down Israeli collaboration with Britain was to be done, but the more extreme suggestions, e.g. that we should drop just one bomb on Tel Aviv, were agreed to be impracticable.

Later the Chancellor sent for me and asked me to make some suggestions (very minor) for the PM's speech. He was very worried about the American reaction, which was much worse than he had expected; he had written to Humphrey, the US Secretary of the Treasury, hoping to put him right. He thought the President was more sympathetic. I said I was deeply worried at the complete division of the country and its possible effects on our whole economic situation. Macmillan said that the trouble was that the people thought oil just came out of taps. Perhaps he should see

Trade Union Congress leaders and explain that we had to struggle to live.

Lunched – by long prearrangement – with Iverach MacDonald and found him in despair. He thought the whole project had been grotesquely mishandled, and above all it was collusive and dishonest. Clearly he had been shocked to the marrow by the revelation of intended duplicity which the PM had made to him – believing that *The Times* was an unshakeable supporter. Iverach had only told Haley – no one else – but he had also urged Haley to go and see the PM and warn him off, but H. had refused to go so soon after his return from the US. But H. was very distressed too.

In the House the almost unbearable tension of the last few days exploded again in a violent scene when the Speaker tried to save Head from his inability to answer the question: what was the status of British soldiers captured by Egypt if we had not declared war? The Speaker suspended the sitting for thirty minutes, which in fact gave time for a very hurried meeting in the PM's room at which an answer was worked out. This was later given in the PM's calm, uninformative speech on the motion of censure. The debate filled the evening and in the end the motion was reasonably heavily defeated, though WM said to me he was voting with the greatest reluctance.

I went back to No.10 where there was a meeting of ministers to decide about how we should react to the UN call for a ceasefire. It broke up after 1 a.m. having more or less decided to go ahead.

Friday, 2 November
I woke up to read of Russia's action in Hungary and the UN's violent reaction to our moves. Before I got to the office I had realized that I was going to resign before long. Still I have no recollection of the decision, only of having decided.

Hard routine work all morning, punctuated by further scenes in the House, and a demand that the House should remain in session over the weekend. An appalling telegram from Hayter (UK Ambassador to Moscow) saying that the Russian change of front in Hungary was largely because they saw us taking the law into our own hands in Suez. This had both frightened and encouraged them.

A lot of time and effort spent tuning up the BBC/TV for a PM's ministerial. It was uncertain whether it would be at Chequers or No.10. Both were tentatively arranged, and at about 5 p.m. I was told Chequers for sure. Charles Hill of the BBC has been called in on the broadcast and we've had words about the script. I suggested that a good deal of emphasis needs to be placed on Eden's record as a peacemonger, but for the first time I found I had little heart for the business.

I lunched with Monckton and told him definitely that I should be resigning when the hostilities ceased. He told me that Tony Nutting (Minister of State for Foreign Affairs) was definitely resigning too, also others including Edward Boyle, Boyd Carpenter, etc. were pretty unhappy. He told me that he had resigned as Minister of Defence because he could not bring himself to press the button for the invasion armada, and he had written all this in his long, unpublished letter of resignation. I couldn't see, from what he said, why he had stayed on in the Cabinet. I also gathered that he had been left out of the latest phase of planning, though he seemed to have been told of the plan of operations when the PM returned from Paris on 17 October. Indeed, that seems to have been what triggered his resignation. 'All that plan with the French,' he said, 'was done by the PM and Selwyn without consulting anyone.' He also said that Selwyn was very very unhappy about the whole thing, but had decided he couldn't stand against it.

Just after the House rose I was called into the PM's room with Selwyn and Brook to discuss the announcement of Nutting's departure. Selwyn said he would be glad to be rid of him and the announcement could be as soon as possible. I said it would be bad to get it in Sunday's papers, but was overruled. So it is to be.

Saturday, 3 November
At our morning meeting with Monckton it emerged that there was considerable military worry about the exact time of our invasion. I was amazed to hear from Chief of Naval Intelligence that the American 6th Fleet had interfered with our invasion fleet on its way to Suez. It had submerged its submarines and so caused us to expect attack until we demanded that they should surface. Then it had constantly buzzed our ships from the air in spite of our warnings that this might lead to accidents. The Americans are clearly even more bitterly opposed than I had supposed. In spite of Hungary, Lodge at the UN is still leading the campaign against us – even though Bob Dixon claims he is basically friendly.

On the political level the great question is: can we get the invasion started in time before the UN makes it too hot for us?

There seems to have been undue delay because though our troops had started before the Israelis invaded (on a 'landing exercise' the Admiralty told me on Monday night) they are not due to land till Monday at the very earliest. Head went off secretly in the early afternoon to Cyprus to have a talk with Keightley to see how the political and military necessities can be married. The government is getting more and more worried about this whole UN affair; the PM keeps on repeating that it is our only real danger now. PM seems calm and spent after all the decisions of the past. Because I feel I am about to abandon him I tend to leave him alone. Selwyn is being very tough. Late tonight I heard him talking to Bob Dixon on the phone and saying again and again, 'We can accept anything from the UN so long as it doesn't stop our troops going in.' Whether he is wise to talk so freely on the open phone to the US knowing what I do about their tapping habit, I very much doubt. But most of Bob's instructions were given on the open phone owing to the extreme pressure of time.

Parliament met again today, and so again I saw the Lobby. I have made it clear to them that with so very much ministerial statement I will *not* comment on events at all.

The rising of Parliament at 3.p.m. was a shambles with Selwyn shouted down, and the whole Labour benches rising and screaming 'resign' at the government front bench. The government, including the PM, walked out looking as nonchalant as possible.

Back at No.10 we pressed on with the broadcast. At the last possible moment – I think it was 3 p.m. – we shifted our plans back to No.10 from Chequers, largely I think because Bobby Allan felt so strongly that the PM should not go away that night even though Clarissa fought for Chequers to the last, even suggesting going down after the broadcast.

David Attenborough of the BBC came to produce at about 5 p.m. and Peter Dimmock struggled to get the cameras etc. ready. Meanwhile there was a nasty business over the right to reply. Grisewood had – foolishly – let Gaitskell know that the BBC would raise no objection to a reply. Ted Heath had blown him up for this and pointed out that the right to reply could only be claimed if it could be proved that the minister had been controversial or biased. The BBC accepted this and told the Labour Party, which then put out a rather nasty (and untrue) piece saying that the government was trying to ban Gaitskell. So Ted and I worked out a careful factual statement of what the situation was. But I realized too that

Ted was under real pressure from PM and party to try and actually stop Gaitskell. I begged him not to try this if only because he was bound to fail. Eventually after the broadcast the Labour Chief Whip phoned from Leicester and claimed the right to reply on the grounds 'that the quotation from Mr Gaitskell's speech had been only partial, and the whole broadcast was one-sided'. Ted refused to accept this, and left it up to the BBC. Cadogan just said he was going to bed, and would decide in the morning. I have heard since that Gaitskell lost his temper over the phone with Grisewood later in the evening and said he would expose the attempt of the BBC to block the Opposition.

I also had to help during the evening to get out a statement by Churchill. Antony Montague Brown rang up about it, said he (Antony, I think) had finished drafting it and it was only a matter of persuading the Old Man to sign it. This was about 6 p.m. so I begged him to hurry or he'd miss the mass of the Sunday papers; would he telephone it to me and I could put it out. But he said it must not seem to be a Downing Street statement. He would bring it up to his flat by car and the press could get it there. After a little thought I felt it was best if this were done by the party HQ and so phoned Oliver Poole who agreed. (In fact the party mucked the whole thing up and it got very bad publicity.) Poole also said that he thought the next week was crucial for the party; if he could stop a split, then all would be well. He feared though that the party had lost for a long time, perhaps for ever, the 'liberal vote'. (This exactly chimes in with what I warned Alec Home of in the August crisis; I think it is correct.)

I gave the Nutting exchange of letters to the two agencies at about 5.15 p.m. and was really shocked when de Zulueta rang me to say the Chief Whip's office was asking if I couldn't hint to the press that Nutting was terribly under the influence of his American mistress and anyway was not quite himself nowadays. I replied bitterly that I thought that was the sort of thing the party did, certainly not me.

I watched the broadcast from the adjoining room with Clarissa and others. It was very effective, though PM read it quite unashamedly. This was the first fruits of all my efforts to get No.10 wired for TV and I think it was technically successful.

In spite of all the activity of the evening I had time to catch up on all the telegrams (what a mass and how politely revealing of the universal antipathy of our action) and to draft my own letter of resignation. But I found this put me in a terrible quandary: I must go, clearly, because I cannot defend a policy I candidly dislike; but I am perhaps being useful in seeing that some truth between government and public remains, also in taking pressure off the BBC, and possibly too in putting forward ideas for ways out of the crisis. Less worthily, I hate the idea of quitting the job, and above all of losing the fascination of watching events unfold at the centre. But go I certainly must when the fighting stops.

Just after midnight the Sunday papers came in. The *Sunday Times* (I'd talked to Hodson in Washington on the phone that morning and told him about our concession to the UNO police force) was friendly, the *Observer* seemed hysterical and I was really too tired to read it, so I took it home and fell asleep reading that Eden must go. But me first.

Sunday, 4 November

I was woken quite late by the phone ringing again and a gay and friendly PM saying that the Sunday papers were really not too bad. He'd looked for me last night to offer me a drink and thank me for everything about the TV – there had been a mass of telegrams supporting him (over 100 before I left last night, including one of humble admiration from Dirk Bogarde!).

I walked to the office feeling very very tired and read a new batch of utterly depressing telegrams. At eleven we had another meeting with Monckton and I walked back with Peter Hope and told him I would be going soon. He was very kind and obviously sincerely sorry. He said there were a great number of extremely unhappy people in the FO and that Nutting's resignation in particular had added fuel to the fire.

Then the routine began again, telephone calls galore. I found there were to be ministerial meetings all afternoon so I asked my deputy Alfred Richardson to come in. I lunched alone at Albany and fell sound asleep afterwards in my chair, to be awakened by the phone again. I realized I was at the end of my tether, rang my nephew Nico at Sheepbrook and asked him to meet the 4.20 train. I went back to the office and sought out Norman Brook and told him I needed to clear my mind by a little rest – so could I go off to the country safely leaving Richardson in charge? He was clearly reluctant but I went.

The week just past has been the worst by far in my life. The knowledge of collusion, the deception, the hypocrisy . . . I am

208

really getting a bit hysterical myself. It seems to me that the PM is mad, literally mad, and that he went so that day his temperature rose to 105°. My mood towards him is extraordinary. I never see him, worn, dignified and friendly, but a surge of deep and almost tearful compassion surges up in me; I leave him and my violent bitter contempt and hatred for a man who has destroyed my world and so much of my faith burns up again. Then I long to be free as a journalist to drive this government from power and keep the cowards and crooks out of power for all time. God, how power corrupts. The way RAB has turned and trimmed.

At High Wycombe Nico met me and I told him my resolve. At about eight o'clock Richard Naish (a country neighbour and friend) dropped in. He was at first anxious to be mildly rude about Eden, but I simply told him my resolve and he then urged me to do it quickly or I would go mad. About 10.30 p.m. I went to bed leaving the phone with Nico and saying I would speak to No. 10 calls and no one else. Almost at once there was a call from de Zulueta: how were they to deal with press calls now that Richardson had gone home? I asked what was up and – on the scrambler – Philip told me: 'It has been the crucial evening, both Israel and Egypt have accepted the ceasefire (though there's some doubt about Israel's conditions) and the question is whether we go ahead. Pineau has come over and urged us that we must or his government will certainly fall. Anyway, we have decided and the landings go ahead at first light tomorrow in spite of the ceasefire.' I spoke to the switchboard and told them to put calls through to Richardson at home – de Zulueta's call made up my mind.

Monday, 5 November

I woke fresh and clear and resolved. I simply waited to get to the office to resign. When I arrived I at once began my letter of resignation, addressed to Brook. With many interruptions it was finished by 12.30, Bobbie typed it on my typewriter (almost in tears) and I sent it across urgently to the Cabinet Office. In it I said I would do what I could to avoid public scandal, and that the announcement should perhaps be delayed till hostilities ended.

What a relief. For the first time in a week I feel reasonably happy, though I now begin to feel like a traitor when I am with colleagues.

The morning was in fact quite busy. Monckton told me that last night's Cabinet had been crucial, the question was 'invade now or never?' He had said 'never' quite strongly and had been supported by Salisbury as well as the much troubled Heathcoat Amory. I told him I was definitely going and urged him to leave too, but he hedged.

There was also a meeting of ministers (I forget whom) because it really appeared likely that Pakistan would leave the Commonwealth. Suhrawardy (Prime Minister of Pakistan) had said he would, but urgent telegrams to Roger Stevens in Tehran managed to bring pressure to bear on Mirza – the President – to reserve this so-called decision. Still the split in the Commonwealth is severe: the Asians are very hostile indeed; Canada is more hostile than America; S.Africa hasn't uttered; New Zealand has insisted on the return of their ship HMS *Royalist* from the Med. task force; only Menzies and his half of Australia support us.

The telegrams from Europe are pretty shocking too: Belgium cannot believe what it hears – which includes the growing rumour that UK and Israel were colluding; Germany is publicly horrified though Adenauer says he will try and support us. At the UN, Lodge refused even to discuss the Hungary resolution with us in advance. From Moscow the story is that the Kremlin is rejoicing in the freedom we have given them. And of course from the Middle East nothing but passionate hatred, and appeals for some help in maintaining the alliance from Michael Wright in Baghdad.

The House was just ninety minutes of hell with the now usual screams from the Opposition and bayings from the Tories. The PM, as dignified as ever, scored a bull point by intervening suddenly to read a flash signal that Port Said has fallen. It was a genuine coup as he certainly did not know it when he went into the House. The Tories cheered themselves hoarse, I felt sick, and rather rashly said to Donald McLachlan sitting next to me: Mafeking. A few minutes later when I went down again the PM was talking to McLachlan in the anteroom and then went into his own room where Haley was. I gathered later that he was telling them both that there was absolutely no split in the Cabinet!

At 5 p.m. Black Rod summoned the Commons to the Lords for Prorogation and I went straight over to Brook's office. I rather dreaded the interview but he was so clearly in full sympathy with me (indeed he said that he realized that no intelligent man could support the policy) that I lost all that. We agreed to defer any announcement – he wanted three weeks, I said a week or ten days

210

was about the most – and not to tell a soul. I suggested that George Christ might succeed me, and that it was absurd to suppose that any neutral journalist would come instead. B. agreed that Eden now would have to have a good Tory and govern with party men in all posts. I said I thought he would fall anyway. He thought not at present though Monckton and Amory were wobbling. I left with almost a light heart for the first time in a week.

Before the end of supper I had been rung up to say that Moscow Radio was broadcasting a very stiff note indeed threatening us with rocket bombs if we did not stop our aggression in Egypt. Eventually Rendel at *The Times* read me the whole thing and I relayed it to No.10 where Freddy Bishop simply said nothing of the sort had been received. I gave this out as our line, but was of course rung up throughout the night.

Tuesday, 6 November

The papers were all full of the Russian note. I hurried into the office and found the stale smell of a bad night. Neil Cairncross, one of the private secretaries, had been up all night and I gathered the PM had had no sleep. The note had arrived at 2 a.m. and I saw a very worrying telegram which had just come in from Moscow, in which Hayter said the Russians are in a very ugly mood, they may really mean to act in accordance with their note; it is imperative that we get back into line with the Americans.

Cabinet was called for 9.45 (at the House because of the Opening of Parliament). As a result I found myself presiding at the meeting in Monckton's room. Just after 10.30 I adjourned the meeting so that we could go to the window 'and watch HM opening the last session of this Parliament.'

I then went over to the House and saw the Lobby. When I went down to the Private Office of the PM's room at the House I ran into Mountbatten. 'You not resigned yet?' he asked. 'Of course I have,' I replied, 'and you?' 'I can't think why they haven't sacked me, I've said such outrageous things.' We then went along to the PO where I gathered from the conversation that a ceasefire was being urgently considered. Indeed Mountbatten was anxious to order the cessation of unloading at once, so that an orderly end could be made to the landing. Of course yesterday's ceasefire at Port Said had turned out to be not so; now it was us who were being defeated by a Russian threat. Not too good.

The telegrams show that the UN has reports that we have heavily bombed the suburbs of Cairo. We have announced that bombing in Egypt has ceased, but I don't know what to believe.

I sent a note to Brook saying, 'If there is a ceasefire I want to go at once.'

The Cabinet dragged on all morning and at the end I gathered things were still not settled, except that RAB would do the Speech and the PM would intervene later. I went and saw Monckton and told him I was going as soon as the ceasefire came. He replied that even the rats ('and I *am* a rat') must stay on the ship now, but the government would fall soon. He was very angry about the report in *The Times* saying there was total unity in the Cabinet. I told him it was just one of the PM's lies.

A few moments later I saw Edward Boyle and urged him to get his resignation over with quickly. He was obviously immensely relieved to find a friend.

About 5.30 I went back to the PO at the House. Gladwyn was on the phone saying that Mollet most urgently requested the PM to put off his statement on ceasefire for thirty minutes at least. I don't think the PM was even told. Then Ike came through on the phone, which the PM took in the PO. From the conversations I gathered that Ike was very stern indeed, insisted on the ceasefire (but agreed to congratulate Eden on it publicly) and insisted absolutely on Anglo-French withdrawal from Suez. 'But it'll take us some time to withdraw even if I survive here,' said Eden. That took till six o'clock and so the PM was a few minutes late in making his announcement of the ceasefire.

I went straight back to No.10 and started to write out my formal note of resignation. Halfway through I was asked to come urgently over to the House again to see the PM. All he wanted was that I should put out the message of congratulation from Ike and make it clear that it came after the announcement of the ceasefire 'or it will look as if he was influencing me'. I gladly told this last lie for the PM.★

I finished my letter and Bobbie typed it. Brook came to my room

---

★'In the afternoon of November 6th President Eisenhower telephoned to me when I was in my room in the House of Commons. He was vigorous and in good spirits. He was delighted by our order to cease fire and commented that we had got what we set out to do; the fighting was over and had not spread.' – *The Memoirs of Sir Anthony Eden, KG, PC, MC: Full Circle* (London 1960), p.561.

and I gave it him with a request to give it to the PM either late that night or preferably next morning.

Then I tidied out my desk, ticked my telegrams, took my secret keys off my chain and left No.10 for good.

Diary ends.

Much mail came in during the next few weeks. The Prime Minister wrote to say that he was 'truly sorry', which was polite if exaggerated. Butler was typically convoluted: 'You know, I think, that I understand – and admire – the reasons which led you to take the course which you did . . . The last few weeks have been neither pleasurable nor – at any rate in a personal sense – profitable. But I felt I was able, and equipped, to do certain things; and the salvage operation here has gone ahead pretty well; perhaps rather better than the more literal one in the Canal . . . For obvious reasons I have marked this letter personal: I know you will understand.' Alec Home characteristically wrote to say that friendship must survive differences of opinion, deep though they may be. From Delhi, a well-placed friend wrote to say, 'We simply will not count any more because we have shown ourselves too out of date and out of touch; the new tie-up between the United States and India is tremendously significant, for London will now be by-passed as a point of interpretation between the new world and the old-new Asia.'

Brian Urquhart, then close to Hammarsjkold at the UN, said that Hammarsjkold sent his regards and 'would have sent his condolences had he not been so marvellously correct'. Urquhart said that 'this *Boy's Own Paper* adventure of Eden's has looked appalling and disastrous from here . . . There is something peculiarly depressing about the "Sapper" atmosphere which emanated from the Anglo-French performance and still emerges from the pronouncements of Tory politicians. They should grow up and try to enter the twentieth century. It is time Ike stopped sulking, the British changed their government, and everyone got down to trying to repair the damage.'

Sympathetic letters also arrived from Arnold Toynbee, Harold Nicolson, and Middle East ambassadors. Joe Harsch was one of the few pro-Suez people who wrote to me, saying that there 'are more people in Washington inclined to approve what the Prime Minister did than there are apparently in London . . . I find myself in the curious position of trying to defend the behaviour of a British government to Britishers here in Washington.' David Butler from Oxford wrote: 'Even when one disagrees with the motives, it is always stirring to hear of resignations on principle; and when one agrees one is doubly moved.' The Curzon Street bookseller Handisyde Buchanan said that Nutting was also a customer and he had had 1,800 letters, and only 35 against; Handisyde, deeply depressed by Suez, added that 'even if, as Jakie Astor said to me, "Everyone intelligent is on our side," it is not much help'. Another friend sent me, after the general withdrawal from Suez, a postcard with a picture of Michaelangelo's Moses: 'Do you experience a fellow feeling with this guy? Another man of immense moral rectitude who got the Israelis out of Egypt.'

Thirty years on, the lessons of Suez are undisputed except by a few backwoodsmen. The most obvious lesson was that it exposed the limits of British power; and thus the illusions of Eden, Macmillan, and Salisbury. The world in which they had grown up was shown to have altered totally. With luck, Britain might have toppled Nasser; but who now believes that we could for any length of time have maintained a 'lifeline of Empire' running through a hostile Arab world supported by Russia?

The other lesson was that the Western democracies could no longer ignore nationalist demands for self-government unless those demands were to be put down by brute force (as in Hungary by the Russians). The colonial world was demanding independence. This was what de Gaulle finally learned in Algeria. This was the 'wind of change' that Macmillan perceived – so that the man who was most wrong-headed before Suez became the most right-headed about its consequences.

And Dulles, the great schoolmaster himself? He saw Britain's actions over Suez as old-fashioned imperialism. But whereas Britain and France rapidly learned and acted on the lesson that Dulles taught them at Suez, Dulles did not heed his own teaching. It was Dulles, by his destruction of the shaky 1954 Indo-China peace settlements, who condemned the United States to learn this same lesson in the far harsher school of Vietnam, at far greater cost over two agonizing decades.

Suez was a great watershed. I remember King Hussein of Jordan asking, 'Weren't you involved in that Suez episode?' and, when I admitted it, adding, 'What a tragedy: the day that Britain finally fell off its pedestal, particularly around here.' The pedestal, he meant, was that of an imperial power which had honourably and carefully decided to lay down power.

When I went to Downing Street I thought over-optimistically of Eden as a man of the future. But he was a man of the past. He was listening to the voices of history. It was he who had negotiated, against strong opposition from his own party, the withdrawal of British troops from Egypt. He thought the Egyptian nationalists like Nasser ought to be grateful; and ought still to behave as if they were part of the Empire. He wholly failed to realize the extent to which the Middle East had moved irrevocably beyond our control. I remember one conversation with him when he talked about the Middle East as lying between the hammer of British power and the anvil of India. India, however, had ceased to be an anvil. Nehru disapproved of Nasser's nationalization of the Suez Canal, but he was certainly not going to allow Eden to use India as an anvil on which to crush Nasser.

Eden was only a blip in the shedding of the Empire. Within six months of Suez we had started the process of decolonization in Africa.

---7---

'The Week'
1957–60

After William Clark resigned from Downing Street at the end of 1956 he rejoined the Observer, *where he remained until 1960. He left no account of these years. John Douglas Pringle and George Seddon have supplied the following portrayal of him as he was then, and of his day-to-day routine at the* Observer.

John Douglas Pringle When I joined the staff of the *Observer* early in 1958, the paper was notable for its many remarkable and exuberant characters. William Clark was by no means the least remarkable among them. He was an extremely intelligent man with a great deal of journalistic experience whom no one took quite seriously largely, I think, because he did not take himself quite seriously. William could never resist a joke and, at his best, he was one of the wittiest men in England. A great many of his jests were directed at himself. He would disarm criticism of his outrageous follies and foibles by making fun of them before they could annoy, and his wit was so quick that one was always left dancing helplessly behind.

William had come back to the paper as something of a hero. The staff of the *Observer* had been united in their opposition to the Suez campaign – or at least as united as they ever were – but it was one thing to write denouncing the Prime Minister and the government for their folly in invading Egypt and another to resign publicly, as William had, in protest against it. It was all the more impressive since it was well known that he had thoroughly enjoyed his job as press adviser to Eden, which brought him so close to the centre of power in Britain. He was seen to be a man who could act with the

216

greatest courage when he believed his principles were at stake.

William's experience both in Britain and the United States was a very useful asset for any newspaper. He knew, or seemed to know, everyone of importance. He had a passion for collecting the friendship of the great. He was an indefatigable name-dropper but he dropped them so lightly and amusingly that it was almost an art form. 'I'm going to Jamaica on Wednesday,' he would tell me. 'I am, of course, staying with the Governor. He has a better table than the Prime Minister.' Once he remarked of some eminent and wealthy industrialist: 'He's so nice I could like him even if he wasn't rich!' I could happily spend hours with William listening to his entertaining flow of gossip.

I got to know William well working with him on a new project. Although the *Observer* was rightly proud of its uncompromising opposition to the Suez campaign, the paper had in fact suffered severely as a consequence. Before Suez the *Observer*'s circulation had been almost level with that of the *Sunday Times* and, as many believed, was on the point of overtaking it, but it had now fallen well behind. Many readers had deserted the paper and many Jewish firms had withdrawn their advertisements. One of the schemes put forward to increase circulation was to publish a weekly summary of news to be written in a lively, simple but well-informed style. It was called 'The Week'. David Astor appointed William to write and edit it and asked me to help him, in addition to my other duties as assistant editor.

George Seddon The idea behind 'The Week' was never better expressed than in a TV commercial which had Fenella Fielding praising it as 'just the thing for busy morons'. Much of its value depended on William's remarkable inside knowledge.

I arrived on 'The Week' at the end of 1959, succeeding Colin Haycraft as assistant to William. I had been introduced to him as a possible successor to Colin by John Douglas Pringle. I had known John since the early thirties when we were on the *Manchester Guardian*, he as a leader writer straight from university, while I was a very junior sub. 'The Week' staff then consisted of William, Ann Taylor, who was officially a researcher but also did a fair bit of writing for the page, William's secretary, and me. We were housed at the top of the Tudor Street building, surrounded by financial and sporting staff and rather isolated from the main editorial stream. Ann and I had a room to ourselves, William had an adjoining one

217

with a glass partition, and his secretary had a small hutch adjoining his. William's temper at this time was often on a short fuse and his reaction to anything disagreeable was immediate and audible. I vividly recall one occasion when he threw several wire correspondence trays at his secretary.

William spent only a part of his days in his room; he was often elsewhere in the building attending one of the endless editorial conferences beloved of David Astor. To quote John Pringle: 'If Mao Tse-tung invented the permanent revolution, the *Observer* in those days perfected the permanent conference.' I think William found them a bore; certainly he often came back from them irritable.

On Tuesday mornings 'The Week' conference took place, at which William, John Pringle, Ann and I drew up a list of possible subjects for next Sunday's page. The major topics were dealt with by William, and Ann would do the necessary research for them. I would be given some of those left over and Ann the rest.

By Thursday morning Ann had completed much of the research that William needed and I was struggling over my pieces, to do them in the William style. Put simply, this consisted of a dramatic opening sentence, a good closing one, with a filling of hard facts leavened by one or two jokes. This sandwich was topped with a clever headline, jokey, punning, or erudite, rather like a good crossword clue.

Friday morning William was in early, scribbling away, his secretary deciphering and typing his copy, which was collected every hour by messengers and carried across to the *Times* building in Printing House Square. Some carbons were also sent to specialists on the paper, for their comments. Friday lunchtime saw one of the more curious of William's 'Week' traditions. He always had lunch in his room with John Pringle. William provided a hamper of food, over which great care had been taken; perhaps a ham from Wiltshire or a game pie, followed by cheese and accompanied by wine. It was a real working lunch and lasted for anything up to two hours. They went through all the carbons of the copy that had been sent to the printers and decided what to do about any adverse comments that came back from the specialists. Much of the lunchtime, however, was spent on the headlines, and progress could be judged by the level of merriment to be heard through the partition.

Before long the proofs arrived from the printers, the changes made by John and William were transferred to them, and Ann and I set off for *The Times* to make up the page. I did not see William again until the following Tuesday. On Saturday morning I was at the *Times* building at eight in the morning to see that all was well with the page, making any late changes if vital news affecting the stories had come in overnight. Occasionally William telephoned while I was on the stone to make some alteration; by then he was usually in the country.

John Douglas Pringle　William rented a small and charming country cottage at Sheepbrook, only some forty-five miles from London and within half a mile of the main road to Oxford, where he often lunched or dined with various dons and undergraduates. Knowing that I had just returned from Australia and was living with my family in a very small flat in Chelsea, William promptly invited us all to spend weekends at Sheepbrook and once or twice lent us the cottage for quite long periods when he was away. He was an extraordinarily kind and generous friend.

It was at Sheepbrook that William was most relaxed. He was not a man for country pursuits and in fact continued to live much the same life there as in London, where he had a set of rooms in Albany, that elegant eighteenth-century building off Piccadilly, which perfectly suited his image as a man about town. But he enjoyed the garden at Sheepbrook, and the peace and privacy which the country alone can give. He used to practise Yoga on the lawn, often changing into a tracksuit to do it (once he changed three times in the course of the morning!).

This was the time when his regular radio talks on the BBC and his television appearances were beginning to give him a modest fame which he thoroughly enjoyed. He had the rare ability to speak eloquently on any subject at any time and was an effective and successful pundit on current affairs. He once said: 'I think the happiest moments in my life are when shaving at 8 a.m. on Sunday mornings when I can watch myself in the mirror while listening to my voice on the radio at the same time!' A typical William jest – half true, half mocking. His appearances on television were a source of great interest, not always uncritical, to the villagers of Lewknor. Once the voice of his old gardener, Mr Cooley, was heard in the village pub silencing argument with the remark, 'That ain't Clark: Clark be fatter than that.'

Well before I myself left the *Observer* in 1963 I was aware that

219

William was not wholly satisfied with his job or indeed with journalism as a career. I think he had two reasons for seeking a change. One was a perfectly respectable wish to improve his financial position. The more important reason was plainly that he wished to devote the rest of his life to Third World affairs. He was deeply committed to the cause of the emerging nations of Africa, Asia and South America, and to the belief that it was in the interests of the wealthy Western nations to give them the economic aid which they so desperately needed. He was against imperialism and colonialism in all its forms and had absolutely no trace of racialism in his own nature. He was as perfectly at ease with African politicians and Indian diplomats as with Oxford dons. He began to plan and work towards what was to become the Overseas Development Institute remarking – another typical William jest – that he had designed the post of Director in such a way that only he could fill it.

My friendship with William did not end in 1963 when I returned to Australia. We continued to correspond and I nearly always met him on my occasional visits to England. I last saw him in 1982 when, with characteristic generosity, he promptly invited me and my wife to stay at his beautiful home at The Mill, Cuxham. In many ways he was unchanged, a little heavier, a little more lame, perhaps a little more serious but just as amusing as ever. I never ceased to be astonished at the range of his gifts. In addition to his work in politics and journalism he had written two novels, one very good, and a successful play. He was an excellent speaker in public on any occasion and, at our last meeting, was hurrying off – not without some satisfaction – to deliver an oration at his brother-in-law's funeral. What a man!

Overseas Development
1960–8

The Overseas Development Institute in London owed its existence to the foresight and energy of a number of eminent men who saw, in the late fifties, before their political leaders, that a wind of change was blowing in Africa and indeed in the whole colonial world. They realized that the crucial challenge facing the second half of the twentieth century was the problem of poverty in two-thirds of the world's population. The bulk of the inhabitants of Africa, Asia and Latin America were still living in conditions of appalling squalor, while in Western Europe and North America most of the people there were living under conditions of affluence. For me, the 'rich white west', as I used to call it, had both a moral duty and a clear self-interest in transferring some of its wealth, both technical and material, to the Third World, to ensure an orderly and civilized process of growth. If this did not happen, I felt sure that there would be a polarization of the poor countries around new centres of influence and/or a degeneration of their societies into nasty and brutish ways of existence. This would not only be an affront in itself but it would rebound very rapidly to our own acute discomfort.

I was much concerned too over the fact that Britain had only recently sloughed off its imperial responsibilities. This created a vacuum in those countries overseas that had recently achieved independence and, more subtle but no less pervasive, in our own psychological make-up. Within an imperial structure we knew for good or ill where our responsibilities lay. In the new age of independence, the relationship between rich and poor on the world stage was far less clear. Nationally we had our welfare state.

Should this not now be transferred to an international plane?

It was with these ideas in mind – many of them extremely inchoate at the time – that the ODI was set up. Its leaders were Leslie Rowan, former private secretary to Winston Churchill and head of Vickers, who became the first chairman; P.M.S. 'Pat' Blackett, a Nobel Laureate soon to become President of the Royal Society; Austin Robinson, one of Cambridge's most eminent economists; Jock Campbell, Chairman of Booker Brothers; Frederick Seebohm, Chairman of Barclays DCO; Donald Tyerman, editor of the *Economist*; Victor Feather, soon to become General Secretary of the TUC.

The whole project would have had difficulty in getting off the ground if Joe Slater of the Ford Foundation had not promised a generous grant payable over three years. Armed with this, the Provisional Council met early in 1960 and advertised an open competition for the Director. There were quite a number of applicants, but by the summer they narrowed down to three: Sir Andrew Cohen, the ex-Governor of Uganda and currently the UK representative on the UN Trusteeship Committee; Flint Cahan, till three months previously the Deputy Secretary-General of the OECD; and myself. To my surprise I was chosen, with Flint Cahan as my deputy (tragically he was killed soon after, and I brought in as his successor Athole Mackintosh who was lecturer in economics at the University of Birmingham); in a year's time the third finalist, Andrew Cohen, was to return to Whitehall as the official founder of what was to become the Ministry of Overseas Development. He was the greatest supporter and closest collaborator of the ODI in all of Whitehall.

The first Annual Report of the Institute for 1961/2 put in prosaic but accurate form what we were about: 'Because of the extreme urgency of the challenge it is of great importance that people in the advanced countries should actively recognize their concern with the economic, educational, scientific, and political development problems of the emergent countries, and with the practical lessons in attempting to solve these problems. For this purpose, the Overseas Development Institute was set up in London in the autumn of 1960.' But these formal words give little hint of the ferment that bubbled up inside the Institute in those early years. Many things were going for overseas development in the early sixties: the Labour opposition's commitment to establish a Ministry of Overseas Development with a minister of Cabinet rank (Harold Wilson, the Labour leader, had been a founder of War on Want a decade earlier), the Freedom from Hunger campaign, the burgeoning of voluntary agencies like Oxfam, Christian Aid and Voluntary Service Overseas – all reflected and contributed to the public's interest in the fight against world poverty. At the heart of all this excitement was the Institute, staffed by a group of energetic and able young people, several of whom had experienced poverty in the underdeveloped countries at first hand.

Our aim above all things was to achieve wise action – in other words, to get things done. But what action? In 1960 there was no established doctrine of economic development of poorer countries. Was it to be industrialization and a trickle down of wealth to the peasants? Or the modernization of agriculture? Or labour-intensive industry? Or heavy external investment? Or the maximization of domestic savings which were then directed to a national plan for development? Could India learn from south-east Asia? Could Africa learn from either?

The ODI, in conjunction with the Brookings Institute of Washington DC and at the request of the US Secretary of State, Dean Rusk, set out on uncharted waters to study the aid givers: Britain, France, Germany, Japan – which certainly showed what very different methods were applied. Then came the turn of the recipients: studies on the impact of aid on Africa, the Caribbean and India. Finally a very detailed study of the impact of aid on various sectors in one country, Uganda. We set up working groups, held meetings, invited a stream of eminent speakers from overseas to meet eminent people in Britain, worked hard (and for the most part successfully) to get the press interested and generally made what Andrew Shonfield, then Director of Chatham House, called 'an enormous amount of noise'.

Our range was wide: we commissioned manuals for developing countries' ministers and officials on such subjects as power supplies, fertilizers and co-operatives – knowing that they would often have to take decisions about these vital subjects with only a little knowledge of them. We compiled a directory of organizations in Britain that dealt with the issues of development – surprising even ourselves by coming up with nearly 200 of them. We wrote a handbook for speakers and writers, simplifying the complexities of world statistics by converting, for instance, maunds per hectare into lbs per acre. We acted as midwife to the Intermediate Technology Development Group and the British Volunteer Programme. We wrote studies of aid programmes, British and foreign, government and private. We wrote policy documents on management and on education. We also gave a platform to leaders such as Pandit Nehru, Kenneth Kaunda, the French Africanist René Dumont, and the Mayor of Berlin Willy Brandt.

We were fortunate in that, before we were a year old, we were able to hold a conference under the chairmanship of Sir William Hayter of New College, Oxford, which was attended by a galaxy of key people in the development world: Mehdi Ben Barka (later murdered in Paris), Raoul Prebisch (then Secretary-General of ECLA), Kenneth Kaunda, Lester Pearson, Iain Macleod (Colonial Secretary), David Bruce (US Ambassador to London), Chief Adebo of Nigeria, B.K. Nehru, Bill Benton, Barbara Ward, and many others. Besides being immensely illuminating for me and the staff, this helped to get us taken seriously by those in power. The ODI was now on the development map.

In July 1961 the British government set up a new Department of Technical Co-operation (DTC). This was the forerunner of the Overseas Development Administration (ODA) which later became the Overseas Development Ministry (ODM). In many ways I think of the establishment of the DTC as ODI's initial success. The very first paper we produced had advocated such a step. From that time onwards, ODI worked in the closest way with successive ministries whose responsibilities were aid and development. As with business houses, we had to make it abundantly clear that we were in no sense a research arm of a government department. Our job was to analyse independently, to dig out the facts and to influence the influential. I regarded my main role as pushing ODI's output into high places. The Institute's reputation, as with any other such organization, depended on the quality of its work. But it was not enough just to be good; we had to be seen to be good and, further, to be seen as such by people who had power and influence. I also felt that it was crucial for those of us dealing with Third World affairs to be out and about in the market place, as it were, and to build a close relationship with the leaders of the countries we were trying to help. My own travels were very extensive, not least to the US which had the leading aid programme in the world.

In 1964 Athole Mackintosh left ODI to head the Overseas Development Group at the University of East Anglia and Tom Soper became my Deputy and Director of Studies. He came from Queen Elizabeth House, Oxford, where he had been Sub-Warden.

I had got to know him well while he was at Oxford and he was familiar with our work as he had written background papers for our 1962 study group on African development. He had a special interest in European Community affairs and the links betwen the EEC and Africa. This balanced my own bias towards the Commonwealth and indeed the US. I felt too that we would get on well together – and we did.

It was around him that the ODI team of young researchers operated and their enthusiasm and skill in presentation was remarkable. It was my policy to let them have their head and they responded superbly. Hours of work and conditions of work were secondary considerations if indeed they were considered at all, and they pushed ahead into this uncharted area of international relations with an energy and a commitment that was astonishing. Adrian Moyes, Juliet Clifford, Peter Williams, John White, Alison Franks, Andrzej Krassowski, James Lambe, Hal Mettrick, Michael Stevens, Michael Cutajar, John Guinness are some of the people who did so much to build up ODI's reputation. The Secretariat of the Institute led by David Wauton relentlessly and efficiently coped with the ever increasing demands of enthusiastic researchers and of those who used our Institute. Lotte Lowenthal, the librarian, built up a superb collection of documents, books and pamphlets in support of our own research.

With Barbara Castle as minister at the ODM and Sir Andrew Cohen permanent secretary, a remarkable phase in aid and development came about. Barbara Castle was minister for a relatively short period, 1964 to 1965, but she, together with her physically and intellectually towering permanent secretary (the new ministry was inevitably dubbed 'The Elephant and Castle'), made a major contribution to Britain's aid programme. The voluntary agencies too played an important and special role in Britain's aid relationship with the Third World and we found our work at the ODI was immeasureably helped by the close links we developed with VSO, Oxfam, Christian Aid, War on Want and others.

It was during these years that people began to question the trade relationship between the advanced and the developing world. In 1964 the first UNCTAD conference took place – a conference that owed much to the then British trade minister, Edward Heath. Just as I feel that the ODI played a significant part in bringing about the establishment of a British government department concerned with aid and development, so too do I feel that we played an important role in nudging the Conservative government of the day towards its constructive and effective attitude towards the very first UNCTAD conference. Interestingly enough, I recall that it took some time to convince our own Council that trade was an essential element in the relationship between the developed countries and the Third World. Twenty years ago there were still those who thought that the way to help the Third World was simply through the re-allocation of financial and technical resources. Trade was regarded by many as essentially a business matter within the framework of government regulations.

Although our studies were mainly concerned with government aid we recognized early on that governments were not enough. In the January 1964 issue of *Progress* I wrote: 'There is really very little chance that governments will be prepared to increase their aid from public funds to fill the gap which might be left by a decline in investment. Nor is it by any means certain that purely government-to-government aid can do the same job of development by itself; certainly it is not an efficient or well-tried method. Traditionally, development has taken place as the result of private investment – that is how the United States, Australia or Argentina were developed; government is the newcomer in this process, made necessary by the demand for speedy development, for cramming a century into a decade.' David Morgan, one of our first research officers, produced a report on *British Private Investment in East Africa* which was a great help in guiding us into the private sector.

Within two years of the ODI being established, we embarked on a new venture which achieved a success and an influence that even in my most sanguine moments I had not foreseen. The Nuffield Foundation made us a grant to enable us to send three fellows each for two years to work in Africa. This was the beginning of what became known as the ODIN Scheme and I cannot help feeling it was one of the most successful ventures I have ever initiated. The core of the problem facing Africa at the time was presented in my address to a joint meeting of the Royal African Society and the Royal Commonwealth Society on 1 February 1962. I said then: 'It would be a sordid ending to a not inglorious chapter of British history if at the close of nearly a century of our rule the economic foundations we had built proved insufficient to take the strain.

'What then are the forces that make a sudden dip in standards appear likely? It is simply this: that European skills are likely to be

226

withdrawn at a rate faster than they can be immediately replaced by African skills. I am not speaking of political skills, which we traditionally regard as innate, but of such skills as being a veterinarian or an electrical engineer, which demand several years of technical training. The East African battle might almost literally be lost for the lack of a horse-shoe's nail, because it is an agricultural economy that is peculiarly dependent on special techniques for keeping the jungle or the scrub at bay.' I was lecturing on the particular problems of East Africa, but my remarks had wider implications, and I continued: 'The nub of the problem, then, is that in the past these skilled technicians have mostly been Europeans and now the Europeans are leaving in large numbers. The criticism that can be made of the colonial past is that the training of African vets and agricultural officers and engineers and so on was left till far too late. It really only began in the last few years, so that now if British technicians leave, as seems likely, in 1962–4 there will be a gap of two or three years before African trainees finish their courses and can even begin to take over.

'How can that gap be filled? To some extent by persuading existing staff not to leave; to some extent by crash programmes of training Africans; and to some extent by bringing in temporary replacements through international agencies such as the UN or through our own British resources.'

It was this last point that was the genesis of the ODIN Scheme. I went on to say: 'One other important category of person who could be helpful is the young graduate who at the beginning of his career would give two years' or more service in Africa. Bright students with qualifications could, with a little training, act as stop gaps in quite senior posts in the administration, or in agricultural and engineering services. In conjunction with the Department of Technical Co-operation and some voluntary bodies, I am trying to see whether, without too much fanfare, we cannot skim off some of the cream of our university graduates for this demanding, exciting work.'

I beat the same drum in two turnover articles in *The Times* in 1962 and 1964, which I concluded by stating, 'Unless the Commonwealth can find some purpose to inspire it during the second half of the twentieth century, and can carry it out in practical ways . . . it will probably wither and die.'

The three ODINs who originally went out started what was to be a regular cadre of brilliant young men working in Africa who made a contribution to developing the continent out of all proportion to their experience and cost. The ODI, through the Nuffield Foundation grant, paid an ex-patriate allowance to the fellows, but their basic pay was that of comparable level Africans, and the local governments had full control of their disposition. As with so much of the early foundations of the ODI, this scheme has prospered and adapted down to the present day, because it is basically about development assistance between private people, friends and colleagues. By 1982 over 150 fellows had served in Africa, and many had continued their careers in Third World affairs. The three ODINs a year had become something nearer ten. I remember Professor Austin Robinson once said that not since Milner's Kindergarten had there been such contribution by young men to Africa. This was high praise but not, I think, unjustified.

By 1967 I was beginning to feel that I should move on from the ODI. There is a limit to the number of years one can put into a small organization and I was starting to be repetitive. Furthermore, by the mix-sixties the Institute had fulfilled its pledges: to provide a centre for work on development problems; to direct studies of its own where necessary; to be a forum where those directly concerned with development can meet others to share ideas and spread the information the organization had collected; above all, to keep the urgency of the problems before the public and the responsible authorities. Financially, although not secure – no institute of this sort can be – we were reasonably well placed. Broadly speaking we had about one-third of our funds from the Ford Foundation, one-third from British foundations, and one-third from British business. We had no funds from government and I think we were right to maintain this detachment.

UNESCO at the time seemed to open possibilities for me but then came a chance to join the World Bank in Washington. Apart from the importance of the work and the high professional qualities of the Bank as a financial institution, its base in the USA was an attraction to me. On 31 March 1968 I left the ODI to take up my position as Director of Information and Public Affairs at the World Bank.

(This chapter has been compiled from notes left by William Clark, and with the assistance of former colleagues at the ODI. Inevitably, and regrettably, it lacks the colour and insights the author would have provided. – Ed.)

The World Bank
1968–80

It is generally not until after the event that one can say for sure whether the declaration of a Year of This or a Decade of That was an act of justified faith or unjustified folly. Such declarations are very much the stock in trade of the United Nations these days, reflecting the Third World's understandable frustrations over what seem to be the permanently receding deadlines for achieving their economic and social objectives. They serve the laudable purpose of focusing international attention on key issues such as the status of women or the supply of clean water, and the achievements within the allotted timetable can sometimes be heartening. But the exercise can be divisive when one party views the objectives as aspirational while the other party insists that they are to be met at all costs. When they are not so met, the recriminations fly and the frustrations multiply. And even in the rare cases where the objectives appear to have been met at least statistically, the uneven distribution of the benefits can be no less divisive.

The First United Nations Development Decade was a case in point. As we entered the sixties, economic growth in many developing countries was proceeding at rates which outstripped anything the industrialized countries had enjoyed at a similar stage in their own history. At the same time, resources were being transferred from the rich to the poor nations on a scale unheard of in previous times. Those who had earlier claimed with great confidence – and there were some very distinguished economists among them – that the developing countries lacked the skills, resources and political stability to make any significant economic advance in the foreseeable future were busy reappraising their too dogmatic assumptions. Thus, when President John F. Kennedy proposed at the 1961 General Assembly of the United Nations that the 1960s be declared the First UN Development Decade, there were high hopes that the relatively modest targets set for the transfer of resources from rich countries to poor, and for the rate of overall economic growth in the latter, could be achieved.

I certainly shared in those hopes and, as it turned out, the overall GNP growth goal of 5 per cent was indeed achieved. But that was about all that could be said for the Decade. Close observers of the development scene, such as myself, could see that at midpoint it was faltering badly. At that stage we were not to know, although we might have guessed, that while the developing countries as a whole were heading for an average growth rate of 5 per cent for the Decade, on a per capita basis income in the poorest countries, with 67 per cent of the population, would have grown at only 1.5 per cent annually. What we could see very well, though, was that the volume of official aid was no longer keeping pace with the growth of the industrialized countries' national product. The donors were tightening their purse strings, and the reasons were not hard to deduce. First, the earlier euphoria had raised unrealistic expectations of the time it would take for development to shrink the gap significantly between rich and poor nations. The mounting evidence that it was clearly going to be a long haul seemed to have escaped, or been ignored by, the believers in 'instant development'. Unfortunately, it was the tendency of bilateral donors to see their largesse as a means of gaining short-term security or trading advantages, precluding in most cases the direction of investment to long-term growth. Thus, in a sense, they became the architects of their own disenchantment with the development effort. It was clear also that in many industrialized nations, eyes were being turned inward on mounting problems at home. In the United States in particular, dealing with domestic poverty and civil rights issues inevitably distracted attention and effort from overseas development. Moreover, the increasingly painful entanglement in Vietnam was hardly an encouragement to the American people to call for deeper involvement in the affairs of far-flung developing nations.

In Britain's case, I was worried that the growing disenchantment would undermine what the nation had with difficulty been accomplishing: its conversion from colonial political master into economic development partner in its recently dismantled empire. The French appeared to have found a position midway between the two in their relations with their former colonies. The British had gone beyond that and could not now step back. It was a partnership or nothing, and with Britain's unrivalled knowledge of the areas it had recently declared independent, there was an ability as well as a moral duty to render whatever service was possible to the new masters.

By 1967, with the Decade definitely out of steam, I turned my mind to what could be done to get the boilers fired up again. Somehow a new sense of urgency had to be injected into the international development effort. As Barbara Ward was eloquently insisting, the population growth rate in the Third World was a ticking time-bomb. If the Development Decade had been launched on the optimistic forecasting of how much could be achieved, the time had now come to broadcast very bluntly to the world at large how much stood to be lost, by developed and developing nations alike, if the effort was not revived. And quickly.

One course of immediate action seemed to commend itself to me. The crisis in the development effort needed a good public airing if anything was going to be done about it. What was needed was an authoritative, well-researched statement, by a panel of disting-uished experts, of the reasons why the Decade was faltering and what had to be done to revive it. I therefore decided to bring together a very small group of people of unquestioned expertise and commitment to the development effort, in the hopes that a brainstorming session might lead us to a plan of action for getting such a statement prepared. Sir Edward Boyle, later Lord Boyle of Handsworth, former Treasury Minister and Minister of Education, and at that juncture Pro-Chancellor of Sussex University, offered his spacious West Sussex home as a weekend venue for such a gathering. Notable amongst the ten or so who accepted my invitation were George D. Woods, President of the World Bank, Barbara Ward, who had just been appointed by Pope Paul VI to the Pontifical Commission for Justice and Peace; René Maheu, Director-General of UNESCO; and Axel Freiherr von dem Bus-sche, one of the earliest and bravest would-be assassins of Hitler, and, more to the point for our purposes, the former founder and first head of the West German Peace Corps and, at that time, an economic development adviser to the World Council of Churches in Geneva.

The weekend discussions, taking place during as well as between the kind of delectable repasts for which our kindly host was noted, raised my spirits considerably. There was no argument about the need to act without delay, and we agreed that Lord Franks, former Ambassador to Washington, and at that time Provost of Worcester College, Oxford, was the ideal person to head a commission of experts. Our choice was Oliver Franks not just because he was probably the best and most experienced head of commissions of enquiry of his day, but also because he had played a major role in setting the Marshall Plan on course.

I duly left the Sussex Downs with a mandate from my friends to write a broad proposal on how we might proceed from there. My first concern was to find a body to underwrite this project which, if mounted properly – of which Franks could certainly require assurance – would involve the hiring of an international staff of experts, travel to the developing world, and other expenses. Fired by George Woods' manifest enthusiasm for an enquiry, I decided to make my first appeal to the World Bank, in the hopes that a positive response from that quarter would obviate the necessity for further appeals in other quarters. I am not by nature a happy fund-raiser, although I have chalked up some successes in my time.

This proved to be one of them. I flew to Washington and found George Woods' enthusiasm undiminished and his willingness to help most forthright. He was due to give an address to the Swedish Bankers' Association in Stockholm on 27 October, and he asked me if Barbara Ward might write him a speech which would effectively rebut the now fashionable cry in the developed world that their aid programmes were so much good money sent after bad. He would then conclude the speech with a proposal to the developed nations that they set up a commission of leading experts in the development field along the lines we had discussed. He would include an offer on behalf of the World Bank to help the commission in every way, including the provision of the necessary finance.

Elated, I returned to London and quickly got Barbara's agreement to work on a speech for Woods. She produced a splendid draft, and cunningly, to lure Oliver Franks, included a passage recalling that before Europe and America could enter wholeheartedly into the experiment of the Marshall Plan, an official body of experts under Franks' leadership had been drawn up from participating nations to study the whole range of programmes and policies required to achieve European recovery. What was needed now, she wrote, was a 'Grand Assize' which should precede any attempt to round off the faltering Decade with a genuine re-formulation of policy.

George Woods duly delivered the speech. It gained considerable publicity, and the call for a 'Grand Assize' was widely endorsed. It was to be Woods' last major speech as President of the World Bank, it being his intention, as he had earlier confided in me, not to make any more once his successor was named. His five-year term would be up on the last day of 1967, and he expected the new President to be nominated by President Johnson well before the turn of the year, and approved by the Bank's executive board, even though he might not be able to take up the reins of office for a few months.

Rumours were already circulating when Woods made his 'Grand Assize' speech that Robert S. McNamara, US Secretary of Defense, would shortly leave the Pentagon and the Administration to take up the presidency of the World Bank. By late November it was becoming impossible for the White House to contain the rumours any longer, and indeed undesirable, since the prospect of McNamara's departure from the Pentagon was stimulating considerable speculation about a consequent change in the character of the war in Vietnam. And so, on 29 November, in a hurry, the Bank's executive board was called into session to consider Robert McNamara's name. There was unanimous agreement to offer him the post, of which he was immediately informed. He immediately accepted, and announced at a Pentagon press conference that same evening that he would not be taking up the post right away, President Johnson having asked him to remain at least long enough into the next year to complete the work on the military programme and financial budget for fiscal year 1969.

I was delighted for the Bank and the development community in general that George Woods was to have such a successor. And my delight turned to considerable excitement when, a few days later, Woods telephoned me asking me if I would like to be the Bank's Director of Information and Public Affairs, a post which he had recently caused to be vacant. Prior to our 'Grand Assize' discussions, I had known Woods only slightly, having originally been introduced to him by my friend Johnny Miller who, at the time of Woods' offer to me, had just retired from his post as the Bank's special representative in Europe. Woods had the reputation of being a rather gruff, occasionally irascible man whom not everyone found easy to work with. He had made his way up from the bottom of the banking profession to the very top, via the chairmanship of the board of the First Boston Corporation. What I had been most pleased to learn about him from Johnny was that he felt sufficiently secure in the investment banking fraternity not to worry at all about what their reactions might be to his determination to turn a cash-flush World Bank into a genuine development financing institution. He knew exactly how far he could go in that direction without jeopardizing the Bank's high credit standing in the financial markets where it obtained its funds. I was able to confirm for myself Johnny's view of the man when I got to know him much better that weekend at Edward Boyle's home. Woods might not be the world's greatest diplomat, but his energy, imagination and political courage were clearly being devoted to turning the Bank, to the real benefit of its developing member countries, into something that it had never been hitherto. I was later to form the firm opinion that Bob McNamara's subsequent huge expansion of the Bank would have been a much tougher and riskier undertaking but for the groundwork laid by his predecessor during a relatively short presidency. Bob was of the same view.

My response to Woods' invitation was that I was certainly very interested in principle, but that I really needed to talk about the scope of the job. We agreed that I should set out in a letter my concept of my duties in that post, and follow this up with a face-to-face meeting in Washington in January if my suggestions commended themselves to him. In the letter I then wrote to him, I told him that I regarded the job as an extension to what I had been doing for nearly seven years at the ODI, which was essentially to create the political will to enhance aid to development. At the Bank I would move into the international sphere from the narrower British base from which I was now operating. I told him clearly that I did not want to be just a press officer reporting to anyone who would listen about the day-to-day accomplishments of the Bank. I wanted to be involved in the Bank management's thinking about the development assistance effort as a whole, and the Bank's role in it. I wanted to put my experience in that field to use in the Bank's efforts as the largest source of development finance to build support for the concept of an international co-operative assault on the obstacles to faster economic development in the Third World. For me, this implied a much wider clientele than just the press. I wanted to include intellectuals and academics and, if I would not be treading on the preserves of other senior Bank officals, the political and business communities as well. 'I am not,' I concluded my letter, 'the international civil service type carrying out a brief handed down. I want to be involved in some aspects of policy-making, and I regard my function as an emissary to leaders of opinion worldwide.'

I felt no need to include in my letter my feelings about the McNamara succession. I had never met McNamara, but I knew enough about him to feel that the arrival of a man of such extraordinary ability and with such an exceptional mind was a stroke of enormous good fortune for the Bank. I had also read a speech entitled 'The Essence of Security' which he had delivered in 1966 to a meeting of the American Society of Newspaper Editors in Montreal. In this speech he had very eloquently insisted that unrelieved poverty in the developing nations was just as serious a threat, maybe a greater threat, to global security than the arms race. This speech had told me a lot about the man which I, and most likely countless others who read it, had not known before.

Woods reacted positively to my letter, and I duly flew to Washington in mid-January to carry the matter forward. He told me that he had anticipated my wish to have Robert McNamara's blessing on the appointment of a Director of Information who would be serving him rather than the President who had hired him. I was therefore despatched to the Pentagon where I had a brief and wholly agreeable meeting with the Defense Secretary. He had clearly studied my credentials with a keen eye, and had, as I later learned, taken the added precaution of seeking an opinion from a mutual friend, David Harlech, who had been Britain's Ambassador at Washington during the Kennedy presidency. It seemed I had passed muster, and McNamara told me that he looked forward to our working together. He informed me he would be free to take up his post at the Bank on the first day of April, and that I might find it convenient to do likewise. I told him that if he had no qualms about our both beginning our World Bank careers on April Fool's Day, I would suppress mine. With happy grins we shook hands on it, and I left the Pentagon entirely satisfied that any lingering doubts I had about leaving England and the ODI were now firmly dispelled. McNamara's transparent enthusiasm for what he was about to embark upon was both compelling and infectious. I knew that this was a man I could really work with.

I returned to London and began to pack up, my enthusiasm for what was to be being tempered with some real sadness at what I was leaving behind. Obviously I had to give up my tenancy at Albany, where I had lived so happily for so long. I just prayed that if things didn't work out in Washington, I would be able to find rooms there again. I had less sad feelings about my beloved country residence, The Mill at Cuxham, near Oxford, for the very good reason that it would be in the excellent care of David Harvey, and ready to receive me on what I intended to be visits of a very regular nature to England on official business.

I arrived in Washington in the last days of March, and was initially installed by the Bank in one of those ghastly Muzak-infested, characterless hotels which give one every incentive to waste not a moment in finding a home for oneself. My search was mercifully brief. I quickly found a charming little house set on the edge of a sloping wooded area in a quiet street in one of Washington's nicest north-west residential areas. It had a wooden deck at the back, nicely tree-shaded in the summer, which became my open-air dining room and study for as many months of the year as the weather allowed, which were not a few. An added attraction was that my old friends Stewart and Tish Alsop lived but a few steps away on Springfield Lane. I therefore declared my search ended and duly purchased 3407 Rodman Street, in which I was to live happily for all of my twelve years at the World Bank.

My next concern was to find a good cook-housekeeper. My favourite method of entertaining has always been to gather a small group of four to six persons around the dining room table where simple but good food and wine can stimulate entertaining and instructive conversation in which all present participate. I therefore needed someone who would be unintimidated by requests, often at short notice, to prepare weekday dinners or weekend lunches as well as keep the house clean and functioning. After one less than happy experiment, I managed to find just the person I wanted. A State Department couple, reassigned overseas, were looking for good employment for their male Chinese cook-housekeeper. Having a great partiality for Chinese food, and finding his references impressive, I hired Kin Tak Luk, who asked to be addressed as Lalu. It was one of the best decisions I ever made. Once I had mastered comprehension of his rather exotic method of expressing himself in English, the wheels of housekeeping began to turn smoothly, and I was able to begin my entertaining. Lalu's Chinese cuisine became a noted feature of the Clark establishment, and was enjoyed by people of great eminence over the years. He was wholly unimpressed by status, and would rate the worth of my guests, whether it be a former prime minister or federal chancellor, solely on the basis of whether they showed appreciation of his dishes.

Putting my domestic arrangements in order had to proceed in tandem with taking over my responsibilities at the Bank. The Information Department, which disposed of a professional staff of twenty-one people plus support staff, had been in the interim care of its deputy director, Lars Lind, since the departure of the previous director, Harold N. Graves, Jr, to a different department of the Bank. I already knew that Lind, a Swede, had had his difficulties with George Woods, but it took me no time at all to conclude that Woods had misjudged his man. I found Lars professionally extremely able, very dedicated and most likeable. He had served in the Norwegian Navy during the early part of the Second World War and had subsequently made a career in the UN system, coming to the Bank in 1964 via the International Atomic Energy Agency, the Food and Agriculture Organization and UNESCO. He was later to succeed me briefly as Director of the Information Department when I was promoted to Vice-President, External Relations in 1974. His final post before retirement was as Director of Information at United Nations Development Projects. One could not have asked for a wiser and more helpful deputy for a newcomer such as myself, and he proved a most valuable colleague and good friend through the seven years we were together.

Also on the staff of the department was someone who had worked for me in London at the beginning of the sixties. I had given Julian Grenfell his first job after coming down from King's, Cambridge, getting him hired by Norman Collins at Associated TeleVision to be a writer and programme assistant on my weekly interview show *Right to Reply*. He later became anchorman of ATV's religious programmes until Paul Bareau, editor of *The Statist*, recommended him to the World Bank as a writer. When I arrived I found him in charge of the department's African interests. He told me that on his first ever visit to that continent in 1966, as press liaison officer on an official visit by George Woods to East Africa, Woods had somehow got the impression that he was a British Member of Parliament who happened to be following the same official itinerary, and had treated him, to Julian's bewilderment, with excessive courtesy and respect until the misunderstanding was revealed. I eventually sent Julian to Paris to head our information and public affairs operations in Europe, and then, during the second half of my stay at the Bank, he was our 'ambassador' to the United Nations in New York.

I was particularly anxious to obtain the services of a first-class secretary who would be of a character to bear with my somewhat informal working habits and who would not mind taking on a few extra responsibilities such as seeing that I paid my electricity bills, replacing lost car keys, or reminding me to make an appointment with my dentist. I found such a person in the Bank in Susan Frampton, a young English lady of great charm, infinite patience and impressive secretarial skills, who carried the added qualification of having worked in the Press Department of the Foreign Office. Happily she stayed with me throughout my twelve years at the Bank and was an unfailingly smiling tower of strength, ruffled by virtually nothing, whether it be the transcription of barely legible notes scribbled down by me at some meeting between McNamara and a head of state, or the deciphering of one of Lalu's less comprehensible communications from the home front. My gratitude to Susan knows no bounds, and I know how delighted my successor, Munir Benjenk, was to have her with him during his own term as Vice-President, External Relations.

On the morning of 1 April, the day I was due to report for duty at the Bank, I breakfasted early in the hotel, watching the amazed commentaries on the TV news shows following President Johnson's wholly unexpected announcement the previous evening that he would neither seek nor accept the Democrat Party's nomination for a second full term in the White House. I arrived at the Bank's 1818 H Street headquarters, just a block and a half from the White House, at a quarter to nine, to find that the other new boy, Bob McNamara, had already been there since eight, a fact of which I took good note. At ten past nine he called me to ask me to attend the 9.30 meeting of the President's Council, a small advisory body for the day-to-day control of the Bank's affairs, and added that he wished me to be a permanent attendee at it. I was flattered and delighted by the invitation; my wish to be a participant in the policy-making was clearly being met.

The council at that time had eight members: the President; the three Vice-Presidents; the Executive Vice-President of the Bank's affiliate, the International Finance Corporation; the General Counsel; the Economic Adviser to the President; and the Director of the Development Services Department. Later that same week, with the arrival of Sir Denis Rickett, just retired as the Treasury's Second Secretary, to take up a World Bank vice-presidency, the number rose to nine, and raised to four the number of non-Americans on the council.

238

At that first meeting, McNamara spoke affably of being a 'new boy who needs to learn', but I couldn't help feeling that he had some pretty decided views on what he wanted to do. He asked all of us to meet again with him individually to tell him of our plans.

I was invited to lunch after the council with Irving Friedman, the President's Economic Adviser, the gist of whose advice to me, the other new boy, was to be aware of the fact that almost nobody else in the top reaches of the Bank was a professional economist. Whether it was intended or not, and I assumed that it wasn't, this information lifted a certain burden from my mind and made me feel much more at home.

I was called back to McNamara's office after lunch, and found George Woods with him. Oliver Franks would be coming in the next day to hear what we had to say about a 'Grand Assize', and we needed to agree on a line. I was greatly heartened by McNamara's enthusiasm for the idea. Woods had courteously and correctly waited until his successor was in office before advancing the matter further, and it was good to know that the latter was anxious to get it moving. The meeting duly took place the next day. Franks was in an enigmatic mood. He showed a keen awareness of the problems such an Assize would have to deal with and an obvious concern that solutions should be found. But he would say neither yes nor no to our offer of the leadership of such an enterprise. I suspected, rightly as it turned out, that he was just too busy to take it on, and I began to think immediately of alternatives.

On the evening of my fourth day at the Bank, I dined with Michael Davie and Nora Beloff. We had just heard that Martin Luther King, Jr, had been assassinated, and I have to confess that while we saw this as a tragic setback for the civil rights movement as well as an appalling crime, it never occurred to us that it could have the immediate violent consequences that now ensued. Throughout the next day, Lars Lind kept coming to my office with fresh reports of worsening rioting in Washington, culminating with the news that Fourteenth Street, just four blocks away on the other side of the White House, was ablaze. It was a strange and uncomfortable feeling, standing there in my office where the quiet of an operating theatre prevailed, watching through the window the black smoke rising from the city streets so close by, and realizing that a very long, hot summer must now be beginning.

At 4.30 that afternoon, McNamara called a meeting in his office to review progress in the negotiations, led by the exceptionally able and charming senior Vice-President, Burke Knapp, on the replenishment of the resources of the International Development Association (IDA), the Bank's concessional lending affiliate. In addition to myself, there were assembled there Denis Rickett, Irving Friedman, and Dick Demuth, the Director of the Development Services Department. Knapp was not far into his report when McNamara's personal assistant, Rainer Steckhan, came in to announce that the Mayor of Washington had ordered a 5.30 curfew for the whole city. Anyone found on the street after that hour would be arrested by the police or the National Guard units that had now been deployed throughout the district. We decided to carry on our discussion of how to get the IDA replenishment through the American Congress. Finally, at seven o'clock, I hitched a ride in Irving Friedman's car to the Alsops' house. The streets were deserted and a pall of smoke darkened the city.

Throughout the evening, both television and radio repeated the curfew order, and somewhat bizarrely the televised pictures of the rioting and looting in the predominantly black quarters of the city were accompanied by assurances that we were being shown them to discourage panic. We also learned that President Johnson had cancelled his imminent mission to Honolulu for Vietnam peace talks, in order to deal with the crisis at home. He looked deathly on the television screen – worse, I thought, than the FDR I had seen in 1945, or the Eden of 1956.

The situation was brought pretty well under control over the weekend, and movement to and from the Bank was back to normal by Monday. On the Tuesday, 9 April, I attended McNamara's first board meeting. The twenty executive directors, representing the 107 member countries, sat around the massive table, their alternates seated behind them. In the back stalls, against the rows of national flags, sat fairly senior members of the staff. On either side of McNamara at the table sat his four or five most senior officers, including, at his side, the Secretary of the Bank. The meeting went extremely badly. One by one, the executive directors attacked a staff paper on the effects of devaluation of the Bank's assets. After ninety minutes, McNamara crisply halted the discussion, withdrew the paper and promised further discussion on the matter at a later date. There ensued a discussion led by the United States Executive Director, Livingston Merchant, in which he roundly criticized certain contract award practices. Finally, under Any Other Business, some questions were raised about the 'Grand Assize', to which the President replied cautiously that the matter was still in the preliminary discussion stage. Meanwhile, a handwritten message was passed to me from Rainer Steckhan relaying Bob's request that I attend a President's Council meeting at two o'clock. Judging by the look on his face at the board meeting, I had a pretty good idea what it was going to be about.

I was not disappointed. McNamara wasted no time in informing the council that he had found the morning's board meeting a pretty horrifying experience. In three hours, nothing had been achieved, and there had been no single mention of development. He had come to the Bank to deal with development issues, he went on, not to participate in a debating society. In future, no proposal should be taken to the board unless it was already firmly established that it had the support of the majority of the voting power. At this point there was much moaning amongst the old hands about the poor state of relations between the Bank staff and the board which the new President had inherited from his predecessor. It seemed there was no doubt in their minds where the blame properly lay. I ventured to suggest in response to this not very edifying indictment that George Woods had spoken up for development, and that this had not commended itself to a board which was afraid to spend money. Surely we should get back to development and try to make a team of the executive directors and the staff. This plea elicited little reaction from my colleagues, and I left at the end of the meeting with the worrisome impression that the majority view was that the best course of action was to keep the board and the staff as far apart as possible as often as possible, in order to avoid conflict. McNamara kept his counsel, and it occurred to me that he was probably happy to let people have their say while he was, at the same time, making up his mind what to do.

Against the dramatic backdrop of Lyndon Johnson's abandonment of another presidential race, the assassination of Dr King, the riots and the curfew, watching Bob McNamara's baptism in the Bank and experiencing my own all added up to a rather memorable introduction to life in the international civil service. Frankly, I was looking forward to a relaxed Easter weekend when I could assemble some thoughts on what I perceived to be the essence of my task: to help create amongst the rich countries that give money and lend money to the Bank a sense of real trust in the institution, and to create that same trust among the developing nations who borrow from it. I needed to start getting a plan of action for my department and myself down on paper, and the Easter weekend would be a good time to start. Or so I thought.

On Thursday evening, however, Bob McNamara told me he had been persuaded to do some short TV tapes for his friend and former Cabinet colleague, Bobby Kennedy, whose drive for the Democratic nomination for the presidency was already in high gear. The tapes, Bob told me, were not intended as an endorsement, and could not be, given his week-old status as an international civil servant. They were simply reminiscences about the Cuba missile crisis days, when Bobby had been absolutely right on how to handle it. I ventured that, in my opinion, he had been rather imprudent to do them as they were bound to be interpreted as an endorsement. On a seasonal note I added that his self-inflicted crucifixion might yet be celebrated as a triumph. He smiled and hurried on.

The next day, Good Friday, I had a midday appointment to discuss information policy with him. We had barely started when Rainer called to say that a Hearst reporter was asking questions about some tapes. I told Rainer to plead ignorance, which he was able to do with a clear conscience. Bob and I discussed the matter further and decided that if I was approached over the weekend, which was most probable, I would say that I had nothing to say. In the meantime, he would draft a brief statement based on what he had told me on the Thursday evening which the press could use.

Despite my having nothing to say to the journalists who called me through the rest of that Friday, the *Washington Post* ran a story the next morning stating that McNamara had taped an endorsement of his close friend, Bobby Kennedy. I went to the Bank early and found Bob alone in his office – he had insisted on his staff not missing their Easter weekend – and before we settled down to talk about the Bank's information policy, we reviewed where we stood on the affair of the tapes. Yes, it was imprudent what he'd done, he told me, but he had felt bound to do it. He had very strong feelings about the exercise of US power. The country and the world could have been destroyed by the wrong use of US power at the time of the Cuban missile crisis. Jack Kennedy, a very wise, very sensitive man, would never have lacked the courage to do what he felt was right, but it would have been very hard for him to oppose a majority decision in his Cabinet. Bobby and he, McNamara, had worked hard not to have the President put in that position, by ensuring a Cabinet majority against a course of action that might have led to disaster. Don't forget, he concluded, that the next US President might well find himself having to make equally fateful decisions in similar circumstances of crisis. Bobby would be okay in that situation. So would Hubert Humphrey. But what if it was Nixon or Reagan?

It was hard to argue with that, and I was both impressed and moved by what had motivated him to do the tapes. I told him so, and we quickly got back to the business at hand.

By Easter Sunday, however, the issue had heated up some more. The press now had Bob's statement, and it appeared in the *New York Times* on Easter Monday morning, along with a statement from the Kentucky Republican Senator Thurston B. Morton calling on him to resign. At our 9.30 President's Council meeting, McNamara said he was sorry that he was cause of publicity about his position at the Bank. He had turned down several offers to write about his years at the Pentagon, particularly the most recent years which were inevitably a part of current politics. But what he had had to say about the exercise of power at the time of the Cuban missile crisis was not. He had felt compelled to say it, and he had therefore said it.

Burke Knapp thanked him for his forthrightness with his colleagues, but I could see that the colleagues were upset. Things did not improve when, as we broke up somewhat dispiritedly, the dean of the executive directors, Dr Luis Machado, a veteran of the Bretton Woods conference and, by coincidence, a Cuban, appeared at the doorway. We were in no doubt as to why he was seeking an urgent meeting with the President.

I later lunched with Marquis Childs, the columnist and Washington correspondent, who told me that the press was pretty well solid against McNamara on the tapes affair, and that our chances of getting the IDA replenishment through Congress had maybe suffered a mortal injury. Trying to keep my spirits up, I returned to my office and arranged to see Bob again at about 4 p.m. I told him about Childs' gloomy report on press attitudes and urged him to talk to the senior staff the next day. He said he already had plans to do so and that he would explain to them that he had ties to the past, and that that was a part of what the Bank was getting with him. But the future of development was what counted, and that was what they must work together on. He then left to convey a similar message to the board who were to meet with him at 4.30.

It was a fairly rough passage for a few more days yet, but McNamara rode out the storm. One could detect a strong feeling in the Bank that although most were unhappy at what he had felt compelled to do, they didn't want this to hobble their new President or mar the Bank's entry into what promised to be an exciting new era. For my part, I had learned more about Bob McNamara and more about the Bank in those dramatic first two weeks than I had ever expected to learn. One thing was abundantly clear: nothing was going to be the same again in the Bank. The development situation demanded that the Bank do a much bigger job than it was currently doing. McNamara was obviously determined to equip the institution to do so, and to carry the member countries with him, especially the major shareholders. There had been, as Harold Macmillan had said in a rather different context, 'a little local difficulty'. It had been overcome, and it was time to move on. And I myself now looked forward to being a participant in what was clearly going to be an exciting endeavour orchestrated by a very remarkable man.

It is not easy to capture in a single chapter, to which time remaining limits me, a twelve-year period of my life which, I have no hesitation in saying, was the most fulfilling I have known. It was my good fortune that my years at the World Bank coincided with Robert McNamara's stewardship, for to be a witness to that stewardship was an experience of extraordinary interest. In recalling those years, I inevitably find my story interwoven with that of McNamara's own odyssey, for I worked with him through twelve of the thirteen years of his presidency, and travelled with him to over eighty different countries. These travels afforded me the unique opportunity, and great privilege, to meet all the leaders of the Third World and to see at first hand what they were struggling to do for their peoples and how far they were succeeding. And, naturally, I was able to observe the lending and advisory operations of the bank at the field level and see what their impact was on the lives of the people we were trying to help.

I will always be especially grateful to Bob McNamara for having me as a regular travelling companion, along with his beloved Marg and whomever was his personal assistant at the time, plus the one or two senior Bank officials whose area of responsibility we were visiting. If I had not been in a position to see and hear what he was seeing and hearing, I would have been hard put to it to discharge my function as Director of Information and Public Affairs during my first five years, and subsequently as Vice-President, External Relations, for the next seven years. As a participant in the President's Council at home and as a member of his small entourage on the road, I was very well placed to fuel the engines of our effort to bring the message of our objectives and philosophy to a global audience.

We had to help convince a sceptical world that development could be made to work and that it was in the common interest of the rich and the poor nations that it should do so. We had to justify our rhetoric by demonstrating through our own operations that it could work. And we had to help persuade both rich and poor that a more equitable global economic order could be brought about, not by confrontation, but only by consensus. That was the burden of the plan I set out for my own operations in the early days of April 1968. Some of my colleagues outside the Information Department, used to a more parochial approach to public relations, found my plans somewhat grandiose. McNamara, I am happy to say, did not. He already saw the Bank as potentially the most important agent of change through consensus. His immediate task was to start equipping it to play that much larger role.

During those first, unexpectedly dramatic, days of April, McNamara found time to pore over the Bank's past lending figures, and was able to draw his first conclusions: the Bank was doing less than it could and should do, and there was a danger that the general paralysis which was afflicting the aid effort in so many parts of the world might soon be gripping the Bank itself. Too many needy countries, especially in Africa, were not being helped by the Bank. The argument that many of them were too backward to prepare projects up to the Bank's high standards left him unimpressed. They could be helped to prepare them. Nor did he buy the argument that the Bank was forced by financial constraints to concentrate its efforts on a limited number of regular customers. There were resources aplenty to be tapped; during the Development Decade so far, the rich countries had added to their annual real incomes a sum of about $400 billion. He therefore gave his first instruction to an astonished President's Council, asking that work be put in hand immediately to draw up a list of all the projects and programmes that the staff would wish to see the Bank carry out if there were no financial constraints. The list would provide the basis for drawing up a five-year programme for the Bank, itself based on individual plans for each country, setting out what the Bank could invest productively in each if there were no shortage of funds. The only limitation would be the capacity of the individual country to use the assistance effectively and to repay the loans on the terms on which they were lent.

This new approach, though welcomed by the great majority of the staff, nonetheless found its critics, among them one senior offical who foresaw 'an awful lot of goldfish at the top of the pool with their mouths open'. But the staff got down to work, and within three months a list was on McNamara's desk. What the aggregate figures suggested very clearly was that the Bank should lend twice as much over the coming five years as it had during the previous five. Bob now had the basis for his programme.

While the staff had been working on its list, McNamara had been laying plans for his first visit to a developing member country of the Bank since assuming the presidency. His choice characteristically fell on Indonesia, one of our poorest and most populous members, which had just returned to Bank membership from which Dr Sukarno had withdrawn the country some years earlier. Indonesia clearly needed urgent and extensive help, and McNamara wanted to see for himself what the Bank could do. General Suharto, who had become President in March, welcomed the suggestion that the President of the Bank pay a visit, and it was duly scheduled for mid-June. To my delight, McNamara asked me to join the mission.

On 4 June, just five days before we were due to leave, Bobby Kennedy was assassinated in the hour of his triumph in the California presidential primary. NcNamara was on a twenty-four-hour round-trip visit to the bankers in Frankfurt when the awful tragedy occurred. We all knew what terrible agony McNamara must now be sharing with the family to which he was so particularly close. On the Saturday I watched on the television at Rodman Street the very moving funeral mass sung for Kennedy at St Patrick's Cathedral in New York, and saw McNamara, his face ashen and weary with grief, helping to bear his friend's coffin. I began to wonder whether he could possibly recover in time to leave the next day for Indonesia. But he did, and the visit, into which he plunged himself with immense energy and concentration, was something of a God-sent distraction.

The long flight took us through Hong Kong and Bangkok on our way to Djakarta, and on the stop for a flight change in Bangkok, I learned something of Bob's determination to be recognized now as an international civil servant and not to let official America treat

246

him as being still one of theirs. As we left the plane to spend a couple of hours before continuing on the next leg, we found an American uniformed military officer saluting at the foot of the aircraft's steps. With the US Ambassador's compliments, would 'Mr Secretary' like to come to the Embassy for a wash-up and a meal and chat? With great politeness, McNamara asked the officer to thank the Ambassador for his courtesy and to explain to him that as he was no longer 'Mr Secretary' but an international civil servant, he would feel more comfortable using the airport's facilities along with his colleagues. A somewhat startled officer saluted smartly and marched away across the tarmac, while we very admiring colleagues accompanied the ex-Mr Secretary into the airport lounge.

The six-day visit to Indonesia was an eye-opener for us. We had, of course, read of its mounting problems under the progressively disastrous rule of 'Bung' Sukarno, but the shape we found it in surpassed our most pessimistic expectations. McNamara immediately offered to establish a resident staff of Bank experts in Djakarta to work along with the government's development planning organization, an offer which was enthusiastically received. Less than two months later, Bernie Bell, the widely respected Deputy Director of Projects at the Bank, was on his way to Indonesia to head a carefully selected resident staff. And by the following summer, $21 million had been lent by IDA to upgrade irrigation and to rehabilitate agricultural estates.

The following month, while the Bank staff were still building up their list, McNamara visited Turkey and Egypt. There had been no lending to Turkey for two years, but there were projects in the pipeline. Egypt, however, had not had a loan from the Bank in eight years, the reason being advanced by the Bank staff that Colonel Nasser's regime had simply not been popular with the United States Congress. Shortly after our visit, appraisal of a Nile Delta drainage project got underway, the first of a long line of projects that would be financed by both the Bank and IDA in the years to come.

I saw in these first forays of McNamara into his Third World constituency the shape of things to come. One of the objectives of such trips was to get to know the rulers of these countries and to let them get to know him. In the early part of his presidency, he had to face the problem that many of the rulers saw him, because of Vietnam, as a militant anti-communist. I remember well President Suharto's efforts to find what he felt must be sympathetic common ground with the new Bank President by stressing the vigour and harshness with which he had dealt with the Chinese communists in his own country who had stood between him and the seizure of power. McNamara let him finish, then asked him how he planned to integrate Indonesia's Chinese into his state, where their skills and hard work were sorely needed.

These meetings with heads of state, which were usually unstructured, were invariably scheduled as the final engagement in the country. This was designed by McNamara so that he could sound out the president or prime minister on where he thought his country was headed and how the Bank could help after he had seen something of the development effort for himself and had had intensive discussions with the ministers and other officials responsible. He paid particular attention to what was being done to meet the basic needs of the poorest sections of the population, and here Marg McNamara played an important supporting role, visiting hospitals, schools and family health clinics, thus enabling Bob to get a good idea of how the reality matched up to the statistical claims of the government.

All of these visits were highly educational for him, and often for his hosts too. He always arrived excellently informed of the state of the economy as seen by the Bank's staff of country experts, and not infrequently astonished departmental ministers with facts and figures of which they themselves appeared not to be personally in possession.

Looking back, I would have to say that our visits to Africa, of which there were many, were the most fruitful. This was the continent where the Bank's help was most urgently needed and it was there that McNamara developed the best relations with leaders. There was mutual admiration, accompanied by plain speaking on both sides, in his exchanges with leaders such as Kaunda, Senghor, Nyerere and Kenyatta. He invariably shunned statistics in such encounters, preferring to discuss Africa's history, culture and current political philosophy. I remember an off-the-cuff talk he gave to Nigeria's Federal Cabinet within weeks of the end of that country's hard-fought civil war. His remarks, drawing on the American experience of binding up the wounds of fratricidal strife, moved several of the generals-turned-ministers to quite unsoldierly tears.

I learned, at the very start of our travels together, that a schedule that confined him to the cities was unacceptable to him. He insisted that at least a full day, preferably two, be spent out in the rural areas. And it was there that he eventually came to the belief that poverty could never really be alleviated except by direct action at the smallholder level. He was able to see that the development projects financed by the Bank in earlier periods, mostly heavily capital-intensive, had certainly helped to modernize, industrialize, and create wealth in the modern sector, which usually meant the cities. They were, by and large, excellent projects. But rapid population growth had swallowed up much of the benefits, and those outside the modern sector, particularly in the rural areas, had been almost wholly untouched in their poverty.

With our return from Egypt in the third week of July, attention had now to be focused on the next major date on the Bank's calendar, the annual meeting in September, at which Bob would be addressing the board of governors for the first time. We were already agreed on what the thrust of his message should be. The income gap between the rich and the poor was increasing, while the political will amongst the developed countries to foster development was diminishing. The Bank would have to provide the leadership. If it did more, others would do more. Now we had to underpin this argument with facts and figures. How much more could the Bank do? In which geographical areas? And in what sectors? And where was the money to come from? To present the outlines of a coherent five-year programme to the board of governors, these questions, and more, had to be addressed in the ten remaining weeks before the annual meeting. The staff's 'wish list' of investments provided the parameters, and labouring mightily through the remainder of the summer, the staff and the President put the pieces in place.

In the meantime, we had not forgotten the 'Grand Assize'. Both McNamara and I were anxious to carry the proposal forward without delay, but, with Oliver Franks' polite rejection of our invitation to head the commission, as I had feared, we needed to find quickly a suitable alternative. We soon settled on Canada's former Prime Minister and Nobel Peace Prize laureate, Lester Pearson. McNamara invited him, and, to our great delight, he accepted on 19 August, and wasted no time in putting together a commission of eight distinguished persons. The seven who joined him were Edward Boyle of Great Britain, Roberto Campos of Brazil, Douglas Dillon of the United States, Wilfried Guth of Germany, Arthur Lewis of Jamaica, Robert Marjolin of France, and Saburo Okita of Japan. A staff of fourteen experts in various relevant fields of development from nine countries in both the developed and developing worlds was then assembled, and the Pearson Commission was eventually able to hold its first meeting that November in Mont Gabriel, Canada. At that first meeting, it was decided to make every effort to have the commission's report in the hands of the Bank at the 1969 annual meeting of its board of governors the following October. Their considerable efforts, I am happy to recall, were not in vain.

We were meanwhile working on McNamara's first annual meeting speech. In the process I began to feel, and so did Bob, that there would be much advantage in having someone to work exclusively as the President's speechwriter. Bob had just the person in mind, and shortly after the annual meeting he despatched me to the Pentagon to have a word with his former speechwriter, Jack Maddux, who was then performing the same literary service for McNamara's successor, Clark Clifford. I was a bit surprised to find a person of Maddux's rather Falstaffian charm and wit engaged in the sombre business of articulating a superpower's defence posture. He joined the Bank to write for his old boss the following January, and proved that he had indeed a remarkable gift for couching the President's messages to the world in appealing, and often very moving, language.

If the first annual meeting speech lacked the Maddux touch, it was nonetheless an effective statement, leaving the governors in no doubt that a new era had opened in the Bank's history. It was the end of September, and the President was by now in a position to flesh out the elements of a five-year programme with some orders of magnitude. The Bank, he told them, should lend twice as much during the next five years as it had lent in the past five years, which would be nearly as much as the Bank had lent since it began operations twenty-two years previously. There would, however, be no derogation from the high standards of careful evaluation and sound financing that were synonymous with the name of the World Bank. On the other hand, we would be looking more and more for projects to finance which would make the most fundamental contribution to the development of the total national economy. And more help would be directed to the poorest countries that needed it most. He went on to remind the governors that the parable of the talents was a parable about financial power, illuminating the great truth that power is given to be used, not to be wrapped in a napkin against risk. At this point in his speech, I noted some senior staff members looking less than comfortable, which did not surprise me. There were some who seriously doubted both the wisdom and the practicality of such a precipitate increase in the Bank's activities.

Bob next addressed the question which by now was surely on the mind of every one of his listeners: where is the money coming from? Acknowledging that there were, of course, certain constraints resulting from balance of payments difficulties, he pointed out that this was a problem of balance among the rich countries and not of balance between those countries as a group and the rest of the world. The Bank had to search the world for surpluses and reserves to be tapped.

This was precisely what Bob had been doing. He had himself been to Frankfurt, Zurich, and many times to New York with his treasurers, and the staff had been looking around the Middle East, notably and successfully in Kuwait. Thus, in his speech, he was able to report that in the previous ninety days the World Bank had raised more funds by borrowing than in the whole of any single calendar year in its history.

As the governors digested this rather startling piece of information, McNamara informed them that there would be considerable changes in the allocation of the Bank's resources, both to geographic areas and to economic sectors, to meet changed and changing circumstances. Noting that the Bank and IDA had tended to concentrate their efforts on the south Asian subcontinent, he expected a further substantial rise in lending to the area in the coming five years. But a greater emphasis would now need to be placed on Latin America and Africa, where activities had been less concentrated, and on some countries in great need of help, such as Egypt and Indonesia, where past activities had been negligible. He therefore foresaw investments in Latin America more than doubling over the next five years, and in Africa more than tripling. In countries where there was no well-established development plan or planning organization, the Bank would try to help put them in place. And special attention would be paid to the Bank's poorest members, who, despite their greater need, had received the least technical and financial assistance from the Bank Group.

He then told them that, among the investment sectors, the greatest increases in investment would be in education and agriculture; a threefold increase in the former, and a fourfold increase in the latter. In the former, the focus would be on education planning, particularly in teacher training at all levels. With regard to agriculture, he deplored the fact that it had for so long been the 'stepchild' of development, despite the fact that two-thirds of the people of the developing countries lived on the soil, and even though these countries were forced to buy $4 billion worth of food annually from the industrialized world. Add to this the widespread dietary deficiency of parents being passed on as mental deficiencies to children, and one had to ask why so little had been done when the problem had been staring the world in the face for decades. Twenty years of research had produced new strains of wheat, rice and other plants that could improve yields by three to five times. Match that to irrigation, fertilizer and peasant education, and miracles could result. There would be setbacks, but the world was now on the brink of an agricultural revolution as significant as any development since the industrial revolution.

Finally, he turned to a subject with which he was to be particularly identified throughout his World Bank presidency, and indeed afterwards: the population problem. It would, he told the governors, be very much easier to leave such a thorny subject alone. But since the rapid growth of population was one of the greatest barriers to the economic growth and social wellbeing of the Bank's member states, it was impossible to brush the subject aside. As a development planner, he had to face the fact that, more than anything else, it was the population explosion that was widening the gap between the rich and the poor nations. As a development agency, the Bank had to take action to help lift the population burden from the backs of many of its member nations. He therefore proposed Bank action on three fronts: to let the developing nations know the extent to which rapid population growth was slowing down their potential development; to seek opportunities to finance facilities required to carry out family planning programmes; and to join with others in programmes of research to determine the most effective methods of family planning and of national administration of population control programmes.

McNamara closed his speech by telling the governors that he had proposed a programme of greatly increased activity because he had faith that the difficulties lying ahead could be overcome. If the Bank showed leadership now, it would encourage those who had begun to lose heart and slackened their pace. The Bank must give this signal to all to rally again to the struggle.

It was a bravura performance which left all of us assembled in the

252

cavernous great hall of the Sheraton Park Hotel a little breathless. I hurried about picking up reactions from delegations and staff, and was able to report later to Bob that the general sentiment seemed to be: good luck to him; we hope he can do it. But there were a few who thought he was about to bite off far more than he could chew. Or, as one highly sceptical staff member put it: 'He's got the trajectory wrong. He's shot the rocket straight up into the air, and it will likely come down on our heads.' This particular critic was clearly not an expert in rocketry, but equally clearly he was not alone in clinging to the conventional wisdom that the World Bank was still essentially a bank, and should be prudent, not pioneering. Among the developing country delegations, however, there was manifest enthusiasm in their discovery that the man from the Pentagon was obviously on their side. The McNamara manifesto looked just fine to them, and all he had to do now was to deliver.

The last three months of 1968 were particularly hectic for me, as for my Bank colleagues. With Lars Lind's help, I reorganized and expanded somewhat my department to reflect the broadening activities of the Bank as a whole. In October I accompanied McNamara to Brazil and Argentina, in the latter of which countries he delivered a speech to the Inter-American Press Association in which, while repeating his intention to have the Bank Group double its lending to the region by 1972, asked the governments to follow economic and social policies which would permit a more equitable distribution of the benefits from increases in production and productivity and to restrain their expenditures on sophisticated military equipment. Having touched two raw nerves, he reached for a third. Reminding them that, at the current growth rate, by the end of the century Latin America's population of 250 million would have risen to 650 million, and would then be growing at a rate of 100 million every five years, he called on the governments to evolve a serious strategy for stabilizing the rate of population growth if they were not to see their development efforts thwarted. It was a courageous speech, and put the governments of the region on notice that the new President of the Bank would not shrink from raising issues that were decidedly thorny if they bore no economic and social development questions of interest to the Bank.

We were home just in time to see Richard Nixon elected President, then we were off on the road again, this time to Afghanistan, Pakistan and India. This was familiar territory to me, but mostly new to McNamara. We travelled from Afghanistan to

253

Pakistan through the Khyber Pass to Peshawar. In an agreeable little ceremony in the Pass, local dignitaries presented the McNamaras with a pair of sheep. I could see that Bob was wondering how room was going to be found for them in our small entourage, so I whispered to him that he was not meant to accept them; in fact it would be an unheard of break with precedent if he did, akin to the Queen deciding after all to accept the Lord Mayor's traditional offer of the keys to the City of London. He looked much relieved and, patting the sheep on the head, restored them to the donors. They were very old sheep, and it may be that they were the same that I had witnessed offered to Anthony Eden in the Pass a few years before.

India and Pakistan had, from IDA's inception in 1960, received about two-thirds of all IDA lending, but both had recently been victims of an acute shortage of IDA funds due to US Congressional delays in making the most recent replenishments of IDA's funds effective. We now had the rather delicate task of explaining to Prime Minister Indira Gandhi in Delhi and President Ayub Khan in Islamabad that, while the expected replenishment – and future replenishments – would be on a scale to permit a steady rising volume increase in IDA lending to the two countries, their combined percentage share was going to have to drop in order to accommodate the needed increased lending to other countries, particularly in Africa. Happily, they took it quite well, and Bob was pleased with his first visit to the area. But the value of it to him, and indeed to myself who already knew India well, went far beyond the establishment of a dialogue with the two leaders (shortlived in Ayub Khan's case – he was ousted early the next year). We were able to get a good idea of just what the introduction of high-yielding new seeds might do for the subcontinent, and McNamara returned to Washington more determined than ever to move his agricultural programme into high gear.

He had also had an opportunity to discuss the population problem, and this was to become the subject of his next major speech. He had told me early after our arrival at the Bank that I should not count on him to make a lot of speeches. His annual meeting speeches would publicly set in place the carefully prepared building blocks of his strategy of development assistance. Only occasionally would he feel the need to address any other audience for the public record. By limiting his statements to occasions when he had something new and of value to say, he could command a more receptive audience. Besides, a great deal of research and analysis would need to go into his speeches, and that in itself suggested restraint. I had to agree with him. Much as he was a fine catch for a public event and a great public relations weapon in our armoury, his scarcity-value argument was valid.

Early in 1969, Father Theodore Hesburgh, president of the University of Notre Dame, had invited McNamara to come to the university to receive an honorary degree and make a speech. Bob knew and much admired the Jesuit academic, and was impressed with the way Notre Dame, under Hesburgh's presidency, had become a catalytic centre of creative thought. On receiving the invitation, he called Jack Maddux and myself to his office and told us that he was accepting it. The degree would be conferred on the occasion of the dedication of a new building to house the business school, and he intended to devote the whole of his speech to the population issue. I caught my breath, but Jack Maddux, himself a former Jesuit seminarian who had left the order to marry and father five children, was chuckling. It was, of course, a bold and brilliant idea. McNamara then charged us to keep the topic of his talk a closely guarded secret from all except those who would be working on the project. To the best of my recollection, we didn't even let Father Hesburgh know until just before the event. It was not that McNamara feared that he might be asked to drop the subject; he simply reckoned, and so did I, that if the press got wind of it in advance, the impact of his statement might be weakened.

Bob, Jack and our population experts got to work and produced an excellent speech in which Bob sought to dispel the 'vague and murky mythology that befogs the issue . . . and builds barriers to constructive action'. He vigorously assailed the myths that more people mean more wealth and cheap labour; that the developing countries have ample uninhabited space for population expansion; that the process of development automatically leads to lower birth rates; that family planning would destroy familial moral fibre. And he vigorously attacked the jeremiahs who would have it that it was already too late for decisive action, and that sweeping famine was inevitable. He dismissed C.P. Snow's prediction that we would watch on our television sets many millions of people literally dying of starvation before our eyes. He, McNamara, was convinced, he told his audience, that there was still time to reverse the situation, if only we would use it, and he went on to lay out what should be done. Then, grasping the nettle of Catholic doctrine, he cited the calls of both the Second Vatican Council and Pope Paul's encyclical 'Populorum Progressio' to solve the population problem as it related to development. Such controversy as remained, he said, was merely about the means, not at all about the end. All had to share in finding and applying the solution.

It was a powerful, carefully reasoned, informative speech for which the students and faculty gave him a standing ovation – some, maybe, for his courage rather than his message. And Father Hesburgh congratulated him on the scholarliness and the thought-provoking content of the address. The following day, 2 May, it was widely reported in the national and foreign press, and McNamara's identification with the issue was now well established.

At the end of the month I went to Tokyo to make a speech to the Japan Economic Association, while McNamara visited Denmark, Germany, Kuwait and Egypt. I spent late June and the early days of July at Biniparell, my summer home on the Balearic island of Menorca, and arrived back in Washington just two days before Bob was once more drawn into a Kennedy family drama. This was the tragic Chappaquiddick affair involving Senator Teddy Kennedy and the accidental drowning of Mary Jo Kopechne. McNamara was in Aspen when it happened, and I was not in the least surprised when we heard that he had hurried to Cape Cod to be with the Kennedy family at this unhappy moment. It was the natural thing for him to do, and when it was reported in the press, no one of any sensitivity at the Bank took the least exception.

Bob's friendship with Teddy Kennedy was to become a matter of comment only once during the remaining twelve years of his term as President of the Bank. That was in 1980, when the Senator appeared to be a formidable threat to the renomination of President Jimmy Carter for election to a second term in the White House. An early-morning television news report on Kennnedy's activities in this regard happened to provide a fleeting glimpse of McNamara leaving the Senator's office. Speculation immediately arose, not least within the Bank, that he might be actively backing Teddy Kennedy's moves to deny Carter the nomination, and even that he might be under consideration for a Cabinet post if Kennedy were to gain the nomination and win the election. On the morning of the newscast, Bob had left early for New York to attend the Administrative Committee on Co-ordination at the United Nations. Duke Merriam – Lars Lind's successor as Director of the Information and Public Affairs Department – reached him by telephone in

Julian Grenfell's office to warn him that the press were asking questions, and a response was needed. This news irritated McNamara, and he instructed Duke to respond to press queries with an unequivocal message from him: he would be making no public statements on behalf of the Senator in either written or spoken form; he had not made and would not be making any campaign fund contributions; and if Kennedy were to win the presidential race, he would not accept a Cabinet post if one were offered. That was that, and I have no doubt that he meant exactly what he said.

Through the remainder of the summer of 1969, we worked on Bob's second annual meeting speech, which he duly delivered to the board of governors in Washington on 29 September. He was able to report that the Bank Group's financing of development projects was up 87 per cent over the previous fiscal year, surpassing the target that had been set. In the world's capital markets, the Bank had been able to borrow $1.25 billion, 80 per cent of it outside the United States, and the most ever borrowed in the Bank's history. And despite an increase in administrative expenses resulting from the greater workload, the Bank had closed out the fiscal year with a record profit of $172 million. The Bank's plans for fiscal year 1970 called for further expansion in lending, to $2.25 billion, with continued emphasis on new areas and sectors. He was confident that the objectives of the five-year programme would be met, and that new financing operations for the period would exceed $12 billion. But, he reminded the governors, the Bank's efforts were not merely, or even mainly, quantitative in their goal. They were above all qualitative, with assistance being provided where it would help most in the removal of roadblocks to development. Nor were we simply searching for good investments in sick economies. We were trying to understand what made economies sick in the first place, so that we could take remedial steps that would encourage recuperation and health.

The bulk of the speech was devoted to the progress being made and the problems still faced in the sectors on which the Bank was particularly focusing, namely population, education and agriculture, urbanization and industrialization. He hammered particularly hard on the unemployment question. Third World unemployment was rising rapidly, especially in urban areas, and about 20 per cent of the entire male labour force in the developing countries was now jobless. Economic growth rates currently averaging 4.5 per cent needed to be raised to 6 per cent, and a better balance between capital- and labour-intensive activities had to be created if the unemployment problem was to be reduced meaningfully. The Bank and other institutions working in that field had to help find solutions to the problem.

Finally, he reviewed the report which the Pearson Commission had, on schedule, just submitted to the Bank. It was, he said, a document of high importance, addressed to the whole world, which deserved the widest possible public dissemination. The Bank would undertake a careful analysis of each of the report's recommendations which bore in any way on the Bank's work, and would submit these analyses to the Bank's board of directors with proposals for appropriate action.

Our subsequent study of the report revealed thirty-three such proposals, the vast majority of which we were able to agree with. One, however, gave us particular difficulty. This was a proposal which, by implication, seemed to be suggesting that our concessional loan affiliate, IDA, should be set up independently, to go its separate way, leaving the Bank to operate as a bank rather than as a development agency. No suggestion could have been calculated to upset McNamara more. The very core of his strategy for the Bank had found expression in a key sentence in his first annual meeting address: 'I have always regarded the World Bank as something more than a bank, as a development agency.' The originator of this new and unwelcome suggestion in the Pearson Report was, we learned, Sir Arthur Lewis, later to be a Nobel Economics Prizewinner. McNamara responded firmly that if there were a choice between effective development and banking orthodoxy, he would choose development. What contributed most to the development of the borrowing country should be the decisive factor in both Bank and IDA operations, and as long as that was the case, there was no justification for splitting them. He repeated this forcefully in his 1970 address to the board of governors, and the matter was not raised again thereafter.

Following the 1969 annual meeting, we were off on our travels once more, this time to Iran and Morocco, and then in a subsequent trip to Venezuela, Guatemala and Mexico. The visit to Iran was the most interesting for me, and for Bob as well, I believe. We travelled extensively through the country during our six days there, and I could see that he was alarmed by the extent of poverty in this oil-rich country and excited by the prospect of persuading the Shah, with whom he had struck up a good relationship, to follow some sound Bank advice on how matters might be improved.

After a moderately relaxed Christmas and New Year in snow-bound Washington, I packed my flight bags once again to accompany the McNamaras to Kenya, Tanzania and Uganda. Kenyatta, Nyerere and Obote were three heads of state whom I already knew, and I was able to give Bob some hints on what to expect. It was certainly one of the most agreeable missions we undertook, and our hosts made time between our myriad engagements to show us something of the wildlife of the region. Bob was impressed by Nyerere, and also by my old friend Amir Jamal, Tanzania's Finance Minister. But I think he got on best with old Jomo Kenyatta. Certainly the venerable Kenyan President took a great liking to Bob and was most unwilling to let their extensive talks come to an end.

In May we travelled to Korea and Taiwan, and in June to Colombia, and I was grateful that that was the limit of my peregrinations as I had my hands very full indeed back in Washington. Every third year, the Bank and the IMF hold their annual joint meetings outside Washington, and that year, 1970, we would be the guests of the Danish government in Copenhagen. Our European office in Paris had been following with growing concern the newspaper and other reports of preparations being made by student and radical groups to demonstrate against and possibly disrupt the meetings of what they considered to be two imperialist organizations, one of them led by the man they saw as the chief architect of the war they particularly hated. I decided that we had better try to take some pre-emptive action, and we set about planning how we could meet with student groups who would be willing to meet with us, and try to explain to them what the World Bank was doing to help the developing countries, and to persuade them that their view that we were motivated by imperialist ambitions was hopelessly wrong. We did indeed find some intermediaries among the student groups who were prepared to sit down and engage in a dialogue, and this we did to some good effect just prior to the annual meeting, using a couple of our younger Scandinavian professional staff members as interlocutors. I myself met twice with the groups and felt that we might have gained some understanding. Earlier, in June, however, we had had a foretaste of the anger of Europe's radical groups when Bob had travelled to Heidelberg for a meeting of the 'Tidewater' group of leading national aid administrators and agency heads, hosted by Germany's Aid Minister, Erhard Eppler.

The demonstrations in Heidelberg were noisy, well orchestrated, and accompanied by the distribution of much anti-Western development aid literature. But the police contained the situation, and the President of the Bank and his colleagues returned home unharmed.

Containing the situation in Copenhagen proved a more difficult task, but certainly not beyond the capabilities of the Danish authorities. The annual meeting was held in a fortress-like building known as the Bella Centre, some way from the centre of the city, and the demonstrations were more or less confined to downtown Copenhagen. But they were extensive and occasionally very violent, and the hotel in which we were staying was ringed with police barriers and anti-riot squads. Protesting groups had travelled from several European countries, including large contingents from Germany and the Netherlands. I and my colleagues from the European office and the Information Department, ably aided by our selected Scandinavian interlocutors, managed to maintain a useful dialogue with some of the more responsible student groups, and I know that it helped take some, but by no means all, of the heat out of the situation.

In his annual meeting address, McNamara spelt out what he saw as the objectives of development in the seventies. I was sorry that the angry mobs downtown would not be taking time out to read what he had to say. It might have made them pause to start reassessing their stand. He catalogued his deep concerns over pervasive malnutrition in the developing world, over high infant mortality and low life expectancy, over widespread illiteracy and endemic and growing unemployment, over skewed income distribution and wealth, and over the widening gap between the per capita incomes of the rich and poor nations. 'At least a quarter of the human race,' he said, 'faces the prospect of entering the twenty-first century in poverty more unacceptable by contrast than that of any previous epoch. Frankly I do not see this as a situation in which any of our shared hopes for a long peace and steady material progress are likely to be achieved.' He then urged that, as a start, the international community should accept the full scale of the crisis and react accordingly. The 6 per cent annual growth rate set as a target for the developing countries for the seventies by both the Pearson Commission and the United Nations had to be met. But growth could not of itself accomplish our development objectives. The resources had to be deployed to achieve the desired growth rate, but we also needed to ensure that in critical fields such as population planning, rural renewal, fuller employment, and decent urbanism, positive policies supported and hastened the social transformation, without which economic growth itself became obstructed and its results impaired.

He then admitted that in all of these critical fields, a great deal of further research and analysis needed to be undertaken to fill the gaps in our knowledge and understanding. But answering the questions would be of little use if the development effort was going to fail anyway for lack of resources. The world was spending $180 billion annually on the so-called security of an ever-spiralling arms race, while the developed nations hesitated to maintain even the present $7 billion of public aid expenditure. There really were no material obstacles to an effective response to the world's development needs. The obstacles lay in the minds of men. We needed to apply at the world level that same moral responsibility, that same sharing of wealth, that same standard of justice and compassion, without which our own national societies would surely fall apart.

It was an excellent speech for the occasion, delivered with much passion, and even US Treasury Secretary John B. Connally seemed moderately moved by it. We returned to Washington happy at least to be free of the smell of smoke and tear gas and the crunch of broken glass beneath our feet.

McNamara's concern that the Bank should be second to none in the scope and excellence of its development economics research and analysis, a concern that he had voiced in his Copenhagen speech, had been very much on his mind. He had now taken steps to meet that concern by hiring Hollis B. Chenery, Professor of Economics at Harvard, to take over Irving Friedman's post of Economic Adviser. Hollis, who became a particularly good friend of mine, set to work to expand the Bank's capacity in the research and analysis field. The small Economics Department was reorganized into three units: the Economics Department, the Economic Programme Department and the Development Research Centre, all of them reporting to Hollis. Many more economists, from around the world, were taken on board, and by 1972 the much expanded complex was renamed the Development Policy Staff, with Hollis as its head.

The staff of the Bank as a whole had been increasing almost exponentially since McNamara's arrival. Not that he had not warned the board of governors of his intentions from the outset.

There had been some strong initial resistance from some board members at the start, but when he was able to show that the necessary increase could be absorbed without letting the administrative expenses of the Bank get out of control, the resistance flagged. In fact, the 767 professional staff he found on arrival in 1968 had risen to 1,654 by the end of fiscal year 1973. It was not just the numbers that had expanded. When McNamara took over, the relatively small staff was about one half American and British, with less than five per cent coming from the Third World. Determined to make the staff more representative of the Bank's worldwide membership, he directed that the recruiting drive correct the imbalance. This was done, and by 1972 over 100 nationalities were represented on the staff.

The year 1970, which marked the arrival of Hollis Chenery, also marked the arrival of a member of the executive board who was to become a close friend and wise counsellor for me. Claude Isbister, a 56-year-old Manitoban with a distinguished career in government service already behind him, took over the Canadian seat on the Bank's board in August 1970. He held it for six years, during which time he stood out as one of the very wisest and farsighted of the directors. McNamara and I had frequent occasion to be grateful for his help and understanding (he could also be a tough but fair critic), and he became a very valued friend.

I was back on the road, or rather in the air, by mid-January 1971, and between then and mid-May visited six more African countries with the President. In four of these countries we were accompanied by the Bank's executive director representing the large group of Francophone African members. Nassim Kochman was an energetic, very likeable young Mauritanian of Lebanese origin who knew his countries extremely well. He served for as long as twelve years on the board (Luis Machado of Cuba had served twenty-four when he retired in 1970) and was still only forty-two when he left in 1974 to become Mauritanian Ambassador to Washington.

Improving relations between the staff of the Bank and the executive board, which had been in a pretty sorry state when McNamara and I had arrived, was something to which I paid a great deal of attention, and in which Bob gave the necessary lead. The sense of greater trust and understanding that was now apparent reflected well on the President as head of the staff, and must have been a factor contributing to the strong consensus that emerged from private soundings amongst the board at the end of 1971 that he should be offered a second term even well before his first five-year term was completed, which would not be until April 1973.

There was, however, one major flaw in the consensus: the United States was not a part of it. Bob's persistent calls for an improvement in what he saw as his own country's lamentable performance in the provision of foreign economic aid were anything but popular with a Congress where aid was seen by many as the quintessential liberal interventionist's tool. Furthermore, and more to the point in terms of his reappointment, he had irked many important leaders in the Nixon Administration who felt that he should be more responsive, as an American, to policy nudges. He had proved again and again that he was not to be nudged. When the Nixon Administration pressed for a cut-off of Bank aid to Chile after the Allende regime came to power in late 1970, McNamara went out of his way to send a private message by the hand of Felipe Herrera, a Chilean and former head of the Inter-American Development Bank, saying that the Bank hoped to maintain relations with the new regime; the fact that this initiative failed was the fault of Allende's own colleagues on the extreme left. American support for McNamara's second term was thus late in coming, and it came only after he had spoken personally with Nixon, who admired him, and after the board had discreetly disabused some Administration people of the idea that the Bank job could be handed out as a patronage plum to a deserving supporter of the President of the United States and his party. With the rather grudging acquiescence of the United States Administration, a second term for McNamara was thus approved early in 1972.

Meanwhile, in September 1971, McNamara had been able to report to the annual meeting, this time held once again in the comparative peace and quiet of Washington, that the five-year programme was well on schedule, and the year's target of $2.5 billion in investments had been exceeded. The staff were now in the process of putting together the second five-year programme. Immediately following the annual meeting, I started work on a paper for McNamara setting out my ideas on a Bank strategy for the rest of the 1970s. I completed it after we had returned from a November visit to four south-east Asian countries and Japan. In essence I told him that we were faced with a splintering world, and that our job was to help reintegrate it, but not on the same pattern as the old. The Bank was an agent for change, and its objective should be to produce a sounder, saner organization of the world economy and

263

world resources. But we could do this from no power base except consent. You, I told McNamara, have not been elected President of the World Bank by the rich nations, nor the leader of the Third World by the poor nations. You and the Bank can be the instruments for carrying out some agreed changes in the distribution of the world's resources – agreed, that is, between the rich and the poor nations. The Bank must always represent all its members.

This left us with the initiative of finding out what was a mutually acceptable degree of change. Our most urgent task was to persuade the industrialized countries to move far and fast enough, while persuading the developing countries to expect and accept less than the optimum. I doubted that the Bank could succeed, but I was sure that if the Bank did not take the initiative, it would not be taken effectively anywhere else; not by the UN, nor by the regional development banks, OECD, UNCTAD, or anyone else. It seemed to me that the sort of changes we were looking for to produce a saner world economic order must include finding a more broadly representative mechanism for running the system, now that its domination by the dollar was on the way out. It could no longer simply be left to the wealthy Group of Ten. Secondly, we would have to try with all deliberate speed to correct the past bias against the poor nations in the flow of resources. For more than a century the world economy had been organized to benefit the highest consumers. This was the origin of the British Empire and the American hegemony. With their passing we must try to substitute a system that was tilted more towards the underdeveloped, low-consuming nations. There should therefore be more automaticity in the flow of resources, such as general trade preference schemes and some sort of special drawing rights link. And the terms of investment, both public and private, in the developing nations needed to be shifted more in their favour.

The Bank, as the representative equally of the rich and the poor nations, was trying to hold together the disparate parts of the world economy so that each could benefit from the other. We faced the incredibly hard task of the political persuasion of sovereign peoples, rich and poor, to accept less than the optimum. And we had to do this with very slender resources for leverage. This threw a great burden on our capacity to be persuasive, and we could not be unless we clarified in our own minds what we thought was truly possible, and then began systematically to publicize it. For that we might need another sort of Pearson Commission, this time numerically dominated by the developing countries.

I further suggested in my paper that we needed to prepare for a deterioration in the investment climate as the developing countries increasingly flexed their muscles with expropriations of assets and repudiations of loans. We needed to be able to show that our AAA bond rating was not based on a perfect record of safe loans, but on a system of prudence, financial strength, and the backing of our shareholders. We could no longer claim that we never invested in a shaky country, but we could claim that our investments were aimed at making the world credit system less shaky.

Dealing with the United States would probably be an equally difficult task, and could not be done at all without a reasonably good relationship with the leaders of the Administration. The Bank would need to be less obviously American-run and yet command American support. To win that support, we would need a real European and Japanese commitment to burden-sharing, and that would in turn be achieved only if we succeeded in making Europe and Japan feel that the Bank Group belonged to them as much as to the US. Europe was building up its own multilateral channels through the European Community, and Japan had a favourite chosen instrument in the Asian Development Bank. These were factors we had to compete with persuasively. But if we succeeded in getting commitment to better burden-sharing, then we would surely find the task of winning American support that much easier. What we needed then to do was to appeal to America's pride as a leader in internationalism and as an economy that could afford massive assistance, rather than seeking to shame them into support.

As for our developing member nations, it was not going to be easy to retain the support of the nations who were the recipients of our loans and our advice, and we needed to stress much more our role as partner rather than 'governess'. Without their manifest support, we could not hope to raise the level of support of the donor nations.

This was the gist of the paper I presented to McNamara in late November 1971, and finding him generally in agreement, I made it the basis of my external relations strategy for the years ahead. With the benefit of hindsight, there is not a great deal I would change. But I was quite wrong on one matter: the People's Republic of China. I suggested that China would make a bid for leadership of the Third World based not on her size and resources, but on the alternative model of development she could boast, a model based on self-help without dependence on the industrialized world. I think I could be forgiven. President Nixon had yet to make his historic visit to China, and few could have foreseen the speed with which that vast country would later open up to the West, or indeed claim its seat in the World Bank or the International Monetary Fund.

As 1971 came to a close, there was one area of my responsibility which still troubled me, and that was McNamara's own relations with the American press. There was a feeling amongst many journalists that he managed the news for his own benefit, and that he was not prepared to waste time with those who might want to know more than just what he thought was right about what he and the Bank were doing. It was an inaccurate perception of the man; he met frequently with individual journalists at their request and was quite ready to answer the most searching questions, provided they were relevant to his position and official activities. But his relations with the American press had suffered a setback in the summer of 1971 with the publication in the *New York Times* of the 'Pentagon Papers', provided by former Pentagon aide, Daniel Ellsberg. As the publication of the confidential papers once again opened all the old wounds of Vietnam, I told Bob that we had to face the fact that we might have a hostile US press to deal with for maybe the next six months. I was not worried, I told him, about the top columnists and editors, who liked and supported him, but about the regular correspondents who were convinced that he slanted the news. I advised him not to withdraw from sight, but to keep contact with the working press, aiming to convince them that the Bank did things that were of interest to them, and that we were interested in what they, as individuals, thought and wanted to know about the Bank. We did not need to push stories of our choosing onto them, but rather stimulate a continuing interest in our work which might bear fruit in friendly column inches at some later date.

I was not so worried about the European press. Much of the 'establishment' press would regard him, I told him, as a fellow aristocrat wrongly guillotined. The left-wing press would join the baying hounds of the American press, but not for long. There were too many juicy European issues for them to get their teeth into. We would, however, need to repair some fences in the Third World. Both the governments and the media had greeted his arrival at the Bank with some misgivings and doubts. Then they had met him and found to their delight that he had no horns on his head, neither was he wrapped in stars and stripes. This favourable view, I now warned Bob, appeared to be in a process of erosion in some Third World quarters as a result of the Pentagon Papers. We would therefore have to put Humpty-Dumpty together again, which should not be too hard. The Bank was a real friend to the developing countries, and we needed now to turn up the volume a little in stressing that our objectives were truly theirs. For his part, I told him, he must strongly re-emphasize his role as an international servant of the world who must stand apart from an America bent on dragging itself through the Vietnam wreckage once more. Our agenda was a different one, and a positive one.

As it happened, he rode out the storm with no great lasting damage done. But his more sceptical view of our ability to win the real trust of working journalists who were chronically more interested in McNamara the former Defense Secretary than McNamara the international civil servant proved closer to reality than my more hopeful view.

Bob began his second five-year term in April 1973, having just completed a major reorganization of the Bank, aimed at ensuring that its structure was better suited to the projected scope and level of its activities. A massive study had been launched in January 1972, led by a well-known international management consultant firm, and try as we did, it was difficult to disabuse many of the staff of their feeling that McNamara knew exactly what he wanted and was merely seeking the blessing of a respected outside expert. In fact, the reorganization made eminent good sense, and if it was indeed all McNamara's idea, more credit to him.

Most of the changes were made in the operational structure of the Bank which had been in place for twenty years. Five regional offices, each headed by a newly created vice-president, were established at headquarters, each office responsible for planning and supervising the execution of the Bank's development assistance programme within its assigned countries. Each now had under its direct control most of the technical, financial and economic experts that had previously been under separate control elsewhere in the Bank. The reorganization also touched my area of responsibility in that I now became Director of External Relations, taking under my wing, in addition to the Information Department, the International Relations Department which dealt with our relations with other international organizations such as the UN, OECD, and the

Commonwealth Secretariat; the Bank's European office in Paris; and the Economic Development Insititute, the Bank's staff college for senior Third World civil servants working in the economic sectors of government. Early in 1974, my rank was raised to Vice-President.

While the reorganization was underway, Derek Mitchell, the British Executive Director since November 1969, completed his term and returned to the Treasury in London as Second Secretary in charge of Overseas Finance. I was particularly sorry to see him go. The British were always excellently represented on the Bank and IMF boards, due to the fact that the Economic Minister and Head of the Treasury and Supply Delegation at the Washington Embassy traditionally took these two board seats. And it was always the true high-flyers at the Treasury who got the Washington Embassy post. Derek was one of the very best, and certainly the best that I knew in my time at the Bank. He was greatly respected and admired in the board and among the senior Bank and Fund staff with whom he dealt, and by no one more than Bob McNamara. Derek became a close personal friend and has remained so, and I have often benefited from his knowledge and wisdom.

Routine seems a scarcely appropriate word to describe my life during Bob's second term, but there was a certain recognizable pattern to each year's activities. There would be the by now traditional January or February foray into our developing country constituencies, as often as not Africa as a welcome escape from Washington's harsh winters. We would usually be on the road again in May, by which time I would be much taken with supervising the writing and production of the Bank's Annual Report which had, by now, become a full-coloured 150-page publication including excellent regional reviews and an extensive statistical annex of economic indicators for which the international development community waited with much anticipation.

The broad dissemination of the fruits of the considerable research undertaken by Hollis Chenery and his experts was to be given a great boost at the end of McNamara's second term with his decision to institute an annual World Development Report, a publication that quickly built up a reputation for itself as an indispensable source for governments, the press, academia and the interested public.

With the Annual Report approved by the board for publication, I could turn my thoughts to the annual meeting speech. Work would have already been well in train for this in various quarters of the Bank since the speech always dealt with one or more substantive development policy issues, in addition to reviewing the state of development generally and reporting on the Bank Group's activities of the previous fiscal year. McNamara took an intense and constant interest in the preparation of his major speech of the year, and it was left to Jack Maddux to take the wealth of material prepared and hew it into a well-worded statement, embellished with the kind of language which lifted what otherwise could have been a too academic lecture to the level of an eloquent, persuasive, carefully reasoned piece of advocacy for the international support we sought for our development strategy.

One such speech was truly a landmark in McNamara's second term. In September 1973 we gathered in Nairobi for our annual meeting, the first time it had ever been held in Africa, and an appropriate recognition of the leading place that continent had assumed in the Bank's new programmes. In his opening address to the governors, after reporting on the successful completion of the first five-year programme, Bob spelled out the objectives of the 1974–8 programme. Bank and IDA lending would expand at a cumulative annual rate of 8 per cent in real terms. Over the five years, $22 billion would be invested in almost 1,000 projects with a total cost of almost $55 billion. But the qualitative changes would be even more significant. The Bank was going to place far greater emphasis on policies and projects which would begin to attack the problems of 'absolute poverty'. This 'absolute poverty' Bob defined broadly as 'conditions of deprivation that fall below any rational definition of human decency'. These conditions would henceforth be the explicit target of new poverty-oriented programmes aimed not at relief but at development to be achieved by making the poor more productive. The phrase 'absolute poverty' was also, in fact, Bob's answer to those who were starting to contend that the developed nations could not afford the increased amounts he was asking because of the need to tend to the poorer elements in their own societies. These, he argued, indeed deserved attention, but their status, by comparison, was one of only 'relative poverty'.

His impassioned plea received an ovation not just from the Third World delegations, but from Western financiers too who were beginning to take an interest in investment possibilities in Africa but had been waiting for signs that the African economies really could be helped to grow from a broader base. At the end of the meeting, the negotiations for the fourth replenishment of IDA's funds, over which the US was stalling, were finally completed, with funding at a substantially higher level than before. This was certainly a vote of confidence in McNamara as he set out on his second term.

But a year later, in his 1974 annual meeting speech, he was to open his remarks by noting that the series of changes that had occurred on the world economic scene had been of a magnitude previously associated only with major wars and depressions. He was referring, of course, to the quadrupling of world oil prices by OPEC following the Middle East war and the Arab oil boycott. As he told the governors, the cumulative impact of these events touched every nation represented in the room. The oil exporting countries and some mineral producers, countries with some 20 per cent of the populations the Bank served, had registered a net gain. The outlook for certain other developing countries with about 30 per cent of the populations looked good in the long term, although they faced serious problems of adjustment to the new conditions in the meanwhile. But for the poorest countries, representing fully half of the populations the Bank served, about one billion people, the situation was desperate. These countries needed promptly some $3 to $4 billion more in concessionary assistance per year. This amount would make the different between decency and utter degradation for hundreds of millions of the absolute poor but was, in relative terms, minute – perhaps 2 per cent of the increase in real income the developed world could look forward to in the remaining years of the decade.

McNamara had certainly been doing everything he could to find the extra $3 to $4 billion. Within weeks of the oil price quadrupling, he had flown to Tehran with his colleague, Jo Johannes Witteveen, Managing Director of the IMF, to talk about an OPEC fund for development. The Shah insisted that if OPEC put up a lot of money for development, OPEC should have a big say in where it went. McNamara insisted that the funds should be allocated to specific projects handled by the World Bank to World Bank standards. McNamara won his point, but OPEC would have one-third of the votes in the body controlling the funds. Unfortunately, he had not reckoned on the US reaction to his tentative agreement with the Shah. The Americans, infuriated by OPEC's price hikes, would have nothing to do with the cartel, and the proposal sank without a trace. It was a major setback for McNamara personally, and for the poorest developing countries as a whole.

A turning point had been reached in McNamara's presidency. The intellectual leadership and the financial clout of the Bank had been firmly established over his six years in office. But with the world in recession and growth in the developing world slowing to a standstill, the debate turned to whether resource flows should be stepped up to meet the needs of a desperate Third World, as the Bank maintained, or whether they should be slowed down to accommodate the industrialized world which was hurting too.

There was an element of compromise in what was to happen, for the middle-income countries, largely in Latin America, were able to borrow substantial amounts from the commercial banking system which had become the repository of huge surpluses accumulated by the oil exporters. But this was of no comfort or use to the poorer nations who had little or no power to borrow commercially. Hence McNamara's conviction that the Bank and IDA had to do more. The United States, however, did not see it that way. William Simon, US Treasury Secretary from May 1974 to January 1977, showed himself adamantly against any sizeable increase in the Bank's activities. As far as he was concerned, it was OPEC which had caused all the economic ills currently plaguing the world, and it was therefore OPEC which should bear the heaviest burden in helping the developing countries they were impoverishing with their oil prices. But it was more than that. Simon was a strict monetarist; he was also quite determined that the United States, as the Bank's biggest shareholder, had a duty to keep the Bank on lines approved by his Treasury. His quite open efforts to control the Bank inevitably led to resentments amongst other groupings on the board, notably the Europeans and the developing countries. In such a situation, McNamara could remain independent and manage by consensus. But for the rest of his term in office, he had to live with the shadow of opposition from the largest shareholder darkening his and the Bank's efforts.

The advent of the Carter Administration in 1977 did not redress the situation. President Carter and his Secretary of State, Cyrus Vance, an old and trusted associate of McNamara from his Pentagon days, were much in favour of substantially increasing

271

what was seen as a shameful level of US development assistance. Carter's intentions were leaked by the White House before Congress had been consulted, and the reaction was, in the light of its now established hostility to aid, quite predictable. To try to retrieve the situation, the Administration, taking up one of Secretary Simon's pet peeves, promised to cut the salaries of the international staffs of both the Bank and the Fund. An eighteen-month investigation revealed that the salaries were comparable with those paid elsewhere in the world by public and private banking institutions, and rather below West European levels. Moreover, the money came out of the Bank's earned income, not out of American taxpayers' pockets. The campaign to cut the salaries thus came to nothing, but not before much mud had been slung at both institutions by hostile legislators and journalists. It is little wonder that the international staff were by now convinced that the United States was looking for ways to destroy or at least dominate the Bank.

Their conviction was strengthened by the growing tendency of the United States to try to limit the use of IDA's funds to purposes which suited individual Congressmen, such as no funds for the development of agricultural products that competed with American agricultural exports. McNamara would have none of this. Nor would he accept the Carter Administration's efforts to enforce its human rights policies through the Bank. The US was free to vote against loans approved by the rest of the board for countries with regimes of which the US disapproved. But the US could not, by itself, prevent those loans from being made.

Despite these problems with the United States, McNamara pressed ahead with his ambitious five-year programme, and kept it on target. At our 1976 annual meeting, held in Manila, he warned of the consequences of continued resource constraints on the Bank and IDA, constraints that would jeopardize the expanded programme. He urged immediate discussion of a further recapitalization of the Bank and a speeding up of the painfully slow progress towards the fifth replenishment of IDA. By the time of the next annual meeting, the IDA negotiations had been successfully completed, and a broad consensus had been reached that there should be an increase in real terms both in the Bank's lending programme and in the expansion of the Bank's capital structure. The uncertainties over future financial operations were therefore resolved, and we all heaved a sigh of relief. As a further manifestation of the easing of our problems with the United States, the Carter Administration backed a third term for McNamara, and it was approved by the board without difficulty that same year.

Early in 1977, McNamara had suggested that there be organized a wholly independent, high-level, but deliberately unofficial commission of experienced political leaders, from both developed and developing countries alike, to assess and recommend feasible alternatives to the current deadlock in North-South relations. The developing nations had achieved a new level of cohesion which was expressing itself largely through the much expanded Group of 77 at the United Nations and in other international fora, particularly UNCTAD. These countries had been making concerted demands for a new international economic order. But some of the terms and structures of this new order did not commend themselves to the industrialized countries, especially not to the United States and the Federal Republic of Germany. And Britain was proving scarcely more enthusiastic. McNamara and I had come to the conclusion that such a commission might be able to show ways to break the deadlock, and we agreed that someone of the political experience and stature of Willy Brandt, now a Nobel Peace Prizewinner, would be the right person to head it.

Brandt was seriously considering it, but he wanted to be sure that there would be no objections from the developing countries who were insisting that the United Nations, where the Group of 77 wielded its power, was the only place where serious decisions could be taken on establishing the new international economic order. There were rumblings that an independent commission could undermine the Group of 77's efforts. It seemed essential therefore that Brandt should seek to convince the Group of 77 that his commission, if he headed it, would be a help, not a hindrance, to future North-South relations, and would in no way replace the continuing efforts in the United Nations. If the 77 accepted his assurances, then Brandt would be prepared to head the commission.

He therefore came over to the United States during our 1977 annual meeting to confer with us, and we then asked Julian Grenfell, at his New York post, to arrange for Brandt to meet as many as possible of the foreign ministers of the Group of 77 countries who were gathered in New York at the moment for the opening of the General Assembly. In a crowded two days, Julian managed to line up thirty-two foreign ministers for individual chats with Brandt, most of them conducted on a sofa just outside the

General Assembly hall as the long general debate got underway inside. Brandt succeeded in allaying their apprehensions, and once satisfied that he had their good will, he called a press conference at the United Nations and announced, to our delight, that he would head the commission.

He selected, with the help of a few suggestions from us, a very strong group of fifteen commissioners, including former President Frei of Chile, once and future Prime Minister Olof Palme of Sweden, former Prime Minister Ted Heath of Britain, Sonny Ramphal, Secretary-General of the Commonwealth, my old friend Amir Jamal from Tanzania, Pierre Mendès-France, and Kay Graham, publisher of the *Washington Post*. The other commissioners were no less distinguished. He appointed as Secretary of the commission Goran Ohlin, Professor of Economics at Uppsala University, and as Director of the Secretariat, Dragoslav Avramovic, the distinguished Yugoslav economist who had formerly been at the World Bank and at UNCTAD.

The commission laboured for the best part of two years and finally approved its report in December of 1979, just after I had returned from what would be my last annual meeting of the World Bank, which was held in Belgrade. It was a lengthy report, addressing the problems of the poorest nations, hunger and food, population, the disarmament-development link, trade, developing country economic policies, industrialization, monetary questions, development finance, and negotiations in international fora. With reference to the Bank, it called, amongst other things, for a doubling of our borrowing-to-capital ratio (which we declined); a substantial increase in programme lending (which is underway); and a greater role for borrowing countries in decision-making and management (which within the constraints of the Bank's constitution is making some headway).

The report was widely publicized and generally well received. But the world was by that time in the throes of the worst recession in forty years, and coping with it allowed little opportunity for much to be done by those urged in the report to take action. Three years later, Brandt followed up with an updated programme, taking into account the events of the intervening years and the worsening of the situation. *Common Crisis*, as it was entitled, was no less compelling than the original report, *North-South: A Programme for Survival*, in its urging that the nations of the world co-operate to find solutions that were truly in the mutual interest. But when my years at the World Bank came to an end in the spring of 1980, as I answered the call of my friend Barbara Ward to take over her International Institute for Environment and Development, I could not comfort myself with any notion that the world was going to do what people like Bob McNamara and Willy Brandt and countless others of like mind were urging. But at least we had tried. And at least we would go on trying.

—10—

Going Home

My final months at the World Bank were not the easiest. I was reluctant to leave so early in McNamara's third term and at a time of increasing stress for the Bank as it grappled with the pressures from its senior shareholder on the one hand and the deteriorating world economic situation on the other. But I could not possibly refuse Barbara Ward's request that I relieve her of her responsibilities at IIED, now that she was clearly so desperately ill. I therefore told McNamara, before we left for Belgrade, that I would like to leave the following April of 1980.

Those same months were even more difficult for McNamara. The issue of America's continuing efforts to select the Bank's beneficiaries came to a head that autumn of 1979. Ironically, the cause of the crisis was Vietnam. Shortly after a united Vietnamese government had taken over the seat in the Bank and Fund left vacant by the defeated regime of the South, the Bank had negotiated an agricultural loan for the country, which was in the midst of a famine-stricken region. With only the United States director objecting, the loan passed the board. Further loans were in the planning stage when, in September 1979, Vietnam invaded Cambodia. Further progress on the negotiation of loans by us was effectively if unofficially halted. But Congress, which was at that time debating the sixth replenishment of IDA, let it be known at the staff level that only a personal assurance from McNamara that there would be no more loans to Vietnam would prevent the defeat of the IDA replenishment bill. The responsibility for dealing directly with the US Congress had always lain with the US Treasury Department, and the Congress should properly have come through

276

the Treasury with their request for a cessation of the lending to Vietnam. But in the confusion and haste of their demand, McNamara was persuaded to sign a letter to the chairman of the relevant House Committee meeting their demand. The letter was immediately made public, and the storm burst upon us. The Bank's board, outraged at this new evidence of United States efforts to politicize the Bank, and distressed by the Bank President's infringement of the rule that the President deal only with the executive branch of member governments, found their confidence in McNamara's ability to defend them from what they perceived as a hostile America badly shaken. To make matters worse, Congress still did not appropriate the funds for IDA, and did not do so for the remainder of McNamara's term as President.

Our troubles were not over. On the eve of the annual meeting in Belgrade, the Group of 77 held a meeting there at ministerial level to co-ordinate their positions before the Bank and Fund governing bodies met. At that meeting, the OPEC countries insisted on pressing a demand that the Palestine Liberation Organization should be an observer at the annual meeting, it having already been admitted to that status in the UN General Assembly and many other UN bodies. At our Belgrade meeting, the issue was finessed by a ruling from the chairman responsive to the American viewpoint. Having the PLO as observers could scarcely have affected the Bank's operations, but everyone knew what the reaction would be in the United States Congress. The matter remains unresolved to this day, it having been subsequently decided by the Bank and the Fund that the only way round it was to suspend the status of observer at our meetings altogether. This has left the PLO at the door; on the other hand it has also left the Administrator of the UNDP, the Secretary-General of the OECD, and many other high international officials languishing there with them.

I was sorry that the Belgrade meeting was to be my last annual meeting as a member of the World Bank staff. And I was very greatly saddened that the meeting should be the occasion of suicide of a valued colleague on my staff who had accompanied us there. I returned to Washington in a dark mood, wondering what else might befall us before my departure. My spirits were lifted, however, by what was to be the last of my travels with Bob and the indomitable Marg who succumbed to her bravely borne illness just a year later. I have nothing but the most wonderful memories of this caring, courageous and absolutely charming person. Between

16 and 24 January we visited Kenya, Tanzania, Botswana, Lesotho and Swaziland, and I returned refreshed and ready to begin the handover to my successor, my good friend Munir Benjenk, then Regional Vice-President in charge of European, Middle Eastern and North African operations. I sold my house in Rodman Street, sorrowfully but well, and said goodbye to the weekend and summer retreat that I shared with Munir on Ella Burling's beautiful Rich Neck Manor estate in Clairborne on the eastern Maryland shore. It had been a happy home away from the city, much visited by our friends, including Jim Callaghan, who, when Prime Minister, dropped in for lunch by helicopter.

And so, on the eve of the twelfth anniversary of my joining the Bank, I took leave of my friends and colleagues. They had been thrilling and extraordinarily stimulating years, which I now recall with feelings of great thankfulness and not a little pride. The experience of working with Bob McNamara was as gratifying and exciting as anything I could have earlier imagined myself doing. When he himself left the Bank a year later, Bank lending was at its highest level ever, work was already launched on a programme of operations in the People's Republic of China, and the Bank's reputation as the largest and most effective development agency in the world was secure. He had performed extraordinary feats, but it was right that he chose to go before his third term was up. He had used the new power he had created in the Bank to full effect, and he left it with its sights trained upwards, leaning into the wind of the world recession, determined to carry the development effort forward, no matter how turbulent the waters. He taught us that it is possible to lift people out of the degradation of absolute poverty, if only we have the will and the energy to do so. He exemplified that will and that energy, and it is sad that he finally left the Bank disillusioned by the failure of too many governments to do what needed to be done to help the process move more determinedly forward.

Shortly after leaving the Bank, I set to work on an article for *Foreign Affairs*, describing the McNamara stewardship of the Bank, and I hope the journal's editor Bill Bundy does not mind that I have drawn on the piece in setting out these recollections of my own days at the Bank. The piece was eventually published in the autumn 1981 issue after some much needed editorial help from Bill, for which I was very grateful. What I did not say in that less personal piece was how deeply I valued Bob McNamara's friendship, formed over our years at the Bank together, and which has continued. It was a privilege and a joy to work with him.

I took up my duties immediately at the International Institute for Environment and Development. I had been associated with the Insititute almost from its creation in 1971 and knew well its work before becoming its President in succession to Barbara. She had created out of it a much respected instrument for focusing the world's attention on the connections between economic development, the environment and human needs; its global audience of government planners, the private sector, the academic community and non-governmental organizations were finding increasing value in its well-researched policy studies and in Earthscan, its international news and information service. The Institute also operated a technical advice and assistance service, the Joint Environmental Service, collaborating closely with the International Union for the Conservation of Nature and Natural Resources. In April 1982 we opened a Washington bureau for Earthscan. This afforded me the opportunity to return from time to time to the city and the friends I had enjoyed through my years at the Bank.

One of my most satisfying undertakings during my five years as President of IIED was the launching in 1982 of the Barbara Ward Fund, the brainchild of a group of her friends who proposed it to carry on the work to which Barbara had devoted her life. Her death shortly after my assumption of her old office had deprived the world of one of its greatest and most compassionate thinkers and doers in the international environment and development field, and it was only natural that those who had known her so well and admired her work so greatly should launch such a fund as a fitting memorial to her. Bob McNamara, Robert O. Anderson, Ted Heath, Abdelatif Y. Al-Hamad and Maurice Strong formed the core of the Fund, and many others have since given generously to it and assisted in making it a flourishing endeavour. It is greatly helping reinforce IIED as a centre of excellence in policy study and aiding in spreading the fruits of our work where it will have real impact and constructive uses.

Early in 1984, I told the board of IIED, at the Institute's annual meeting held in our new Washington office, that having just begun my fifth year as President, we ought to choose a successor to take over at the end of it. The choice most appropriately fell on Brian Walker, former Director-General of Oxfam, and a man exceptionally well versed in the realities of grass-roots development.

279

By the time I handed over to him, I knew of my terminal illness, and my first concern now became to use what time I had left to me on writing my memoirs, for the undertaking of which I had always assumed sufficient time in my dotage. With the help and encouragement of Jane Heller, my talented and patient editor at Sidgwick and Jackson, and a number of friends, the work has been able to go forward. There were some events in my varied life that I felt worth recording, and I have tried to select those experiences and the people connected with them, the recalling of which might shed a little extra light on some of the events and developments that have helped shape our history over the past fifty years. I was lucky to be in some interesting places at some interesting times with some interesting people.

Postscript
by
David Harvey

William's secretary at the *Observer* was not the only one to duck before a flying letter tray. Old habits died hard with William and right until his last office role, as President of the International Insitute for Environment and Development, his acute and sudden bursts of frustration vented themselves upon some unfortunate girl who clearly 'knew not Moses'.

The host of secretaries were really the people who kept the William Clark show on the road – all the way from the *Britannica* days, on the *Observer*, at No.10 (he was quite shameless about availing himself of his contacts in the telephone room for years after he left), his own Overseas Development Institute, the World Bank and, finally, the IIED.

However, this book sees the light of day because of the dedicated friendship of two men in particular: Michael Davie and Julian Grenfell. As they saw William's strength flag so they harnessed his notes and instructions into chapters which hold together the narrative of an extraordinarily active life.

A glance at William's old engagement diaries suggests that he was quite as busy as any politician, which, in a way, he was. He spent every moment of the working day meeting people. 'Breakfast, dinner, lunch and tea,' he would opine – in his lifelong adherence to Bellocian principles – 'is all the human frame requires', but William needed people as well. And if they could not be persuaded to his office, or to Albany, or to Rodman Street in Washington DC, then they had better be in reach of a telephone.

The late Christopher Rowlands described William as 'the switch-board operator of the Establishment' and, certainly in his own 'development era', William was a voracious collector of names. But he was also planting seed corn, as well he knew. He could not resist a new face and, in consequence, many people in the front of British life today owe their start to William's help and encouragement.

In the early sixties, as William began to explore the new territory of development and 'Third World studies', he met some young graduates who, straight from school, were determined to do something practical about the poor four-fifths of the world. Their impatience and iconoclasm often gave him a very hard time but now, I think, most of them will allow that William was a major adult support to their beliefs, not least because he clearly inhabited a much wider world than their own. He was conscious of the limits of power as much as of the possibilities, and his whole career was a remarkable example of Disraeli's dictum of the 'art of the possible'.

This period was a crucial moment in the careers of two young men: Adrian Moyes, currently at Oxfam, who was his first personal assistant at the ODI; and Peter Williams, now Director of Education at the Commonwealth Secretariat, who became an early ODIN. In spite of their now extremely busy lives they have fleshed out William's rather bald account of the first days of the Institute. Tom Soper, William's deputy during most of his period at the ODI, took considerable trouble to compile an account of the ODI's work during William's tenure, for which the publishers and I are more than grateful because, fifteen years later, original records are sparse.

Curiously, William's greatest mentor, David Astor, was not able to tell much about this period and William's hope of heading a new institute to study development problems. The origins of the ambition are not recorded. One laconic reference to the topic was made by William in a diary for 1960 (which, unfortunately, he only kept for a few days). In that he noted a visit to a lecture at Chatham House where he heard that there were plans by 'Pat Blackett and others' to set up an institute to study Third World problems and that Andrew Cohen was likely to head it. He recorded neither comment nor conjecture about this 'chip of news'.

As both John Pringle and George Seddon make clear in their vivid accounts of 'William at work', it was the chips of news and the nuggets of revelation which made William's journalism work. 'Chips of news', incidentally, is another Clark memento, owed in this case to the title of the gossip column in his home town's weekly paper, the *Haltwhistle Gazette*. (He religiously subscribed to it even

282

after his elevation to Washington and deeply resented its eventual merger with the *Hexham Courant*.)

In one sense, this memoir is all chips. As William himself said on the fateful All Hallows Eve when Dr Ball told him the bad news, he felt himself 'falling down a lift shaft'. But he controlled what must have been a terrifying sense of panic and set to with energy and efficiency to organize his papers. He had thrown nothing away; neither school notebooks nor household bills. By and large, they were all neatly labelled – except the photographs, that is. William was an inveterate 'snapshotter' with a reporter's eye if not a photographer's sense of composition. Alas, very few of the thousands of prints and transparencies are captioned. With his own sharp eye for posterity he must be extremely vexed at his own laxity and my failure to listen. No Boswell me.

Friends anticipated William more for his gossip than his view on world affairs, with the possible exception of Harold Nicolson. Agog to hear William's account of the disastrous Paris summit between Khrushchev and Eisenhower (spoiled by the U–2 cock-up), he demanded: 'Will there be war?'

There is no question that a great fund of gossip and anecdote is lost. He was himself a 'Boswell' of the post-war period and many of us are guilty of taking it for granted. Yet, when confronted by his death-line with the choice of deciding the framework of his testament, he reacted quite sharply against the idea of an anecdotal memoir on Nicholson or Channon lines.

As a formidable student of history William saw clearly the drift of events whilst at No.10. (The months of relatively humdrum press adviser chores – nowhere so highly developed or cynical as the Westland affair or *Yes, Prime Minister* now suggest – are not included.) But his guests for years afterwards rocked with astonished laughter at stories which, it would now appear, will not stand the test of print.

How sad, for example, to consider that it may not be true that Her Majesty signed an emergency Order in Council on the rump of her racehorse in the Goodwood paddock – with a flustered scratch group of Privy Councillors clustered around her. Nor that Anthony Eden considered control of the BBC would be any problem since the 'DG was my fag at Eton'.

William used to have it that he was 'allowed' to go on holiday at the critical Suez build-up period to get him out of the way – but somewhere where he could be reached by a secure telephone. So he had to put up with a holiday in Gibraltar. His subsequent stories about his return to a very different atmosphere at No.10 pivoted on the theme of having had his office moved downstairs to the Garden Room (re-dubbed by me over years of repetition as 'the boot room story'). It was there that ministers, admirals and generals kicked their heels, he would say, and thus inadvertently spilt the beans on what was going on 'upstairs'. His private accounts of the affair also suggested a much more positive role on the part of the Queen, with the implication that if the Cabinet was resolved upon a military solution the Prime Minister should inform the Leader of the Opposition.

'Tut, tut! What a disaster', quietly spoken, betokened events of a truly cataclysmic nature – perhaps the loss of an air ticket or the collapse of Sunday lunch on the kitchen floor. One knew better than to proceed with other than the greatest tact and sympathy. The phrase did not recur after All Hallows Eve. William resorted to a determined stoicism which few of his friends and acquaintances would have expected but which he had shown at least twice before when facing excruciating operations on his injured knee (including the removal of the knee cap). This remarkable inner strength was clearly sustained by the stream of visitors and shoals of mail (unleashed by his valedictory New Year card).

One such tribute, which gave him particular satisfaction, came from William P. Bundy, former editor of *Foreign Affairs*. 'Surely the Lord does move in mysterious ways,' he wrote, 'or perhaps wish to apportion the burdens of responsibility more widely. Certainly you have done much more than your share, and would fairly be entitled to rest from your labours. But not this way, and not now.

'Apart from the wider debts we share with literally millions of others, my mind goes back to many happy and rewarding times . . . you have been the truest of friends, with whom one picked up just where one had left off, regardless of interval or distance . . .

'I think of laughter, of insight, of warmth and caring – of all that binds together the members and candidate members of E.M. Forster's grouping of the sensitive, the considerate and the plucky (if I have it right).

'So now, as you exercise to the fullest the last of these, our hearts are with you daily. At times like this one does return to the prayer book, asking that this burden be lifted from you or at least made lighter. But whatever may come, be sure, dear friend, that you have done nobly, and that it has been of very good report indeed.'

When William died there were yet more letters. Tarquin Olivier touchingly evoked his feelings for William and voiced some of the influence William obtained over people who sought him out: 'He, more than any other, seems to have been in the background of my own career development, ever since 1963. He was always *there*, kind, supportive and deliciously ridiculous. So many of his absurd sayings have become part of my daily thoughts.'

Had William seen these memoirs to a proper completion I suspect he would have started this chapter with a phrase such as: 'A hearty vote of thanks to the Headmaster, the School Prefects and all who made it possible.' The line came from his Oundle schooldays.

William could run a whole day on his bizarre bank of clichés. 'Welcome to our happy home'; 'I'm so low I could sit on a ha'penny stamp and dangle my legs' (usually reserved for the secretaries – as was 'Where's my cup of tea?'); 'Isn't it a lovely day. Good old God!'; 'Who would like a glass of delicious and refreshing . . . (whatever)'; 'Where was I when I was so rudely interrupted?' (usually by his beloved telephone); and . . .

'Backward they looked o'er the whole state of paradise, so late their happy home' (misquoted but invariably uttered after lingering over a beautiful view or a satisfactory outing). The lines are by Milton and quite by chance (good old God or a school prefect?) I re-played a recording William made in Washington of some of his favourite poems.

What I heard was: '. . . the last lines of "Paradise Lost", which I wrote out on the day that I left No.10:

> So spake our mother Eve and Adam heard,
> Well pleased, but answered not; for now, too nigh
> The archangel stood, and from the other hill
> To their fixed station, all in bright array
> The Cherubim descended; on the ground
> Gliding metérous, as evening mist
> Risen from a river o'er the marish glides,
> And gathers ground fast at the labourer's heel
> Homeward returning. High in front advanced,
> The brandished sword of God before them blazed
> Fierce as a comet; which with torrid heat,
> And vapour as the Libyan air adust,
> Began to parch that temperate clime; whereat

In either hand the hastening angel caught
Our lingering parents, and to the Eastern gate
Led them direct, and down as fast
To the subjected plain; then disappeared.
They, looking back, all the eastern side beheld
Of Paradise, so late their happy seat,
Waved over by that flaming brand, the gate
With dreadful faces thronged and fiery arms.
Some natural tears they dropped, but wiped them soon;
The world was all before them, where to choose
Their place of rest, and Providence their guide:
They, hand in hand, with wondering steps and slow,
Through Eden took their solitary way.'

This spiritual element in William was usually encompassed by his relish of nature. Gazing out at the daffodils in The Mill garden he remarked to a young red-headed Scottish friend, 'It is so nice, dying slowly.' Above all, his love of hymns – muddled with a good deal of sentimental recollection of his schooldays. He insisted that 'hymns are the folk songs of the English'. And he took his Master's degree at Chicago University – since he was obliged to do some teaching as a visiting fellow – in theology.

Thus he joined two aspects of his American experience with a quote from De Tocqueville shortly before he was confined to his bedroom: 'I am reminded of what he said when the priest and clergy assembled around his death bed with bell, book and candle. As they started on the last rites by abjuring him to renounce the Devil and all his works he wagged an admonitory finger: "Tush! This is no time to make new enemies!" '

Nevertheless, I doubt if there is a friend of William who does not, at some moment of the day, beset by frustration or the absurdity of events, give vent to his echoing cry: 'For God's sake . . .'

The Mill
Cuxham
28.1.86

Index

Index

Index

Index

291